ABCs
of
WEST COAST
GARDENING

ABCs
of
WEST COAST
GARDENING

MARY PALMER

HARBOUR PUBLISHING

Published by

HARBOUR PUBLISHING

P.O. Box 219, Madeira Park, BC Canada V0N 2H0

www.harbourpublishing.com

Cover and page design and composition by Martin Nichols
Front cover background photo of *Wisteria floribunda* and *Viburnum japonica* by Adam Gibbs; front cover inset photo of Gold Nugget Squash by West Coast Seeds, title page photo of Dahlias, Cosmos, Ami Majas, Sweet peas, Deep Stocks by Bob Cain; author photo by Benson View Photographic Arts

Printed in Canada

Harbour Publishing acknowledges the financial support of the Government of Canada through the Book Publishing Industry Development Program (BPIDP) and the Canada Council for the Arts, and the Province of British Columbia through the British Columbia Arts Council, for its publishing activities.

THE CANADA COUNCIL | LE CONSEIL DES ARTS
FOR THE ARTS | DU CANADA
SINCE 1957 | DEPUIS 1957

National Library of Canada Cataloguing in Publication

Palmer, Mary, 1920–
    ABCs of west coast gardening

    Includes index.
    ISBN 1-55017-253-0

    1. Gardening—Northwest, Pacific. 2. Gardening—Pacific Coast (B.C.) I. Title.
SB453.2.N83P34   2002 635'.09795   C2002-910678-8

for my husband Al

Acknowledgements

Thanks to Mary Schendlinger for editing, and to Howard White, Peter Robson, Martin Nichols, Helen Godolphin and all the good people at Harbour.

C O N T E N T S

PREFACE

Gardening books, like gardens, are as individual as the people who created them. This book is no exception. After six decades of gardening—running a nursery in Seattle, working as the gardening columnist for the Seattle *Times*, then homesteading on a Canadian Gulf Island—I have developed a passionate interest in the possibilities for West Coast gardens. Given the right mix of work and knowledge, any piece of West Coast ground can be made endlessly bountiful, productive, glorious and satisfying. I know, because I've done it. Several times.

It is up to you to do the work. But a lot of the information you'll need is to be found in the book that is in your hands. *ABCs of West Coast Gardening* is a broad-spectrum gardening book: general enough to guide beginners beyond the two-marigolds-in-a-pot stage, yet packed with the kind of detail on new plant varieties and horticultural tips that will have master gardeners dog-earing its pages.

Let's say you have just bought your first home. To save a little money you decided to do the landscaping yourself. You stand in the middle of the bare lot and wonder, what's next? *ABCs of West Coast Gardening* offers a step-by-step guide to improving the soil, starting a lawn, selecting trees and shrubs—in short, all aspects of gardening that you need to turn a new house and yard into your own beautiful *home*.

Or perhaps you have recently retired and moved from a large home and garden to "scaled-down digs." You need to make the garden smaller so your back muscles are not overtaxed. Sections of this book will help you set up a low-maintenance, small-space garden that produces prodigiously.

Perhaps you are a seasoned gardener flummoxed by a gardening problem: bolting cabbage, anemic roses, cranky ferns. Check out the relevant sections in the text. Chances are that a remedy (or better yet, a prevention) is described in plain, no-nonsense language.

ABCs of West Coast Gardening is foremost a practical book. If there is much of my philosophy in the text it emerges tangentially. But I do want to pass on one story—perhaps *parable* is a better term—that encapsulates my feelings about gardening. It dates to the years when my husband Al and I were living on Jedediah, a 256 ha (640-acre) island in the Strait of Georgia. We had acres of orchards, flowers and vegetables—in part to feed and keep ourselves, in part to sell and maintain our farm tax status. It was an unimaginable amount of work (and joy), but sometimes the setbacks were almost too much to bear. Like the year the crows started harvesting the crops before us. We were at wit's end with these black-feathered raiders when our friend, the famous coastal log salvager Sam Lamont, dropped anchor in nearby Home Bay. Al and I made our way to the bay to greet him.

Sam took one look at us and asked (in his characteristically shy fashion), "What the hell's the matter with you two?"

The garden on Jedediah Island. Mary Palmer photo

Al explained, "Sam, the damn crows are getting the best of us."

Before Sam could answer, Al spotted a lamb squeezing through a distant fence and dashed off. Sam watched him go and said, "I'll tell you what to do. Mary, have you got any of Al's good Scotch around?"

I nodded.

"Pour a big bowl of that Scotch and put it where the crows can have their fill," he said.

I was shocked. "Not Al's best Scotch, Sam!" I protested, thinking of the very long swim I'd have to make off the island if Al were to discover me offering his good Scotch to...*crows*.

But Sam was adamant. "You want to get rid of the crows," he said. "After they fill up on Scotch they will be in a drunken stupor and you and Al can do them in."

The next morning I stealthily poured some of Al's favourite Scotch in a bowl and placed it in the orchard. Soon the crows were toasting each other, calling and coaxing in a frenzy. A wild erotic party was in play. Some had already passed out under the trees. I was enjoying the show when Al appeared. I told him about the ploy and, after uttering a few blasphemous phrases, he settled down and we went outside. What to do? Zonked-out crows and a single raven lay all around, waiting for us to dispatch them. Menacingly, Al hoisted a fallen limb over his head. The solution to our woes was at hand. But he let the limb drop harmlessly.

"I can't kill the damn things," he choked out.

Neither could I. We passed the rest of the day watching the crows' revelry, mindful that while it is good to enjoy a garden's bounty, it is even better to enjoy gardening itself.

Good digging and good luck!

CHAPTER 1

Getting Started

Improving the Soil

THE LIFE OF ANY GARDEN IS IN THE SOIL. A gardener's first task, then, is to make sure the soil is as healthy as possible. Most home gardens are not naturally fertile, loose, friable and teeming with micro-organisms. Often during construction of new homes or other buildings, earth-moving machines remove most of the topsoil and expose hardpan or a sand-and-gravel pit.

Foxglove. Adam Gibbs photo

The first step in soil improvement is to examine the soil to a depth of at least 60 cm (2 ft). Test its structure by taking a handful and squeezing tightly. Then open your hand. If the soil remains in a tight ball, it is mostly clay. If the ball falls apart, the soil may be too light and sandy for many plants. If the soil holds together but falls apart when you touch it, then it has the right texture for growing most plants.

If a garden soil is sticky when wet and bakes hard when dry, it is a clay soil. Heavy clay soils are characterized by a degree of compactness, which makes cultivation difficult and interferes with the oxygen supply to the root zone. Heavy clay soils restrict the movement of water and air, which encourages poor drainage in winter.

Light, sandy soils dry too rapidly because the particles are large and water passes through them quickly. These soils do not retain nutrients well, either.

Heavy clay or sandy soils are improved with generous additions of organic materials, mainly through the release of plant nutrients caused by microbial actions and the ability of the organic matter to form healthy chemical compounds. As well, organic materials can break down vital nutrients such as nitrogen and phosphorus that are sometimes "locked" in the soil, and release them to the plants.

Experiments have shown that decayed organic material, known as humus, supplies plants with 95% of the nitrogen, up to 60% of the phosphorus and up to 80% of the sulphur and minerals they need. In addition, organic material greatly improves the structure and condition of the garden soil. As the matter decays and dissipates, the soil opens to penetration of water, air and fertilizers, thus stimulating root development.

Plowing soil. Mary Palmer photo

Readying soil. Mary Palmer photo

Compost

Humus, or organic material, is the life of the soil, and the compost pile is the gardener's best source of humus. Material from the compost heap acts as a sponge, absorbing water and holding plant nutrients in the soil. Leaves, grass clippings, faded flowers, vegetable parts, kitchen wastes, seaweed, wood ashes and other organic materials placed in the compost heap will decompose and be returned to the soil as nourishment.

A compost pile is usually built in layers. The bottom layer should contain coarse material such as heavy sod, plant stalks and twigs. The next layer is soil. Add layers of soil several inches thick alternately with layers of vegetative matter, then sprinkle a bacterial compost maker over the vegetative matter to hasten the decomposing process. Avoid adding large, mature weeds or diseased plants.

Cover the compost heap with heavy black plastic sheeting. The covering intensifies the heat for decomposition and keeps weed seeds from germinating.

Plastic moulded compost bins are also available from garden supply stores. They need only chopped vegetable matter and a sprinkle of sand or soil.

Several commercial bacterial compost makers are available, or you can make your own by mixing 13.5 kg (30 lbs) of sulphate of ammonia, 11.3 kg (25 lbs) of ground lime-stone, 6.8 kg (15 lbs) of super-phosphate, and 6.8 kg (15 lbs) of muriate of potash. This amount of material is sufficient to treat 450 kg (1/2 ton) of vegetative matter. Sprinkle it on top of vegetative matter layers throughout the compost heap at the rate of 4.5 kg (10 lbs) per cubic yard.

Most material will decompose thoroughly in 3 to 12 months. When the compost is ready to use, it will resemble soil, dark in colour and light in texture. It will have a clean, woodsy odour.

If adequate space for a large compost heap is unavailable, composting may be done in a 122 litre (32 gal) black plastic garbage bag. To hasten the decomposing action, keep bags in a warm garage or basement. Place a couple of shovelfuls of garden waste into the bag, then sprinkle a high-nitrogen fertilizer, such as 10-6-4, over the material, at the rate of 125 mL (1/2 cup) to 2 shovelfuls of garden waste. Continue to add wastes and a sprinkling of fertilizer until the bag is full. Add about 1 litre (1 qt) of water to the material and tie the top of the bag securely. In several months the composted material will be ready for the garden.

Green Cover

Green cover or green manure crops provide another satisfactory and inexpensive means of conditioning the soil. Sow clover, vetch, rye or alfalfa thickly in the late fall. Before turning over the cover crop in the spring, add a complete 5-10-10 fertilizer over the area. Use 900 g (2 lbs) of fertilizer to 9 m² (100 sq ft) of green cover space.

Animal Manure

Animal manures are useful sources of organic matter. **Poultry manure** is highest in fertility. It is loaded with nitrogen, but low in phosphorus and potash. Use it with caution when fresh—it can burn or otherwise injure plants. A top dressing of 5 cm (2 inches) of animal manure is best for most crops. Add poultry manure to the compost or incorporate it thoroughly into the soil, and wait several weeks or months before planting.

Sheep manure is a relatively quick source of nitrogen, but it loses nitrogen rapidly when exposed to air and should be turned into the soil promptly.

Horse manure generates a great deal of heat during decomposition and is commonly used in the bottom of hotbeds in place of electric-heat cables for starting seeds and cuttings. Fresh horse manure is rich in ammonia and offers more plant nutrients than cow manure. Horse manure is also useful as a top dressing over vegetable or flower beds in the late fall or winter.

Cow manure is low in plant food elements, yet it is useful because it creates large amounts of organic humus when decomposed. 900 kg (1 ton) of cow manure contains approximately 4.5 kg (10 lbs) of nitrogen, 900 g (2 lbs) of phosphorus and about 3.6 kg (8 lbs) of potash. Cow manure should be composted to destroy weed seeds. Dry or pelleted forms of cow manure may be applied directly to the garden.

Seaweed

Gardeners on the West Coast are fortunate to have an abundance of seaweed available. Seaweed is filled with many minerals and has an aggregating quality and growth-promoting substance. A substantial quantity of potash is found in seaweed. Seaweed decomposes rapidly into gases and soluble compounds, so don't expose it to the elements for long periods. Apply it to the soil or work it into the compost heap immediately after gathering it. A top dressing of 7.5–10 cm (3–4 inches) each fall and spring is beneficial. Asparagus plantings benefit greatly from seaweed.

Peat Moss

Peat moss is the partly decomposed remains of plants accumulated over centuries under airless or nearly airless conditions. Although peat moss does not contain nutrients, it aerates the soil, improves drainage and retains water when needed. Ultimately it helps plants absorb nutrients from other materials.

Peat moss often cakes or dries out on the surface of the soil and draws moisture from the ground. Before spreading peat moss, open the bale and allow water from a slow-running hose to penetrate the dry material. Apply a covering of 5 cm (2 inches).

Wood Matter

Ground bark, wood chips and aged sawdust can be used as mulches or turned into the soil to raise its humus content. These materials aerate the soil and improve moisture retention. Any of these wood materials also makes a decorative and useful top dressing.

As wood matter decomposes it uses nitrogen, because the micro-organisms in the soil that break down the wood matter feed on nitrogen. For each .76 m^3 (1 cubic yd) of ground bark, wood chips or sawdust applied to the garden, use 1.5 kg (3^1/$_2$ lbs) of sulphate of ammonia, or a fertilizer with a high nitrogen content.

To Lime or Not to Lime

Before you consider the use of lime, test your soil to determine what it requires. Soil-testing kits are available in garden centres and nurseries. Or you can hire a commercial soil-testing firm to provide accurate soil tests and recommend ways to correct any deficiencies.

A soil test will tell you how acid or alkaline your soil is, by measuring the pH. On the pH scale, 7 is neutral, neither acid nor alkaline. Below 7 indicates acidity, above indicates alkalinity. Most garden plants develop best in a soil with a pH of between 6.5 and 7. As well, soil with a pH of 6 to 8 usually contains a larger population of soil organisms, which make plant nutrients more available and prevent "lockup" of trace elements such as iron.

The heavy rainfall on the West Coast causes most soils to be acidic, because carbonates (salts) are carried away in the runoff and the alkaline elements are replaced by hydrogen ions from the water. Some mulching materials also affect the pH of the soil. Peat moss, oak leaves and pine needles tend to reduce the pH and increase acidity.

If your soil tests acidic, you may want to add a substance to make the soil more alkaline ("sweeter"). But first, make sure the balanced pH is the right level for your soil.

Getting Started

Acid-loving plants include azalea, rhododendron, holly, camellia, heather, blue hydrangea, *Magnolia grandiflora*, *Soulangiana* and *Stellata*, *Pieris*, skimmia, cypress, hemlock, pine, spruce, Scotch broom, dogwood, styrax, kalmia, strawberry, blackberry, currant, gooseberry, blueberry, tomato, rhubarb, grape, cucumber, pepper, parsnip, pumpkin, squash and celery.

Plants that thrive in an alkaline soil include peony, iris, abelia, daphne, sweet pea, clematis, astilbe, lilac, delphinium, gypsophila, rose, plum, apple, wisteria, sweet-gum tree, pyracantha, clover, cabbage, asparagus, artichoke, beet, carrot and onion. Hydrangeas that grow in alkaline soil usually produce pink blossoms.

If you do decide to lower the acidity of your soil, there are several additives you can try: finely ground oyster shells, wood ash and marl have been used to good effect. Dusting, or powdered sulphur, is another dependable material to lower soil pH. It works slowly but has a lasting effect. Spread 450 g–1.35 kg (1–1 1/2 lbs) of powdered sulphur over 9 m² (100 sq ft) of area. Turn the sulphur into the soil and water in.

But the most common way to lower soil acidity is to add lime, a white caustic substance that is obtained principally from deposits of limestone. Some types of lime are produced as by-products of the chemical industry. Garden lime usually is obtained by grinding either calcium carbonate or dolomite. The finer the lime is ground, the faster the reaction in the soil. The fineness is expressed on the package as a percentage: at least 50% should pass through a 100-mesh screen or sieve.

Dolomite lime is composed chiefly of carbonates of magnesium and calcium and is recommended for use in this region. Hydrated (wet) lime is effective immediately when applied to the soil; however, it is leached from the soil quickly and is ineffective after a short time.

The amount of lime to apply is determined by the texture and moisture content of the soil and the change in pH level that is required by specific plants. To raise the pH of a dry, sandy soil by one point, add approximately 16 kg (35 lbs) of dolomite lime to each 90 m² (1,000 sq ft) of area. On medium loam soil, use 22.5 kg (50 lbs) of lime, and on a wet, heavy clay soil, incorporate 31.5 kg (70 lbs).

As well as adjusting the soil pH to a level more favourable to most plants, lime helps make soil more fertile. It allows nitrogen, phosphorus, potassium and sulphur in the soil to be more available to plants. It also increases natural bacterial activity in the soil, which decomposes plant residue and releases nutrients. As well, lime adds calcium and magnesium to the soil. (Calcium deficiency is apparent when young leaves and growth buds become bent and die back to the tips and along the margins, and the leaves are wrinkled. Magnesium deficiency causes a general loss of green colouring, which begins in the bottom leaves and moves up the stem of the plant, while the veins of the leaf remain green.)

It is important to note that lime is a soil conditioner and additive, not a fertilizer. Do not use fertilizers for 2 to 3 weeks after applying lime. If the two are applied simultaneously, the lime may "lock" some nutrients in the fertilizer, rendering it less effective.

If you want your soil to be more acid, you can add ferrous sulphate. To lower the reaction of the soil from pH 8 to pH 5, which is a sufficient degree of acidity for azaleas, spread 900 g (2 lbs) of ferrous sulphate over each 9 m^2 (100 sq ft) of soil. Turn the material into the soil thoroughly. Ferrous sulphate can also correct iron deficiency in soils, indicated by plants with pale yellow needles and leaves.

Watering the Garden

The application of water to plants requires more understanding, judgement and skill than most other gardening chores. Plants absorb their nutrients in the form of a solution, so when moisture is unavailable, plant growth and productivity suffer.

During dry summers, the soil supporting plants needs a phenomenal amount of moisture. In a single summer day, a mature tomato plant may transpire as much as 4 litres (1 gal) of water. A giant shade tree in full leaf often takes 530 litres (140 gal) of moisture from the ground in 24 hours. Lawn grasses need at least 5 cm (2 inches) of water every 4 days in dry summers. Long-established trees require less watering than young trees or recent transplants. Newly transplanted trees or shrubs should be watered 1 to 2 times a day in summer until their roots are well established.

Broad-leafed evergreens, such as rhododendrons, will develop scorched leaves if they are unable to absorb water through their roots and leaves on hot, dry days. In hot weather, water every part of these plants early in the morning. Wash the leaves down and use a soil soaker or wrap a perforated watering hose around the base of the plants.

Small annuals and perennials may be watered more frequently, even daily. They are best watered in the morning to keep them fresh and growing actively. Plants in hanging baskets, window boxes and other containers may require watering 2 to 3 times daily if they are in the direct sun.

The moisture requirements of plants in the vegetable garden vary. Onions need less water than squash or cucumber plants. Vegetable or berry plants that are filling out or expanding need more water. Ample water is necessary when pea pods are beginning to fill, or corn cobs to swell. Once the crop begins to mature or ripen, avoid overwatering. Tomatoes will split, onions rot and potatoes become watery if they take in too much moisture late in the season. Water vegetable soil in the early morning. The moisture is absorbed quickly with rising temperatures and sunlight. Wet soil in the evening encourages mildews and other plant diseases.

The amount and frequency of watering depends on plant requirements, rainfall, temperature, winds and soil. Different types of soil have different percolation rates and moisture-holding properties. The rule of thumb is: the larger the soil particles, the less water the soil holds.

Sandy soils are made up of large particles, so water penetration is relatively fast. A block of sandy, light soil 3 m (10 ft) square and 60 cm (2 ft) deep can hold 456 litres

(120 gal) of water. This type of soil, which allows the water to enter quickly and drain readily, needs frequent watering.

Clay soils are made from small, compacted particles, so they require fine, slow watering over a longer period of time than sandy soils. A heavy clay block 3 m (10 ft) square and 60 cm (2 ft) deep will absorb and hold 1,216 litres (320 gal) of water.

Organic mulches, such as peat moss, ground bark, decomposed sawdust and aged manure, increase the capacity of the soil to retain water. Organic mulches contain spongy reservoirs that hold moisture—sometimes more than their weight in water—until needed by the plants. Moisture held by organic particles in the mulching material is given grudgingly to the summer wind and sun, yet is yielded eagerly to the roots of plants. Mulching materials also add nutrients and cultures of helpful bacteria.

When watering any plant, water deeply to the full depth of the rooting zone without flooding or waterlogging the earth. Shallow, frequent watering discourages deep roots, encourages surface roots, and tends to build a suffocating thatch on lawns.

Water should not be applied more rapidly than it can be absorbed. Slowly soak the soil until it is saturated deeply. Then allow the ground to become almost dry again before applying more water. Overwatering combined with inadequate drainage results in a waterlogged soil that will exclude air from the roots and the plant.

Some symptoms of overwatering or underwatering of plants are weak, stunted growth; yellow or reddish foliage; few flowers, berries or fruits; frequent wilting; and dieback of twigs and branches.

Propagating Plants

Seeding

In nature, seeds fall to the ground in autumn and are covered lightly with leaves. They spring to life when the soil and air become warm. Gardeners hasten this natural process by planting seeds indoors during February and March, but whatever way you choose, remember that timing is everything. If the seeds are activated too early in the season, seedlings develop too large and spindly for satisfactory transplanting by the time the weather outdoors is frost-free.

Select fresh, vigorous seeds. Old seeds germinate slowly and produce inferior seedlings, or none at all. For practical purposes, consider three years the limit for most garden seeds to germinate and grow vigorously. Note, however, that this does not apply to notoriously hardy weed seeds. Records show that some weeds have germinated readily after fifty years of dormancy. The record for seed viability is held by an Oriental water lily called Indian lotus (*Nelumbo nucifera*), one of whose seeds was known to be at least 400 years old. It was found by a Japanese botanist in a former lake bed in Manchuria. At the other end of the longevity scale are the seeds of certain orchids, some maples, Para rubber trees, wild rice, willows, birch, elm, chestnut, oak and poplar. They live only a few weeks after release from the parent plant. If the seeds from these plants cannot be sowed at once, they should be stored briefly in moist sand in a cool place.

The seeds of carrot, onion, parsley and parsnip will not germinate quickly or successfully if they are more than a year old. Always plant fresh seeds of delphinium, African daisy, geranium, gerbera, larkspur, regal lily, lunaria, pansy, phlox, pyrethrum, salvia, schizanthus and verbena.

Commercial seed firms collect all seeds from nurseries and garden centres at the end of each planting season, and replace them with fresh seeds the next spring. However, gardeners often keep their own seeds for planting and need to be aware of the viability of these seeds. You can test the viability of seeds by placing a few on a piece of moist blotting paper laid in a shallow pan and covering the pan with glass or plastic. Keep the seeds at 16–21°C (60–70°F). If most of the seeds germinate in a few days, the remaining seeds are likely worth planting.

For a jump on garden season, start seeds in cold frames, in the greenhouse or on a windowsill. Many gardeners use a fluorescent tube as a light source. For proper intensity, place the seedlings 15 cm (6 inches) below the light tube. Most plants develop best if they are grown under short-day conditions, such as 10 to 12 hours of light each 24 hours.

To germinate, seeds need adequate light, warmth, an even supply of moisture, free circulation of air, a sterile starting medium and basic viability. Containers for starting seeds must be sterile, deep enough for the seedlings to root and with adequate drainage in the bottom. Wooden or plastic flats, peat pots, or milk, egg or cottage cheese cartons are excellent containers for starting seeds.

All containers and tools must be sterile. First wash them in hot soapy water, then soak them in undiluted pickling vinegar for 1 to 2 hours.

Your seed germination mixture must be light and porous, like leaf mould or peat moss. It must also be sterile, to prevent damping-off, a disease that flourishes under damp, stuffy conditions and can cause young seedlings to topple and die within hours. Sterilize your seeding medium in a 175°C (350°F) oven for 1 hour or purchase sterile perlite and vermiculite, which are satisfactory because they are light and yet retain moisture. If the seeds have been treated with fungicide by the seed firm to prevent damping-off, the packet is so labelled.

Fill the containers about two-thirds full of soil mixture or other starting material. Level and firm the material well with a wooden board or brick. Soak it with water. Then sift more soil or other material over the first wet layer to fill the container to within 6 mm (1/4 inch) of the top.

With a ruler or piece of wood, make furrows in the soil to receive the seed. Follow the directions on the seed packet as to depth and spacing between the rows. If directions for planting are unavailable, plant the seeds according to type and size. Fine seeds such as ageratum, petunia and lobelia are broadcast over the surface and barely covered with sand, perlite or charcoal dust. Large seeds such as squash, cucumber, marigold and zinnia are planted in the starter mix at a depth twice the diameter of the seed. Always sow seeds sparingly and leave enough space between the tiny starts to allow for free circulation of air and spreading of the leaves. If sown too thickly, they will fail from overcrowded conditions.

Mist the seed lightly with water, then cover the planting with transparent plastic wrap or a pane of glass to keep the moisture in. The seeding will not require watering again until germination. Many gardeners slip the entire planting into a plastic bag, which provides each batch of seeds with a private greenhouse.

When the first signs of green appear, remove the bag or covering and place the planting in a bright spot with filtered sunlight if possible, or under fluorescent light. One of the most important factors in the successful raising of seedlings indoors is the temperature. If it is warmer than 21°C (70°F), seedlings will grow too tall, weak and spindly with almost no roots. Temperatures between 13° and 18°C (55–65°F) encourage plants to develop slowly with strong root systems and squat, fat, compact top growth.

Water the seedlings just enough to keep the soil surface moist. Turn the planting frequently to keep the young stems growing straight.

After the seedlings have produced a true set of leaves, apply a liquid plant food every 10 days. Make a solution of 15 mL (1 tbsp) of a 5-10-10 or equivalent commercial fertilizer in 4 L (1 gal) of warm water.

When the young seedlings develop and grow and the second set of leaves appears, they are ready to be transplanted. The first thinning and transplanting generally is done from 15 to 20 days from seeding. The young plants are transferred into flats or into individual 5 cm (2-inch) peat, plastic, fibre or clay pots.

Special potting soil for the transplants is available at garden centres and nurseries, or mix 2 parts of garden loam, 1 part peat moss and 1 part coarse sand for the transplants.

Carefully remove the thinnings to be transplanted. Prick out each seedling by gently inserting the pointed end of a thin stick or pencil point alongside the plant and lifting the soil gently. This loosens the roots so that you can pull up the plants. If the seedlings are quite small, move them in clumps of 2 or 3. They are separated easily when transplanted. With your fingers, press the soil around the remaining plants firmly to seal any air spaces around the roots.

Do not allow the roots of the uprooted seedlings to dry out, and don't let the sun strike them.

After the seedlings perk up, fertilize them with a solution made of 15 mL (1 tbsp) of a commercial 5-10-10 plant food in 4 L (1 gal) of water. Use this on the growing soil every 10 days for vigorous development. Commercial starters and booster formulations are also available at garden centres.

Water the transplants lightly yet frequently to maintain a moist growing soil. Avoid waterlogging the soil.

Prepare the garden for bedding or seedling plants thoroughly in advance. Turn in organic material such as peat moss, ground bark and aged manure. Rake it level and water well. Spread a special transplanting fertilizer over the area.

Before seedlings are planted in the garden, they should be hardened off, or accustomed to outdoor conditions. Expose them to cool temperatures for 7 to 10 days. In the daytime, place the flats or pots outdoors in a semi-sunny, sheltered spot. At night, take them back indoors. Water lightly to discourage soft growth and avoid the use of fertilizer.

Transplant the young plants out into the garden on a cool, cloudy day, in the late afternoon or evening. Shade the young plants from the direct sun for a few days to prevent them from wilting before they become reestablished.

Replant the starts in their new quarters individually, setting them in the soil at approximately the same depth as they stood in the original container. Prepare a pocket for each plant and fill it with water. Set the plant carefully into the hole and firm the soil around the base. If plants have been grown in fibre pots, remove the paper from the outside of the root system before setting the plant in the prepared hole. If plants have been started in peat pots, set the entire pot in each planting hole. The peat pot will break down in the soil and improve it. Avoid covering the lower leaves with soil. An exception to this rule is tomato plants: remove about a third of each plant's lower leaves and bury the plants 5 to 8 cm (2–3 inches) deep in a horizontal position. In a few days they will straighten toward the sun, and a more vigorous root system will develop. Soak the soil around the roots with a rooting hormone and water mixture. Leave a small depression around the plant base to retain water.

If you selected your seedlings from a garden centre or nursery, transplant them to the garden in the same manner as those raised indoors at home.

Grafting

Grafting is a method of propagation in which a piece of one plant is transferred to another and eventually becomes a part of it.

Grafting is useful in the propagation of plants that fail to grow well on their own root system. Grafting may also improve the form and colour of flowers and alter the growth habits of the plant by producing dwarf or weeping varieties.

Home gardeners with limited space for fruit trees can develop an "orchard" of considerable variety by grafting several varieties on to 2 or 3 trees. Grafts make it possible to grow as many varieties of a particular fruit, such as pears, apples, peaches, plums, cherries or apricots, as there are branches on the tree.

Grafting is also useful on ornamentals such as dogwood, rose, quince, lilac and pyracantha.

For the graft to be successful, the transferred part, called a *scion*, must be taken from a plant that is a close botanical relation to the rooted section, or *stock*. A pome fruit such as an apple will unite with other apples, and a stone fruit such as a peach will grow on a peach, plum, almond, cherry, apricot or other stone fruit. However, a pome fruit will not unite with a stone fruit.

The scion, usually a bud or twig, is taken from the plant to be propagated and it becomes the top part of the new plant. The stock may be only the root of a plant, or it may include the tree framework.

The main objective of grafting is to bring together the *cambium*, that thin layer of cells between the outer sapwood and the inner bark, of the stock and the scions so that a strong union takes place. The growing tissues of the scion and stock must be flush or in close contact for the parts to unite.

Simple or whip grafts are used to expand small shrubs or trees. They are successful in either winter or early spring. A section of 1-year-old growth about the thickness of a pencil is diagonally cut into sections, each of which contains 3 to 5 growth buds, with a razor sharp knife. A long, sloping cut is made on a branch or trunk of a tree or shrub at the same thickness as the scion wood. Then the scion is bound closely to the understock: the cambium layers of the two pieces are joined together tightly at all points. Tie or bind the graft with raffia or tape and cover with grafting wax.

Cleft grafting is perhaps the most common method used to change one variety of tree to another. It is the method used to top-graft many fruit or ornamental trees and shrubs. Cleft grafting consists of cutting off the stock, splitting the stump at the cut end and inserting 1 to 2 wedge-shaped scions into the split.

Begin by smoothing the edges of the cambium with a sharp, clean knife, so that it can be seen easily. Place a chisel on the centre of the stump and drive it into the stock 8–10 cm (3–4 inches) with a wooden mallet. Then prepare scions. Choose parts of the previous season's growth, from the outside of the tree where it is vigorous. A scion should be about 12.5–15 cm (5–6 inches) long, and spaces between buds should be about 1 cm (1/2 inch). Cut off the tip of the scion and make a second cut 1 cm (1/2 inch) below the third bud, making a tapering wedge.

Trim 1 or 2 scions and fit them snugly down into the cleft at the outer edges, so the cambium bark of the scions meets that of the understock on the outside. Remove the chisel. Cover the cut area immediately with grafting wax, as exposed grafts invite insects, disease and excessive moisture.

Cleft grafting is most successful with apples and pears, but difficult with plums and cherries and almost impossible with peach trees.

Fruit trees may be changed from variety to variety by **bud grafting**. Budding is usually done during July, August and September. By midsummer the buds have matured and the stocks are in active growth, making the bark peel more easily. The bud sticks are taken from new growth, and only the mature buds are selected for use. The bud, including the stick, should be about 8–10 cm (3–4 inches) long. It is cut in a shield shape, including a thin layer of bark.

Clean the rootstock near ground level. With a sharp knife make a horizontal cut

1.2–2 cm (1/2–3/4 inch) through the bark, but not deep enough to enter the wood. Then make a perpendicular cut about 2.5 cm (1 inch) long from the centre of the first cut, making a T shape. Very carefully lift up the right-angled corners and insert the shield-shaped bud. Slip the shield-bearing bud into the incision on the understock. Tie in place with raffia or an elastic band. When the graft is set into place and secured, all the surfaces including the tip end must be covered with grafting wax.

Taking Cuttings

The wonder of watching part of a plant take root and grow into an entirely new plant is one of the gardener's great satisfactions. Cuttings have the same characteristics as the parent plant. Working with cuttings is an especially good way of propagating hybrids and desirable forms of plant species, as they are not likely to reproduce true from seed.

Plants reproduce from **stem cuttings** most readily in summer. They have finished their exuberant spring advance and any new foliage is beginning to mature. The time to take cuttings is when the new shoots of the present season's growth are brittle, and snap when bent.

Summer flowering plants such as fuchsia, carnation, delphinium, chrysanthemum and many houseplants may be propagated in summer from cuttings.

Woody ornamental plants that root and grow readily from cuttings include arborvitae, evergreen azalea, barberry, cotoneaster, euonymus, mahonia, osmanthus, pieris, heather, forsythia, daphne, yew, juniper, holly, rhododendron, camellia, ginkgo, tamarix, liquidamber, photinia, pernettya, gaultheria, hypericum, ceanothus, ivy, jasmine, honeysuckle, wisteria, passion flower and hydrangea.

Take softwood stem cuttings in the early morning, from mature plants that are healthy, vigorous and well branched. Brittle shoots or slips that snap when bent are best for cutting material. Select stem cuttings from lateral shoots with a small section of the previous year's growth attached, if possible.

Stem cuttings vary in length, depending on the plant. Generally a cutting is 5–20 cm (2–8 inches) long, with at least two or three leaf nodes or joints.

Make cuttings with a sharp, clean razor blade or knife. Dip the cutting tool in a disinfectant before using.

Make the cut just below a leaf node or joint. Remove the lower leaves from the cutting and allow one or two leaves to remain at the top. If the leaves are large, as with rhododendrons, cut the leaf about halfway across, at an angle. This makes it easier for the cutting to support the leaf and develop roots at the same time.

Encourage the growth of roots by dipping the cut end in a hormone rooting powder containing indolebutyric acid. Root the cuttings in a mixture of half peat moss and half sand, or in either vermiculite or perlite. Water the planting thoroughly before the cuttings are inserted. Insert the cutting into the rooting mixture so that it stands erect with 1 to 2 nodes buried. Press the soil down around the cutting after it is planted.

Plant the cuttings far enough apart to accommodate the size and spread of the leaves: 5 cm (2 inches) between cuttings and 8 cm (3 inches) between rows is usually adequate. Water the planting thoroughly once more.

Enclose the entire planting inside a clear plastic bag and fasten tightly. The rooting medium should be kept moist, but the cuttings should not require watering until after they are well rooted. The plastic bag forms a miniature greenhouse that is vapourproof. Place the bagged cuttings in a bright spot but out of direct sunlight. Keep the planting at 16–21°C (60–70°F).

Cuttings of most plants will root within 2 months. Success is indicated by new top growth and a well-developed root system. If cuttings fail to root, the top will turn brown, then black.

When the cuttings have rooted, lift the new plants from the starting medium and plant in a fibrous loam and sand mixture in individual containers or out in the garden in a permanent place.

Root cuttings offer a means of propagating some trees, shrubs and plants that produce root suckers or a heavy tuberous root, including Oriental poppy, pernettya, sumac and some barberries and lilacs.

Lift the plants from the soil and cut the roots into sections with a sharp spade. Sections or cuttings should be about 6–20 mm ($1/4$–$3/4$ inch) in diameter and 10–15 cm (4–6 inches) long. Plant the cuttings immediately in a fine sandy soil and keep the planting moist. Generally a number of shoots develop from one root cutting. When they are 2.5–5 cm (1–2 inches) high, thin until only one plant remains in each space.

Many varieties of ornamentals, fruit trees and berry canes are propagated by **hardwood cuttings** taken in late autumn when the plants are dormant. Grape, forsythia, holly, viburnum, currant, hydrangea, weigela, mock orange and many other deciduous shrubs and trees are easily reproduced by this method.

Select only healthy, vigorous stock as a source of cutting material. Make a clean, slightly diagonal cut just above a bud at the tip and just below a bud at the bottom of each cutting to yield a 23 cm (9-inch) long cutting of the twig or branch with a portion of the older wood at the base. Wood with long joints, such as grape, should be cut to include at least two growth points or buds. Cuttings of most plants will be about the thickness of a pencil.

After making the cuttings, tie them in bundles of ten cuttings or so, with the lower or butt ends even and the cuttings facing in the same direction.

Bury them outdoors in a light sandy soil, below the frost line, about 60 cm (2 ft) deep. Place them in the ground in a vertical or slightly horizontal position.

By spring a callus will have formed on the ends of the cuttings. Take up the bundles and plant each cutting in the garden individually. Plant the cuttings deeply, almost to their entire length, in sandy soil in dappled shade. New plants soon will form that can be planted in their permanent places.

Cuttings Through the Year

(H) = Hardwood cuttings, (R) = Root cuttings, * = Difficult subjects, small percentage of success, (G) = Greenhouse subjects (tender tropical plants that need warm, humid conditions year-round). All others are softwood cuttings.

January

Abies (fir); *Acacia* (mimosa); *Andromeda polifolia* (H) (bog rosemary); *Arbutus unedo* (H) (strawberry tree); *Arctostaphylos* (H) (manzanita); *Aucuba* (H) (spotted laurel); *Callicarpa* (H) (beauty-berry); *Calluna* (H) (heather); *Cassiope* (H) (white heather); *Chamaecyparis* (cypress); cotoneaster (H); deutzia (H); *Drimys* (G) (winter's bark); *Elaeagnus* (H) (Russian olive); forsythia (H); *Ilex* (H) (holly); *Juniperus*; *Kalmia* (H) (mountain laurel); leucothoe (H) (lily-of-the-valley); *Lonicera* (H) (honeysuckle); *Osmanthus* (H) (butcher's broom); *Pernettya* (H) (prickly heath); *Picea* (spruce); *Pieris* (H); *Pinus* (pine); *Rhododendron laponicum* (H); *Sciadopitys* (umbrella pine); *Taxus* (H) (yew); *Thuja* (arborvitae); *Tsuga* (hemlock).

February

Arctostaphylos (H); *Aucuba* (H); *Calluna* (H); *Cassiope* (H); *Chamaecyparis*; *Erica* (H) (heath); fuchsia (H); *Garrya elliptica* (H) (silk tassel); *Hydrangea macrophylla* (H); *Juniperus*; *Osmanthus* (H); *Picea*; *Pseudotsuga menziesii* (Douglas fir); *Tsuga*.

March

Caryopteris (H), (blue beard); *Cassiope* (H); *Chamaecyparis; Juniperus; Tsuga*.

April

Androsace lanuginosa (rock jasmine); *Caryopteris* (H); *Cassiope* (H); *Daboecia* (H) (heath); *Hedera* (ivy); *Lippia* (lemon verbena); *Lonicera* (H); *Syringa* (lilac) (immediately after flowering); *Vaccinium* (H) (huckleberry); yucca (lift plants and remove toes or small buds at base of stem and rhizomes; dip into dry wood ashes to stop bleeding).

May

Calluna; Daboecia; Enkianthus; Erica; Exochorda (pearlbush); forsythia; fuchsia; *Halesia* (silver bell); *Hydrangea petiolaris; Jacobinia* (G) (shrimp plant); *Lagerstroemia* (crape myrtle); *Menispermum* (moonseed); *Myrica* (Pacific wax myrtle); *Osmarea* (x *Osmanthus*); Paulownia (R) (Empress tree); penstemon; prunus (cherry); *Rhodotypos* (white kerria); *Sarcococca; Ulmus* (elm).

June

Acacia; Acer (maple); *Actinidia* (kiwi); *Andromeda polifolia*; azalea; *Callicarpa; Callistemon* (bottlebrush); camellia; *Caryopteris; Cercidiphyllum* (katsura tree)*; *Cercis* *canadensis* (redbud); *Chimonanthus* (winter sweet); clematis; *Clethra* (sweet pepper bush); *Cornus* (dogwood); *Corylopsis* (witch hazel); cotoneaster; *Davidia* (dove tree); *Deutzia; Enkianthus; Erica; Exochorda;* forsythia; fothergilla; fuchsia; *Gaultheria shallon* (salal); *Ginkgo* (maidenhair tree); *Halesia; Hamamelis** (witch hazel); *Heliotropium* (heliotrope); *Hydrangea petiolaris; Hypericum* (St. John's wort); *Hyssopus* (hyssop); *Kerria* (Japanese rose); *Lagerstroemia; Leucothoe; Lonicera; Malus* (crabapple); *Menispermum; Myrica; Osmanthus* (Sweet olive); *Penstemon; Pieris; Potentilla* (cinque-foil); *Prunus; Punica* (pomegranate); rhododendron (small-leafed and very early blooming forms); *Rhodotypos; Rhus cotinus* (smoke tree); *Ribes* (currant-gooseberry); *Salix* (willow); *Sambucus* (elderberry); *Sarcococca; Spiraea* (bridal wreath); *Stewartia; Styrax* (Japanese snowbell); *Tamarix* (tamarisk); *Thuja orientalis; Tilia* (linden); *Ulmus; Vaccinium; Viburnum* (snowball bush); *Weigela.*

July

Abelia; Actinidia; Abutilon (G) (flowering maple); *Acacia; Acer; Ampelopsis* (blueberry climber); *Andromeda polifolia; Arctostaphylos;* azalea; *Berberis; Buddleia* (butterfly bush); *Calluna; Calycanthus* (spice bush); camellia; *Campsis* (trumpet vine); *Ceonothus; Celastrus* (bittersweet); *Ceratostigma* (G) (plumbago); *Cercis canadensis; Chaenomelis* (quince); *Choisya* (Mexican orange); clematis; *Clethra; Cornus; Corylus* (filbert); *Corylopsis;* daphne; *Davidia; Deutzia; Empetrum* (crowberry); *Erica; Escallonia; Eucryphia; Euonymus* (spindle tree); *Eurya;* forsythia; *Fothergilla; Franklinia* (Franklin tree); fuchsia; *Garrya; Gaultheria procumbens* (wintergreen); *Genista* (*Cytisus*: Halesia snowdrop tree); *Hamamelis; Hedera; Helianthemum* (sunrose); *Hoheria* (New Zealand lacebark); hydrangea; *Hyssopus; Ilex; Jasminum; Kalmiopsis; Kadsura* (scarlet vine); *Kerria; Kolkwitzia* (beauty bush); *Laburnum* (golden chain tree); *Lavandula* (lavender); *Ledum* (Labrador tea); *Leiophyllum* (sand myrtle); *Leucothoe; Ligustrum* (privet); *Liquidambar* (sweet gum); *Lithospermum* (use soft young shoots); *Lonicera; Loropetalum;* magnolia; *Mahonia* (Oregon grape); *Nandina* (heavenly bamboo); *Nothofagus* (not a true beech); *Olea* (olive); *Olearia* (tree aster); *Osmanthus* (holly olive); *Oxydendrum* (sourwood); *Pachistima* (Oregon boxwood); *Pachysandra* (Japanese spurge); *Passiflora* (passion vine); *Pelargonium; Penstemon; Periploca* (silk vine); *Pernettya; Philadelphus* (mock orange); *Phlomis* (Jerusalem sage); *Photinia; Phyllodoce* (mountain heath); *Pieris; Pittosporum; Potentilla; Punica;* rhododendron (small-leafed); *Rhodotypos* (jetbead); *Rhus; Ribes; Rosa* (right after blooming); *Silix; Sarcococca; Senecio; Spiraea; Stachyurus; Stewartia; Styrax; Stranvaesia; Symplocos* (sapphire berry); *Ternstroemia; Teucrium* (G) (germander); *Trochodendron* (wheel tree); *Umbellularia* (California laurel); *Vaccinium; Veronica; Viburnum* (evergreen and deciduous); *Vitex* (chaste tree); *Vitis* (grape); *Weigela;* wisteria.

Getting Started

August

Abelia; *Abutilon*; *Andromeda*; *Arctostaphylos*; azalea (evergreen); *Berberis*; *Bruckenthalia* (close to erica); *Buddleia*; *Buxus* (boxwood); *Calluna*; *Camellia* (*japonica* and *sinensis*); *Campsis*; *Caragana* (pea tree); *Carpenteria* (bush anemone); *Cassiope*; *Ceanothus*; *Chimonanthus* (fringe tree); *Choisya*; *Cistus* (rockrose); *Clethra* (white alder); *Colutea* (senna); *Cryptomeria* (Japanese cedar); *Cupressus* (cypress); *Cytisus*; daphne; *Davidia*; *Epigaea repens* (trailing arbutus); *Escallonia*; *Eucryphia*; *Euonymus*; *Eurya*; *Fabiana* (G) (heath-like); *Fatsia* (aralia); forsythia; *Franklinia*; *Garrya*; *Gaultheria*; *Genista*; *Gordonia*; *Halesia*; *Halimium* (helianthemum); *Hebe* (veronica); *Hoheria*; hydrangea; *Ilex* (holly leaf sweetspire); *Jasminum*; *Kadsura*; *Kalmia*; *Kerria*; *Kolkwitzia*; *Lavandula*; *Lavatera*; *Laurus* (bay); *Ledum*; *Leptospermum* (tea tree); *Leucothoe*; *Libocedrus* (incense cedar); *Ligustrum*; *Liquidambar*; *Loropetalum*; magnolia; *Mahonia*: *Metasequoia*; *Myrica*; *Nandina* (early August); *Nothofagus*; *Olea* (G); *Osmanthus*; *Pachistima*; *Pachysandra*; *Parrotia*; *Pelargonium*; *Penstemon*; *Pernettya*; *Philadelphus*; *Phlomis*; *Photinia*; *Pieris*; *Pittosporum*; *Podocarpus* (fern pine); *Potentilla*; *Pyracantha*; *Quercus* (evergreen only, use half-ripe wood growth with thin heel of old wood); *Raphiolepis* (India hawthorn); rhododendron (medium-leafed); *Rhus*; *Sarcococca*; *Sciadopitys*; *Schizophragma* (vine hydrangea); *Senecio*; *Skimmia*; *Sophora* (Japanese pagoda tree); *Sorbaria* (false spirea); *Stranvaesia*; *Ternstroemia*; *Tsuga*; *Umbellularia*; *Vaccinium*; *Veronica*; *Viburnum*; *Vitex*; *Vitis*; *Weigela*; *Zenobia* (related-heath-heather).

September

Ampelopsis; *Andromeda*; *Arbutus unedo*; *Arctostaphylos*; *Artemisia* (wormwood); *Aucuba*; azalea (evergreen); *Benzoin* (spicebush); *Buxus*; *Calluna*; *Camellia japonica*; *Cassiope*; *Ceanothus*; *Cistus*; *Colutea*; *Cryptomeria*; *Cupressus*; *Davidia*; *Epigaea repens*; *Escallonia*; *Euonymus*; *Felicia* (blue marguerite); forsythia; *Gaultheria*; *Genista pilosa*; *Halimium*; *Halimiocistus* (X-cistus); *Hebe*; *Helianthemum*; *Hoheria*; *Ilex* (hollyleaf sweetspire); *Itea*; *Kerria*; *Laurus nobilis*; *Lavandula*; *Ledum*; *Leiophyllum*, *Metasequoia*; *Morus* (mulberry); *Olea*; *Osmanthus*; *Pachistima*; *Penstemon*; *Pernettya*; *Photinia*, *Picea*; *Pieris*; *Pimelea prostrata* (related to daphne); *Potentilla*; *Pyracantha*; rhododendron (medium- and large-leafed); *Rosmarinus* (rosemary); *Salvia* (sage); *Sarcococca*; *Skimmia*; *Sophora*; *Stranvaesia*; *Taxus*; *Ternstroemia*; *Tsuga*; *Vaccinium*; *Veronica*; *Viburnum*; *Vitis*.

October

Andromeda; *Arbutus unedo*; *Arctostaphylos*; *Aucuba*; *Benzoin* (H); *Berberis* (H); *Buddleia* (H); *Callicarpa*; *Callistemon*; *Calluna*; *Camellia japonica*; *Chamaecyparis*; *Choisya*; *Cistus*; cotoneaster; *Cytisus*; *Daboecia*; daphne; *Dimorphotheca* (cape marigold); *Erica*; *Escallonia*; *Eurya*; *Euonymus*; *Felicia*; *Fuchsia*; *Gaultheria*; *Genista*; *Halimiocistus*; *Helianthemum*; *Hypericum*; *Ilex*; *Juniperus*; *Kalmiopsis leachiana* (rhododendron relative); *Kerria* (H); *Lavandula*; *Laurus*; *Leptospermum*; *Lonicera*; *Lycium* (matrimony vine); *Morus*; *Muehlenbeckia* (wire vine); *Osmanthus*; *Pachistima*; *Pachysandra*; *Paulownia*; *Pernettya*; *Phillyrea*; *Photinia* (H); *Phygelia capensis* (cape fuchsia); *Picea**; *Pieris*; *Pimelea*; *Pyracantha*; *Raphiolepis*; rhododendron (medium- and large-leafed); *Ribes*; *Rosa*; *Rosmarinus*; *Salvia*; *Sarcococca*; *Skimmia*; *Sophora*; *Stranvaesia*; *Taxus*; *Ternstroemia*; *Tsuga*; *Vaccinium*; *Veronica*; *Viburnum*; *Vinca*.

November

Abelia; *Arbutus unedo*; *Arctostaphylos*; *Aucuba*; *Benzoin*; *Berberis*; *Buddleia*; *Calluna*; *Camellia sasanqua*; *Cassiope*; *Cedrus libani*; *Ceanothus*; *Chamaecyparis*; cotoneaster; *Cytisus*; *Daboecia*; daphne; *Deutzia* (H); *Drimys*; *Elaeagnus*; *Erica*; *Escallonia*; *Euonymus*; *Garrya* (H); *Gaultheria*; *Hebe*; *Hedera*; *Hypericum*; *Ilex*; *Jasminum* (H); *Juniperus*; *Kalmia* (H); *Kerria* (H); *Laburnum*; *Laurus*; *Leiophyllum*; *Ligustrum* (H); *Lonicera*; *Loropetalum* (H); *Nandina* (H); *Nothofagus* (H); *Osmanthus* (H); *Pernettya* (H); *Photinia* (H); *Picea**; *Populus* (H) (poplar); *Ribes* (H); *Rosa* (H); *Salvia*; *Sarcococca* (H); *Skimmia* (H); *Sophora* (H); *Stranvaesia* (H); *Taxus*; *Ternstroemia* (H); *Tsuga*.

December

Abies; *Acacia* (R); *Aesculus* (R) (horse chestnut); *Ailanthus* (R) (tree of heaven); *Aralia* (R); *Arbutus unedo* (H); *Arctostaphylos* (H); *Aucuba* (H); *Calluna* (H); *Camellia sasanqua* (H); *Cassiope* (H); *Catalpa* (R) (Indian bean); *Cedrus libani*; *Celastrus* (R); *Chamaecyparis*; cotoneaster (H); *Dendromecon* (R) (poppy tree); *Drimys* (H); forsythia (H); *Ilex* (H); *Jasminum* (H); *Juniperus*; *Koelreuteria* (H); laburnum (H); *Laurus nobilis* (H); *Ligustrum* (H); *Lonicera* (H); *Nandina* (H); *Paulownia* (R); *Philadelphus* (H); *Picea**; *Pinus**; *Platanus* (H) (sycamore); *Polygonum* (H) (knotweed); *Populus* (H); *Rhododendron lapponicum* (H) (Lapland rhododendron); *Rhus* (R); *Romneya* (matilija poppy) (R): *Rosa* (H); *Rubus* (R); *Salvia*; *Sciadopitys* (H); *Spiraea* (H); *Tamarix* (H); *Taxus* (H); *Thuja*; *Tsuga*; *Vitex* (H).

Layering

Layering is a simple and dependable method of plant propagation. Plants multiply in nature when low-growing branches lying on the ground get covered with fallen leaves and soil and take root. Essentially the difference between layering and a cutting is that the layering remains attached to the parent plant until it is rooted. Cuttings are severed from the plant at the outset.

Layering is best done in early summer. The first step is to prepare the soil around the base of the parent plant. Work compost and other organic material into the soil. This aids the development of a healthy root system on the branch to be placed in contact with the soil.

Common methods of layering are mound layering, tip layering, trench layering and air layering. **Mound layering** is done by heaping soil over the lower plant stems.

Forsythia, lilac and quince are easily propagated by mound layering. Mound layering is done in late spring and early summer. Lightly scar the bark of the stems that are to be under the soil and prepare a mounding soil containing peat moss and sand. Prune the parent plant severely of top and side growth. Then mound soil around the parent plant to about a third of its total height.

Tip layering, which consists of holding down long, curving tips with rooting soil, is useful on plants that have long, flexible, drooping branches, such as raspberry, climbing rose and pyracantha.

In early summer, select desirable branches and bend them to the ground. At a point 15–30 cm (6–12 inches) from their tips, scar or ring the bark of each branch. Then lodge the scarred portion a few inches under the rooting soil. Allow the tip to protrude from the soil a few inches. By the following fall, most branches will have formed roots. Sever the rooted branches from the main plant and set them out on their own. Several branches may be rooted from one plant at the same time.

Trench layering is done by laying long branches in trenches, then covering them with soil until roots form and new shoots start to grow. Use this method on plants with long, slender, flexible stems, especially grape, blackberry, dwarf pear, willow and viburnum. In midsummer, strip all the leaves from long branches that are to be rooted, except a few at the tip. Then scar the bark lightly on the branch in two or three places where leaves were pulled off.

Lay the branch in an open, shallow trench about 15 cm (6 inches) deep. With wire holders, fasten the branch in the trench in the shape of a large hairpin. Cover the branch with 8–10 cm (3–4 inches) of sandy soil, leaving the tip of the branch exposed. Roots usually form at the base of the branch along where the bark was scarred. When roots have formed, carefully uncover the entire branch. Cut the individual plants from it and plant them on their own.

Air layering will produce roots on a growing stalk or stem of a parent plant. It is done by slitting or scarring the bark of a stalk or branch, wrapping the scar with moist moss and enclosing the operation in plastic.

Indoor foliage plants such as dieffenbachia, or rubber plants that become too tall and leggy, are made more decorative by air layering. Many garden plants such as rhododendron are increased by air layering. Hybrid tea roses whose top growth is grafted on stronger root systems will not air layer successfully.

To air layer, remove the leaves and twigs along a 10 cm (4-inch) section of stalk or branch, some 30–38 cm (12–15 inches) from its tip. Peel off or scar a 1.3–2.5 cm (1/2–1-inch) ring of bark in the middle of the defoliated section down through the cambium, which is the light green layer just under the outside bark. Rub the scarred part with a root-inducing hormone powder. Wrap a handful of wet sphagnum or woods moss over the cut area and tie it around the stem with soft string. Cover the moss tightly with plastic wrap. In 2 or 3 weeks, most plants will form roots, which can be seen through the plastic. Once the roots have formed, cut the new plant from the parent, just below the new ball of roots. Plant it out on its own.

Hybridizing Plants

A rose is a rose is a rose—until a creative gardener comes along and improves it by hybridization. In the plant world, hybrids are crosses between selected parents of different varieties. The outcome is unpredictable, yet often rewarding.

Hybridizing consists of taking pollen from one flower and placing it on the stigma of another flower. The seeds that result from the cross occasionally produce plants that are superior to the parents.

The gardener who wishes to play the role of the bee must select suitable parents for the cross. Parents are chosen according to what is desirable: the female rose parent determines the strength and vigour of the plant, while the male parent brings in colour, fragrance and form of the bloom. Widely different plants will not cross with each other. Crosses between two different genera are rare. Even two plants of the same species sometimes fail to cross. They are known as cross-sterile plants.

Plants such as pines may have male flowers in one place on the tree and the female elsewhere on the same tree. This type of plant is known as monoecious. When a plant has all its reproductive organs in one flower, as in a rose, it is called perfect.

The stamens, the male part of the bloom, carry the pollen. The stigmas, or tips of the pistils, in the centre of the bloom, are the female part. They receive the pollen.

Timing is important. Hybridize on a dry, calm, sunny day. The pollen from the flower can be days or weeks old, but the flower that the pollen is placed on should be newly opened, with the stigma just mature enough to be receptive.

To prevent self-pollination, remove the stamens from the flower you have chosen as the mother. Prevent wind or bees from taking other pollen to the mother by covering the bloom with a plastic or paper bag. Leave the bag over the operation until the stigma is receptive: it appears moist, sticky and expanded when ready for the pollen. At this point, take pollen from the flower selected as the male parent and transfer it to the stigma of the mother.

The pollen germinates on the stigma and works its way down to the ovules, which form the seed. You will know that fertilization has been successful when the seed receptacle becomes swollen as the seed grows.

Rose hybridization is simple and affords a good example of the hybridization process. Work in late July. First take male pollen from the rose blooms not fully opened. Remove the petals; then, with a sharp knife, cut off the anthers, which are found around the rim of the bud (they produce pollen). Place the anthers in a shallow container with the pollen and keep covered in a warm, dry place, until dry.

Select a bloom on the mother plant that has just begun to open, yet whose bud is too tight to allow the entrance of bees or other insects. Remove petals, sepals and anthers of the maternal bloom, leaving only the pistils. Leaving the stripped flower on the plant, dip or dust it in the dry pollen in the container. Cover the pollinated flower with a plastic or paper bag. Make pin-sized holes in the bag to allow air circulation.

In early October, remove the rose hips from the plant that was hybridized. Keep the hips in a cool, well-ventilated place until the end of December. Then open them, wash them in cool water and extract the seeds.

Place the seeds in cool water, and discard any seeds that float. Seeds that sink are ready for planting. Plant the rose seeds indoors in a sunny window or warm greenhouse. In spring, tiny plants appear. Then in midsummer a few will show flowers. This is the time of great expectations for the hybridizer.

Big Mac

Coast gardeners cherish ripe, red cherries from their own trees. So do raccoons, deer, crows and robins. Lots of experts and just plain folks recommend covering the entire tree in discarded fish nets, to discourage the critters.

My husband Al and I scrounged around for fish nets, poles, ladders and ropes to do the job, sharing the orchard with our herd of cattle. Bovines are curious creatures, and our prize bull, Big Mac, rushed right over to inspect the project. Immediately he put down his horns and became entangled in the net. Big Mac was a free spirit: he resented gates, fences—and now fish nets. He thrashed, snarled and snorted to try to release his horns from the net. The harder he struggled, the more entangled he became. His harem of cows soon circled about in wonderment. Big Mac was a proud fellow. He resented being caught by a fish net, and he was furious.

In fact, he was out of control—a raging spectacle. Al came down from the ladder and yelled at me to get some tranquilizer pellets the veterinarian had given us for emergencies.

I left the panic area in a full run, reached the barn, hastily threw some pellets into a bucket with some grain, and ran back, weaving my way among the onlookers—cows, sheep, dogs, and even a few crows that were circling overhead.

Al grabbed the bucket and dropped it in front of Big Mac, who slurped up the lot. Al asked me how many tranquilizer pellets I had put in.

"I'm not sure," I said. "Just a handful or two, I think."

"Oh my God," said Al.

Then we both watched as Big Mac's eyes began to roll around in all directions, then to close. His knees sagged and he fell to the ground. Now he was ours. We both began to untangle the net from his horns, as the animal audience lost interest and took off for better pastures. We watched over our bull all afternoon while he slept. The tree was unnetted, and all shared the ripe, red, juicy cherries.

Vegetables, Herbs and Fruits

WEST COAST GARDENERS OFTEN ENVY THEIR EASTERN COUNTERPARTS for consistently hot summers; on the other hand, eastern gardeners often envy west coasters for their long growing season. Coastal gardens produce bountifully in spring, summer and fall. And provided with cold frames, clear plastic shelters or unheated greenhouses, the same gardens can produce in winter as well. A year-round growing season is the West Coast gardener's greatest advantage.

Jim and Pam Gordon's leaf lettuce. Bob Cain photo

Veggie garden. Mary Palmer photo

But the coastal grower must also make full use of what sunshine there is. Gardens should be located to get the fullest sun exposure—away from trees, tall shrubs or buildings. The garden should also be on high ground, because an excess of water in the spring keeps the ground cool and delays seeding. At the same time, the garden should be sheltered from wind. Gardeners in some blustery coastal areas joke that their plots are subjected to such gusts that even carrots must be staked. If those prerequisites—exposure and protection—sound exclusive, that's because they are exclusive. In almost any kind of gardening, finding the best location is a matter of balancing divergent needs.

Vegetables

When it comes to soil, any plot can become a vegetable garden. Some soils require more work than others. If the vegetable garden site is on bare earth, add aged manure, peat or compost. If the site is on sod, remove the sod in cubes and reuse it as lawn elsewhere, or stack the clods grass side down, let them decompose, then add aged manure, peat or compost to the recently exposed soil. It can take several years to amend heavy clay coastal soils and make them friable.

Once established, a vegetable garden requires an annual boost of organic materials and fertilizers. Aged manure and other organic material such as peat moss, compost, ground bark or old sawdust should be spread evenly over the garden. Then rake in a 5-10-10 fertilizer applied at a rate of 1.3 kg (3 lbs) for every 18 m² (200 sq ft) of seed bed. If a good rain does not follow the fertilizer, water deeply. The end result is a healthy, nutrient-rich soil that is ready to seed.

To determine if the garden soil is ready for early spring seeding, squeeze a handful of soil tightly into a ball and break it apart with your fingers. If the earth stays in a tight ball it is still too wet; if it crumbles it is ready.

Before you plant, make a garden plan so that tall plants will not end up shading smaller plants in the vegetable garden. Arrange the garden so that corn, sunflowers, pole beans and other tall species do not cast shadows over such smaller sun-loving crops as tomatoes and cucumbers. Using the same plan can help keep the soil producing for as long as possible in the season, and over the years. As soon as the early crops are harvested, plant more seeds in their place. For example, some early peas mature in 70 days. When they are finished, plant late beets, turnips, beans or spinach in their place. The garden will also benefit if crops are rotated; that is, don't grow the same type of plant in the same place year after year. Soil nutrients can become unbalanced and certain soil-dwelling pests can build up.

Many seeds come with detailed planting instructions. As a general rule, seed is planted to a depth about 3 times its diameter. Avoid the common mistake of planting seeds too deep. After planting, firm the soil well with a board, brick or the back of a flat hoe.

If young seedlings get too crowded they need to be thinned. And remember, some thinnings such as onions, beets and lettuce may be eaten if you pull them from the row when they are large enough for use.

Artichokes: Globe and Jerusalem

The globe (or French) artichoke is a hardy and decorative perennial vegetable (it stays in the ground season after season). The plant grows 1.5 m (5 ft) high and wide, and resembles a giant thistle. It produces a globe-shaped vegetable and then a spectacular purple flower.

Artichokes require fertile, well-drained soil. Before planting, turn the ground thoroughly and work in generous amounts of organic humus. Add 900 g (2 lbs) of combined blood meal, bone meal and wood ash for each 18 m² (200 sq ft).

Globe artichokes may be started from seed, but this is extremely difficult. Artichokes rarely reproduce true from seed and do not produce a crop for at least 2 years after planting. It is much more common to propagate artichokes from parts of the old plants, in one of two ways: by transplanting sections of rootstocks (called "stumps"), or by planting rooted offshoots from the bases of old plants. Rootstocks produce larger, earlier plants because a number of offshoots are immediately forced. To obtain root sections from an old plant, pull or cut off the base of the stem to secure a planting section several inches in diameter and 15 cm (6 inches) or more in length. The pulpy stock stores nutrients, which are used for new leaf and root growth. Sections of rootstocks or offshoots are often available in the spring at garden centres or nurseries. Or a friendly gardener may be willing to share extras.

Plant the stumps about 15 cm (6 inches) deep, with the tops above the ground. Space the young starts at intervals of 2 m (6 ft) in rows 2.4 m (8 ft) apart.

Artichokes die or do poorly if water freezes around their roots and crowns. Before heavy frosts, cut the plant to ground level and spread decomposed manure liberally over the crowns. Mulch over the planting area heavily with a piece of thick roofing paper or with wire mesh covered with leaves and evergreen boughs, to a depth of 30 cm (1 ft). One foot of insulating material is a minimum. In the spring, after heavy frosts are finished (usually about the middle of April), remove the winter insulation. Then spread near each plant 125 mL (1/2 cup) of a nitrogen fertilizer such as ammonium nitrate, ammonium sulphate or calcium nitrate. If the soil is too acidic, turn into the ground approximately 250 kg (8 oz) of ground limestone for each mature plant.

The portion of the artichoke eaten as a vegetable is the undeveloped flower head. Gather the heads when they are young and in bud. When the flower stems are cut close to the ground, tender shoots will spring up rapidly and may be cooked as greens or eaten fresh like celery, asparagus or chard.

Jerusalem artichoke (also called sunchoke) is not a true artichoke, but a species of sunflower native to North America. Traditionally it was cultivated by Pacific Northwest aboriginal people for its nutritive qualities. The French call it *topinambour*. In Italy it is *girasole*, or sunflower. The pronunciation of *girasole* (je-RAS-o-ly) may be the reason this plant became known as Jerusalem artichoke.

The Jerusalem artichoke can be started like a potato, from cut sections of the tubers. One tuber section planted in the spring will multiply and produce 5 to 8 artichokes.

Prepare the soil as if for potatoes. Dig and work the soil to about 45 cm (18 inches) until it is loose. Incorporate organic humus. Heaps of old straw, ground sawdust or decomposed compost turned into the ground are beneficial. Avoid using manures or lime on the growing soil.

Plant the tubers in a long row against a fence or as a border, as the plants grow over 2.4 m (8 ft) tall in loose, fertile soil. Many gardeners plant the tubers in a trench 30 cm (1 ft) deep in rows 60 cm (2 ft) apart. As you dig the trench, move the topsoil to one side. Use it to cover the shoots as they appear until a hill is formed over the planting.

Water the plants regularly when they are flowering, as they are forming new tubers at the same time. Keep the area weeded well and continue to hill up the planting as it develops.

In late summer the plant begins to bloom, like a small sunflower. In late October, when the flower and stems have dried, dig the artichokes out of the ground and wash away the dirt. (A good blast from a garden hose does the job well.) Dry and store as potatoes, but put a few in the refrigerator, as the chill brings out the delicacy of the flavour.

Jerusalem artichokes are tasty when cut raw for salads, baked in casseroles or steamed and mashed like potatoes. In Chinese dishes they are a good substitute for water chestnuts.

It is not a good idea to leave Jerusalem artichokes in the garden over winter. They may not survive, and if they do, they will multiply too rapidly and become as over-adventurous as a weed.

Asparagus

Asparagus embodies the spirit of spring. Tender, green spears thrust through the frosty ground with gusto. Yet it is also one of the most wholesome, appetizing and versatile of vegetables. If grown near the sea, where kelp, seaweed and wind-blown sea salt get added to the soil, asparagus can be amazingly prolific.

Asparagus is a permanent planting that requires an open sunny area. With good cultivation, asparagus roots will produce spears for up to 15 years. Forty plants will supply a family for one year (fresh, frozen and canned asparagus).

Prepare the planting area thoroughly for the deep-reaching roots. Turn and till the soil at least 45 cm (18 inches) deep. Asparagus requires an alkaline (sweet) soil with a pH reading of 7–8. To the loosened earth, add 1.8 kg (4 lbs) dolomite lime for each 9 m^2 (100 sq ft) of planting area, and work in several inches of seaweed and aged manure. Dig a trench 30 cm (12 inches) deep and 30 cm wide for the roots. In the bottom of the trench, add super phosphate or a complete fertilizer, high in phosphorus, at the rate of 1.8 kg (4 lbs) to 9 m (30 ft) of trench. Cover the fertilizer with 5–8 cm (2–3 inches) of fine, sandy soil.

Select vigorous 2-year-old roots from healthy stock. Place the roots in the trench, 35 cm (14 inches) apart. Fan the roots out well and fill in the trench with prepared soil. Cover the crown (the part where the roots join the top part of the plant) with 5 cm (2 inches) of soil. Remember: better too shallow than too deep!

As the plant grows, add more soil around the tops until the trench is filled in to the level of the surrounding ground. Water the new planting deeply and side dress along the rows with additional organic material such as kelp, seaweed, manure and compost. Keep the young planting fertilized, well watered and weed-free (asparagus enjoys a life of solitude—it resents competition from weeds and other vegetation) to encourage rapid, sturdy growth. As new growth appears in early spring apply a 5-10-5 commercial fertilizer at the rate of 2.3 kg (5 lbs) to each 9 m^2 (100 sq ft) of planting.

Asparagus should not be harvested the first year. Allow the stalks to grow and the plants to establish themselves. In the fall, when the tops have turned brown, cut the foliage. In the second year after planting 2-year-old stock, harvest the spears when they are 15–20 cm (6–8 inches) high and before the branches toward the tips begin to show. Cut the spears with a sharp knife, just below the ground. Continue to gather them for 3 weeks, then allow more shoots to develop. The asparagus harvest season is generally 6 to 8 weeks long. Do not cut top growth after June 20. If you allow the tops to grow and mature, the plant will repay you with years of produce.

Beans: Broad (Fava) or Windsor

One of the earliest vegetables that can be planted outdoors on the coast is the broad or Windsor-type bean. You can seed these beans in October or November, or in early February and March.

In autumn, prepare the soil by digging deeply and filling with organic material such as aged manure and compost. Sow the seed at 23 cm (9-inch) intervals, 7.5 cm (3 inches deep) in rows 45 cm (18 inches) apart. When the plants are in full flower, pinch out the tuft of leaves at the top of each one to discourage blackfly.

Popular broad bean varieties include:

- Witkiem. Matures in 75 days. The earliest of the broad beans. Each long, full pod contains up to 6 large, flat beans that are excellent fresh or frozen.

- Broad Windsor. 240 days. Requires 240 days if overwintering, or 130–150 days if the seed is spring planted. Plants grow to 90 cm (3 ft) in height. Each light green pod produce 6–7 green seeds.

Jim and Pam Gordon's broad beans. Bob Cain photo

Beans: Bush

Bush beans are an excellent source of vitamins A and C and dietary fibre. They are a warm-season crop that requires heat to germinate and set flowers. Beans prefer a sandy loam enriched with organic material. They need mildly acidic soil, so do not seed them on soil that has been limed during the past 2 years. Seed in mid-May to June, when the sun has warmed the soil. If the soil is soggy and cold, the seed will fail. Do not soak seed in water before planting. Sow the seed 2 cm (3/4 inch) deep, and 5–10 cm (2–4 inches) apart.

Bush beans. Mary Palmer photo

Fertilize the planting when the sprouts show 4 to 5 leaves each, and again when pods begin to form. Sprinkle a 5-10-10 fertilizer thinly along the rows or around the hills. Water deeply. Be careful not to overfertilize, or you are likely to get large plants with small sets of pods.

To prevent the spread of plant diseases, avoid cultivating and walking through bean plants in the morning when the dew is on the leaves.

Bean plants require moisture throughout their growing season. They are sensitive to both too much and too little water. Dry conditions will cause pods to drop or shrivel, and wet soil will result in pod drop and stunted plants. Avoid spraying water directly on the leaves, which discourages flowering and encourages disease.

Harvest beans frequently to encourage more to follow. If the pods become too full, the plant will stop producing flowers and pods.

Popular bush bean varieties include:

- Dutch Princess. Matures in 50 days. Flavourful, green stringless pods are especially great for freezing.

- Blue Lagoon. 55 days. Tender, dark green 15 cm (6-inch) pods with a very sweet flavour grow on sturdy, upright plants. Recommended for canning, freezing or cut green beans.

- Jade PvP. 53 days. A heavy-bearing plant, producing extra-long, 17.5 cm (7-inch) pods. Pods are slender and green. The pods remain fresh and crisp for several days after harvesting.

- Mirada PvP. 52 days. Medium-sized, green, round, straight, 15 cm (6-inch) pods appear on strong upright bushes. Very resistant to bean mosaic (a virus causing mottled leaves).

- Horto. 70 days. Great flavour as fresh green beans or dried winter beans (picked when mature). The dried beans are quite showy with red stripes.

- Cannellini. 85 days. Produces gourmet beans that are the mainstay of Tuscany-style minestrone soup and other hearty dishes. Looks like a small white kidney bean.

- Slenderette. Splendid for home gardens and small organic market growers. Slender, dark green stringless 12.5 cm (5-inch) pods on vigorous plants that grow to 50 cm (20 inches). Pods grow on upper half of bush for easy picking.

Beans: Pole

Pole beans love to climb. Grow them beside a high fence or arrange rough poles of fir or alder in a teepee structure that the plants can snake up. Prepare the soil as for bush beans. Plant 5 to 6 seeds around each pole. Water and fertilize as for bush beans.

Popular varieties include:

- Blue Lake. Matures in 70 days. This older variety is excellent for freezing and canning. Stringless green pods about 15 cm (6 inches) long are fleshy and tender. They have white seeds. It is important to keep picking the mature beans to encourage heavy yields.

- Blauhilde. 65 days. A stringless blue pole bean with long, fleshy pods 23 cm (9 inches) long. Beans turn green when cooked.

- Cascade Giant. 70 days. An improved version of the popular northwest bean, the Oregon Giant. Thin, stringless pods 20–30 cm (8–12 inches) long display scarlet and purple stripes.

Blue Lake pole beans. West Coast Seeds photo

- Liana. 90 days. Also called the Oriental Yardlong Asparagus bean. Plant in warm soil with full sun exposure. Delay planting until June 1. The plants produce dark green, flavourful beans up to 90 cm (3 ft) long on tall vines. Pick them when they are as thick as a pencil and gather carefully, as the vines are delicate.

Beets

Beets are grown for early greens, bunch or baby beets, and mature beets. In all cases, quality depends on rapid plant development encouraged by a fertile, moist soil.

Beets are sensitive to soil acidity. Test soil for pH before seeding. If needed, apply lime to the soil at the rate of 1.8 kg (4 lbs) to each 18 m² (200 sq ft). If the soil lacks lime the stems grow pinky-red and the leaves are reddish. Beets thrive in a deeply prepared soil. Turn the soil and work in generous amounts of organic material.

Plant the small seed clusters 2.5 cm (1 inch) deep in rows 45 cm (18 inches) apart. Try not to let the soil dry during root development. After the seedlings develop a few green leaves, add a complete fertilizer low in nitrogen and high in phosphorus and potash. Thin for greens or bunching beets until the plants are 10 cm (4 inches) apart— these will be the main crop. Apply 450 g (1 lb) of fertilizer to each 3–4 m (10–12 ft) of row.

Beet varieties to consider:

- Kestrel F1. Matures in 53 days. Excellent as a baby beet with smooth, round roots and a small crown. Very sweet red roots mature early.

- Early Wonder. 60 days. Produces a semi-globe-shaped red root. Grows quickly in cool spring weather.

- Winterkeeper. 60 days. Produces unusually large round roots. Seed in mid-July for winter keepers. With a covering of mulch, the roots remain healthy in the ground over winter.

- Moneta. Does not produce multiple plants from one seed like other varieties; therefore thinning is not required. Bright green 30 cm (12-inch) leaves; deep, dark red roots.

- Bull's Red. Cooked tops are excellent. Roots are flat globes with alternating red and white zones; the ultimate for adding zest to salads.

Broccoli

Broccoli can be found in home gardens everywhere, yet thirty years ago it was considered a specialist's plant and avoided or ignored by amateur gardeners. Broccoli is high in vitamins and minerals, and it is easy to grow.

Seed broccoli from April through mid-July. A July sowing of late-maturing varieties produces broccoli in late fall. For early spring harvest of overwintering types, purchase plants at the nursery and start transplants in June and July. Space plants at intervals of 40–45 cm (16–18 inches), in rows 90 cm (2 ft) apart. Plant the broccoli in light, sandy soil. Water the plants on the foliage and keep the ground moist.

Broccoli also requires light fertilization. Spread 125 mL (1/2 cup) of a complete fertilizer around each transplant 1 to 2 weeks after the young plant is set out. Avoid the use of fertilizers high in nitrogen, as they encourage hollow stems.

Overwintering plants need the boost of a complete fertilizer in February. Fish meal or liquid 5-10-10 is ideal. Apply 60 mL (1/4 cup) fish meal to the base of each plant, or dilute fertilizer to half strength and apply as per package directions. Space young plants as for summer varieties. Broccoli thrives with ample elbow room.

To harvest, cut off the middle head, leaving as much stalk on the plant as possible. New side shoots will appear at each leaf joint. Maintain a productive plant by keeping the centre heads cut before any yellow flowers appear.

Broccoli: Everest. West Coast Seeds photo

Some popular broccoli varieties:

- Rapini. Transplants mature in 45 days. Does not form a centre head, but produces small florets. Take these when they are young to prevent bolting.

- Everest F1. Transplants mature in 80 days. A mid-early variety with a domed, small-beaded 15 cm (6-inch) head on a 55 cm (22-inch) plant.

- Green Valiant. Transplants mature in 92 days. Develops monstrous, tightly budded green heads, and a very strong root system with many side shoots.

Broccoli: Rosalind. West Coast Seeds photo

Broccoli: Purple Sprouting. West Coast Seeds photo

- Rosalind. Transplants mature in 60–65 days. Purple-tinted heads thrive in the heat of summer, and tolerate cool fall and winter conditions.

- Purple Sprouting. Matures in 220 days from seed. Must overwinter before it can be harvested in March and April. Start seed in mid-July. This variety is easier to cultivate than spring-started plants. Tall plants are filled with sweet-tasting purple shoots, which become green when cooked.

- Windsor. 62 days. A new hybrid with large, heavy blue-green domes and medium-small beads. Resistant to downy mildew, brown bead and head rot.

Cabbage

Cabbage may be started from transplants purchased at the nursery, or seeded directly in the garden. Seed early varieties in succession from late February to July. Seed later crops in early summer for autumn or winter use.

Cabbage responds to a loam soil well supplied with nitrogen, phosphorus, potash, boron, calcium and magnesium. Test the soil and if necessary, supply the calcium and magnesium by using generous amounts of dolomite lime. Add borax to increase boron.

Cabbage seed is sown 6 mm (1/4 inch) deep in rows 75 cm (30 inches) apart. Keep the soil moist at all times. A thin sprinkling of a complete balanced fertilizer with an analysis of 5-l0-10 should be applied every 2 to 3 weeks while the plants are developing. To keep cabbage heads on fast-growing varieties from bursting, twist the tops of the plants to break a few roots when the plant is nearing maturity.

There are dozens of varieties of cabbage, including early, red and autumn or winter varieties. Earlies include:

- Golden Acre. Transplants mature in 70–75 days. An early variety for coast gardens, it also works for fall planting. Oval heads are large and green-leafed.

- Charmant F1. Transplants mature in 60 days. Light green outside leaves and yellow-white interior. Heads are small and tight.

Cabbage: Charmant. West Coast Seeds photo

- Jingan. Transplants mature in 55 days. Jingan produces 900 kg (2-lb) heads of cabbage exceptionally early in the season. Leaves are bright green with a small centre core.

Good red cabbage varieties include:

- Red Express. Transplants mature in 65 days. An early, red compact cabbage. Interior is solid; head is oval and reaches .9–1.3 kg (2–3 lbs).

- Ruby Perfection Hybrid. Transplants mature in 85 days. Firm, dark red head weighs about 2.3 kg (5 lbs).

- Red Rodan. Transplants mature in 140 days. A huge grower, reaching almost 30 cm (1 ft) in diameter. Hard, firm head is tender and flavourful. Overwinters well.

Some autumn and winter cabbages:

- January King. Matures in 60–210 days from seed. Plant in early July. Heads remain unspoiled in the garden until March. Head is flattened with purplish markings on the leaves, to 2.3 kg (5 lbs).

Cabbage: January King. West Coast Seeds photo

- Desmond Hybrid. 95 days from seed. A medium-sized cabbage. Blue-green leaves cover the head, which weighs 1.4–1.8 kg (3–4 lbs).

- Glory of Enkhuizen. 90 days from seed. Prized for kraut making. Large, oval heads have light green leaves.

- Tundra. 180–220 days from seed. A recent introduction from England. When seeded in June and July, it can be harvested from October to April. Withstands severe winters.

Carrots

Carrots, like most root crops, require deep, well-worked soil. The delicate root system will not penetrate soggy, stiff clayey soils: the taproot will not grow well and the hair-like feeder roots will not find enough oxygen. Fine carrots grow in fertile, humus-filled, well-drained sandy loam.

Spade the carrot-growing area at least 25 cm (10 inches) deep when the soil is on the dry side. Break clods and remove rocks. Forking of carrots is caused by the taproot encountering a rock, then splitting to form two branches.

Jim and Pam Gordon's carrots. Bob Cain photo

Plant carrots only when the spring weather has warmed (on the coast, early April is the usual time to seed carrots) and avoid planting when the days are cold and the soil is wet and sticky. Before planting, sprinkle a 5-10-5 fertilizer over the seed bed at the rate of 900–1,350 g (2–3 lbs) to 9 m² (100 sq ft) and water well. Avoid using manures unless they were incorporated into the soil during the previous fall. Fresh manures cause hairy, rough roots with splits. Well-composted humus, aged sawdust, ground bark, peat moss and kelp create an ideal growing medium for carrots.

For a small family, seed a 3 m (10 ft) row and follow it every 3 weeks with another 3 m row for a continuous supply of carrots all summer and fall. Many gardeners seed carrots in late August or early September to avoid insects and diseases. If you do so, cover the planting with several inches of mulch for overwintering.

Maintain an evenly moist seed bed with daily sprinkling from the day the seeds are planted until the carrots are harvested. If possible, water from overhead as this results in better root formation and flavour.

The carrot rust fly is a real pest on the coast. Carrot fly larvae are attracted by the smell of the carrot leaves, so you can prevent some damage by mounding soil over the leaves with only 2.5–5 cm (1–2 inches) showing, or by covering the planting with a floating row cover such as Reemay.

Store carrots in the garden through the winter by covering them with several inches of a mulch of straw.

Mainstay carrot varieties include:

- Autumn King. Matures in 90 days. Sow in August and harvest all winter.

- Danvers Halflong. 65 days. Thrives in heavy soil, producing broad, tapered roots. Thin plants early to give the roots a chance to develop. Carrots keep well in the garden at maturity.

- Flyaway. 75 days. Shows some resistance to the carrot rust fly. Carrots are sweet and crisp.

- Healthmaster F1. 110 days. Contains more vitamin A than most carrots. Great flavour when cooked, served raw or juiced.

- Mignon. 45 days. A baby carrot that keeps its small size in the ground. Bright orange, with a sweet flavour.

- Thumbelina. 55 days. A petite carrot that should be thinned in the row to 30 plants per 30 cm (1 ft). Small and round, and will grow in heavy soils. Favoured by gourmets.

- Canada Gold Harvest. 65 days. Vigorous in growth and uniform in size. Carrots are 23 cm (9 inches) long, deep orange with smooth skin, and store well.

- Vita-Treat. Smooth, long, tapered roots. Has relatively high beta-carotene content.

- Idaho. 78 days. A premium storage root that keeps well through the winter. Strong, stocky carrots, tender with excellent flavour.

Cauliflower

This cool-season vegetable grows well given the right conditions. It needs a fertile, enriched soil filled with organic humus such as aged manure, and it needs regular watering, especially during hot summer days. If soil becomes nutrient-deficient or dry, bolting can occur. Cauliflower must have slow, even growth from seeding to harvest to produce full heads.

Soil pH should be 6.5–7.0. If a recent test shows the soil is more than that, incorporate dolomite lime. If it shows the soil is too alkaline, add cottonseed meal. Apply the neutralizing materials into the soil before seeding or planting transplants. As a rule, soils along the Pacific Northwest coast are slightly acidic and require lime if cauliflower is to thrive.

If your soil is boron-deficient, cauliflower may become bitter and the leaves may grow narrow and turn brown. Correct the deficiency by applying 28 g (1 oz) of borax to 6 m (20 ft) of row.

Seeding may be done as early as January in a cold frame, or in April outdoors. Set out seedlings or transplants in the garden in early May. Plant at 60 cm (2-ft) intervals, in rows 60 cm apart. After the young transplants have been growing for 4 to 5 weeks, a light application of liquid fish fertilizer is needed every 2 weeks until heads form.

Proven cauliflowers include:

- Snow Crown F1. Matures in 50 days from seed. Vigorous and rapid growth produces 900 g (2-lb) heads with large curds of a mild flavour. Long wrapper leaves fold over to protect heads. One of the quickest and easiest of all cauliflowers to grow.

- Ravella F1. Transplants mature in 65–85 days. An import from Holland, great for seeding from early March through June. Produces many snow-white heads. Plants are vigorous and sturdy in cool weather.

- Andes. 65 days from seed. A main-season cauliflower producing large white heads protected with strong wrapper leaves.

- Brocoverde. 75 days from seed. Produces large, dense, lime-green heads that remain green when cooked. Flavour is mild and inviting.

Many gardeners successfully overwinter cauliflower. Overwintering varieties are the slowest to mature: they do not form curds until after the first fall frost. Start from seed in mid-July. Hold back fertilizers until spring. Then give an abundance of fertilizers high in nitrogen, such as fish meal. Place 15 mL (1 tbsp) of fish meal around the base of each plant in late February. Two weeks later apply a complete fertilizer around the plants and water well. Winds on the coast often stress cauliflower. Protect them with a windbreak.

Cauliflower: Purple Cape. West Coast Seeds photo

Two popular varieties of overwintering cauliflowers:

- Purple Cape. Transplants mature in 200 days. Heads are ready in mid-March. Produces sweet, bright purple curds.

- Veitch Autumn Giant. A snow-white type that can be seeded in mid-June. Produces large heads from October to January. August seeding will yield heads from March to May. Plants seeded later in the season produce smaller heads.

Corn

Corn is a great summer and autumn crop on the coast. Start corn outdoors in mid-May. If planted too early it will fail. If early corn is a must, cover the seeded rows with clear plastic and remove the covering just when the seed germinates. Some home gardeners try for early corn by planting the seed indoors in March and transplanting the starts in May, but the results are inconsistent at best.

Plant corn in an open, sunny site. Corn benefits if planted in an area where beans were grown during the previous season, or where a cover crop of alfalfa, clover or other green manure was recently grown.

Dig the ground deep and manure it well. Make a planting furrow 25 cm (10 inches) deep. Add fish meal, wood ash and kelp, cover with organic materials such as humus and compost, then plant the corn. When it is 60 cm (2 ft) high, apply a commercial fertilizer high in nitrogen along the rows.

Most corn requires cross-pollination. Plant seed in blocks of at least 4 or 5 rows of the same variety. Corn is wind-pollinated, so single rows of corn often produce a crop of empty ears. Plant seeds about 25–30 cm (10–12 inches) apart at a depth of 2.5 cm (1 inch) with rows 75 cm (2 1/2 ft) apart. Expect 30 to 36 cobs per 3 m (10 ft) of row.

Keep the patch free of weeds when the corn is young, but avoid cultivating near mature plants: the roots are close to the surface and are damaged easily. To discourage weeds, seed white or ladino clover over the corn patch. The clover will not interfere with the corn crop and may be tilled into the soil later as a green manure.

Corn requires a light daily watering, preferably in the early morning.

The corn is ready for harvest when the tassel at the top of the cob turns brown. It tastes best immediately after picking, when the sugar content is at its highest.

Fine corn varieties include:

- Precocious F1. Matures in 65–75 days. The earliest yellow corn with main-season quality. Ears to 17.5 cm (7 inches), each with 14 to 16 rows of sweet kernels.

- Kandy Kwik Hybrid. 65 days. A variety with sugar-enhanced genes. Early to mature with 17.5 cm (7-inch) cobs, each with 14 to 16 rows of extra-sweet kernels.

- Peaches and Cream Mid Hybrid. 85 days. A bi-colour variety producing sweet kernels on 20 cm (8-inch) cobs of 16 to 18 rows each.

- Super Sweet Hybrid Corn. Do not plant this variety near other varieties of corn that mature at about the same time. Nearby varieties should mature 12 to 15 days before or after the super-sweet types otherwise they will interfere with the sweet flavour of Super Sweet Hybrid Corn by cross-pollination.

- Kandy Corn F1. 89 days. Produces extra-sweet, tender

Jim and Pam Gordon's corn. Bob Cain photo

and juicy ears. Ears to 20 cm (8 inches) long, each filled with 14 to 16 rows of yellow kernels in red striped husks on 2 m (7-ft) stalks.

- B1-Time Hybrid. 78 days. A new generation of bi-coloured super-sweets. Cobs are 23 cm (9 inches long) with 18 rows of kernels.

- Chinook. 80 days. A unique ornamental variety with stunning decorative colours from dark maroon through tan, with shades of red and bronzy orange. Each plant bears 2 ears on the main stalk. Great for holiday decorating.

Kohlrabi

Kohlrabi looks like a turnip growing on a cabbage root. The young tops are used as greens, though it is the white, green or purple bulb—really a swollen stem—that is prized. It tastes somewhat like cauliflower.

Seed and cultivate kohlrabi as for turnips, but you can grow kohlrabi in a dry soil. Like cabbage, kohlrabi needs boron, so test the soil and add borax if necessary. Avoid the use of manures on the growing area.

Plant seed about 8 mm (1/3 inch) deep. Thin the plants to 30 cm (1 ft) with 60 cm (2 ft) between rows. Sow seed from April to June. Harvest the bulb when it is about the size of a tennis ball.

Top kohlrabi varieties include:

- Kolpak. Matures in 50 days. Produces uniform bulbs that are slow to become pithy or fibrous.

- Superschmeltz. 60 days. Very sweet and tender for a giant variety of kohlrabi.

- Purple Vienna. 40 days. An older variety that has bulbs with purplish skin and white inner flesh.

- White Vienna. 42 days. The most commonly grown kohlrabi on the coast. Marked by white outer skin and white flesh.

Lettuce

Lettuce, like other leaf crops, must grow rapidly without a setback in development.

Plant the seed in thoroughly tilled, organically enriched, moist soil. As soon as the soil is workable in early spring, seed lettuce in rows 38 cm (15 inches) apart and thin to 30 cm (12 inches) between heads. Barely cover the fine lettuce seed with light soil, and gently press it down into the seed bed with the back of a hoe. Fertilize along the rows with a high-nitrogen fertilizer every 2 weeks until the plants are 10–12.5 cm (4–5 inches) tall. Keep the soil around the base of the plants evenly moist at all times. Bitterness in the leaves is usually due to fluctuation of water. Seed germinates in 7 to 10 days in spring.

Lettuce seed planted in July and August often fails to germinate due to high temperatures. To solve the problem, soak seeds for 12 to 16 hours in cool water, then air-dry on newspaper for 2 hours before sowing.

There are many varieties of lettuce. Of the butterheads, consider:

- Arctic King. Matures in 4–5 months. Grows successfully in the severest coastal winters. Seed under shelter in September and October; plant matures February through March. Light green outer leaves and a tender, crisp and juicy lime green centre.

- Sangria. 4–5 months. A summer butterhead lettuce that is slow to bolt. Leaves are thick and tipped with rosy-red edges; heart is light green.

- Buttercrunch. 4–5 months. A dark green butterhead type with a showing of yellow inside. Slow to bolt in summer heat.

- Esmeralda. 4–5 months. A new variety. Firm, crisp, light green 450 g (1-lb) heads form on large plants with sturdy bases. Plant is resistant to tip burn, bolting, mildews and mosaic (a virus that causes mottled leaves).

Crisphead (or Batavian) lettuces to watch for:

- Minetto. Transplants mature in 80 days. An early crisp variety with firm heads of dark green.

- Cardinale. 48 days. A new French crisp leaf lettuce. Leaves are thick, dark, brilliant red and curly.

- Sierra. A cut-and-come-again harvesting lettuce. The bright green, densely leaved head is tinged with red.

- Nevada. Deep green upright leaves that do not go brown or wilt when cut. Plant resists bolting, tip burning and mildews. Grows to 25 cm (10 inches) tall.

Leaf lettuce varieties do well in all seasons. Pick leaves each day for salads, or gather whole plants at once. Some top varieties are:

- Simpson Elite. Matures in 45 days. Large, crumpled light green leaves with a tender texture. Slow to bolt.

Jim and Pam Gordon's leaf lettuce. Bob Cain photo

- Grand Rapids. 45 days. Suitable for outdoor seeding; also excellent in greenhouse or cold frame. Curly light green leaves are crowded on the stem.

Oak leaf lettuce has deeply notched leaves with rounded edges. These plants produce best when the leaves are picked daily. Some excellent choices are:

- Royal Oak Leaf. Matures in 45 days. Very productive. Harvest outer leaves continually or the entire plant at once. Leaves are dark green with thick midribs.

- Brunia. 74 days. A deeply lobed French variety with long, slender, red-tinged leaves and a green base. A crisp gourmet lettuce.

- Red Salad Bowl. 50 days. A French variety with large, open heads and deeply lobed brilliant red leaves. Slow to bolt in summer. Keeps its mild, non-bitter flavour even when mature.

Lettuce: Red Salad Bowl. West Coast Seeds photo

- Bionda di Quercia. A new organic with light green leaves, similar to oak leaf varieties. Grow it for salads.

Onions and Their Relatives

Onions are a cool-season crop. Plants grow according to the duration of light and dark periods: the onion top develops until a critical light duration is reached, then it bulbs. The size of the bulb is directly proportional to the size of the top, so the vegetable attains maximum size when the plant is sown as early as possible in spring, after the last hard frosts, and allowed to develop all through the late spring and summer.

Onions love open, sunny growing sites and light, sandy soils enriched with compost and aged manure. Seed them 1 cm (1/2 inch) deep in rows 45 cm (18 inches) apart. As the

Jim and Pam Gordon's onions. Bob Cain photo

young plants grow, side dress the rows every 3 weeks with fertilizers high in nitrogen and potash (10-5-10). Use 225 g ($\frac{1}{2}$ lb) fertilizer for each 3 m (10 ft) of row, and water it well into the soil. Wood ash sprinkled between the rows is beneficial. Thin plants to 7.5 cm (3 inches) apart when the tops are 8–10 cm (3–4 inches) high. Onion roots are shallow and require light, frequent watering in summer. An oversupply or lack of water checks growth; subsequent regrowth encourages the plant to go to seed. Once the plant has bulbed, stop watering.

Green onions can be grown quickly from seed in the early spring. Seed, side-dress and thin green onions as for onions.

For a continuous supply of onions, plant sets, which are grown in furrows about 4 cm (1$\frac{1}{2}$ inches) deep. Press them into the topsoil so only their tips are showing. If both green and mature onions are needed, space the sets 2.5 cm (1 inch) apart. As they grow, pull every other onion as a green onion, leaving the others to mature. One pound of sets will usually yield 13.5–18 kg (30–40 lbs) of onions.

Popular green onion varieties include:

- Yellow Dutch. Matures in 60 days from sets. Sets are highly recommended for both cooking onions and green onions. Stores well over winter.

- Yellow Spanish. 60 days from sets. Sets produce flavourful spring onions.

Multiplier onions, which furnish early spring green onions, are both hardy and perennial. Multipliers generally are planted in September from the top sets or from division of the bunch of onions that develop. They may remain in the vegetable garden all year round. The original bulb splits into many bulbs. Only a few yards of a row are needed in the average home garden for multipliers.

Fine varieties include:

- Egyptian. An excellent multiplier onion, known as the "walking onion" because at maturity the stalk falls over and the bulblets take root and "walk," or spread. Replant the tiny bulblets about 2.5 cm (1 inch) deep. Pull and use as other onions.

- Catawissa. 250 days. A new variety of fine green onion that grows tall with small bulblets on top, which sprout while in mid-air.

Onions for storage such as Copra, First Edition Hybrid and Cardinal Red F1 ripen in early September. When the bulbs are ripe, the tops yellow and fall over. Bend the tops toward the north, which will keep them from shading the bulbs. Scratch away some of the soil from around the tops of the bulbs so they are sitting on the surface, fully exposed to the sun. Insert a garden fork in the soil along one side of the onion and gently lever the fork until the roots on the opposite side are broken. Two weeks later, break the roots on the other side. A week after that, remove the onion from the ground and lay them on wire mesh a few inches above the ground to dry. Remove all foliage but leave the papery wrappers on the bulbs. They contain an enzyme that naturally inhibits sprouting during storage. When the onions have dried outdoors for 10 days, place them in open net sacks and keep in a cool (but not freezing), dry, well-ventilated place.

Some storage varieties are:

- Norstar. A fast and vigorous grower, with white globe-shaped bulbs. May be pulled fresh or stored for a short time in fall.

- Red Wing Hybrid. Deep red exterior and interior rings. Keeps longer than any other red onion.

- Greek Salad Hybrid. Hard, flattened round onion with medium-low pungency and good storage qualities. Developed for salads and prized for its large, red bulbs with thick rings.

- Blanco Duro. Matures in 120 days. Bears large, 10 cm (4-inch) white globe bulbs. Tangy but sweet enough to eat raw.

- Copra. 104 days. Highly recommended for winter storage. Medium sized yellow-skinned onions are sound and flavourful.

- First Edition Hybrid. 105 days. Firm globe-shaped bulbs with pungent, cream-coloured interior flesh. A good storage onion.

Onion: First Edition. West Coast Seeds photo

- Cardinal Red F1. 300 days. Mild flavour with a flattened globe shape. Stores well for several months.

- Walla Walla. 300 days. A huge, mild, sweet Spanish. Seed in August for harvest in late June and early July. May also be sown in spring for fall harvest (spring sowing results in a more pungent taste). Has a short storage life of 2 to 3 months.

Chives

Chives (*Allium schoenoprasum*) are grown for their onion-flavoured leaves and their fluffy, round lilac- or mauve-coloured blossoms. Chives are perennial. Divide and replant mature clumps every 3 to 4 years to renew. Cut tops frequently. Plant bulblets in the early spring or fall. Set them at 20 cm (8-inch) intervals in rows 30 cm (12 inches) apart. Alternatively, you can sow seed outdoors in early spring. Cover the tiny seeds lightly with 1 cm ($1/2$ inch) of sand.

Like other members of the onion family, chives thrive in a sunny site, yet manage to produce well in shadier areas. Give them a light, well-drained, sandy soil enriched with organic humus. Chives require more water and fertilizer than other onion-like plants as they are eager producers of succulent green leaves.

Water the planting deeply every 10 days during dry spells. In early spring, spread a 10-5-5 fertilizer at the rate of 900 g (2 lbs) per 9 m² (100 sq ft) of planting. A fall feeding of organic material such as kelp and manure is beneficial.

Garlic

Garlic (*Allium sativum*) has been a centrepiece of cooking since ancient times. There is even a Talmudic rule that decrees that garlic be used in certain dishes. Ramson, or wild garlic, which grows all over the Gulf Islands, got its name from the ram—an allusion to the plant's strong scent.

Garlic is more exacting in its cultural requirements than onions. Give the plants a place in full sun, and a light, sandy soil. Garlic is planted outdoors between September 1 and March 15. Select bulbs that are large, firm and healthy. Separate the bulb into cloves and discard the centre stem, but leave on the papery skins. Plant each one separately, with the pointed end up, 7.5 cm (3 inches) deep and 7.5 cm apart, in rows 30 cm (1 ft) apart.

When green shoots appear, fertilize the new planting with a 5-10-10 fertilizer, or use organic fertilizers such as blood meal, bone meal or fish meal. Use 1.3 kg (3 lbs) for each 9 m^2 (100 sq ft) of row. As the plant grows, remove any flowering stalks. This forces the plant's energy into growing the bulb. When the tops have ripened or turned brown, and several dry, sunny days are expected, dig the bulbs and allow them to dry outdoors for a few days. For winter storage, hang them in a cool, airy, frost-free location.

Proven garlic varieties, which mature from bulbs or divisions in several months, include:

Dried garlic at Hornby Farmer's Market. Bob Cain photo

- Silverskin. Planted in February or early March. Prized for its long storage capacity and decorative strong stems that are suitable for braiding. A strong-flavoured garlic.

- White Music. Best planted in early October. Large, pungent cloves. An excellent winter keeper.

- Elephant. Develops an enormous bulb with a mild flavour similar to leek. Fall plantings are ready by August.

Leeks

Leeks, another member of the onion family, have a mild, sweet flavour and are used in salads, soups and stews, or cooked as vegetables. Leeks were first grown in the Mediterranean but they have adapted to the Pacific coast and have become a superior winter vegetable.

Leeks prefer a sandy loam enriched with organic material. The soil must be moist, with adequate winter drainage. Seed leeks in late February in 10–15 cm (4–6 inch) deep rows and thin them as they mature. Thinnings may be eaten fresh, or transplanted into 15 cm (6-inch) deep trenches, with 23 cm (9 inches) between plants and 45 cm (18 inches) between trenches. As the leeks grow, fill the trenches with soil gradually, creating long, succulent, blanched stems. If you grow them at ground level, mound earth around the stems as they grow.

Leek flower. Chuck Heath photo

Top leek varieties:

- Durabel. Matures in 125 days. A hardy winter leek, tender and mild. Bulb is slow growing but remains firm until late April.

- Jolant. 75 days. A summer leek only. Long white shafts are topped with blue-green leaves.

- Autumn Giant. 85 days. A huge leek for fall use. Long, large, creamy white shanks and green leaves enfold the plant.

- Laura. 120 days. Thrives in cold temperatures. Produces thick, medium-length shafts with dark blue-green leaves.

Shallots

Shallots (*Allium cepa*) are grown infrequently although they are delicious and not hard to cultivate. They look like small tulip bulbs, with a shiny brown skin that when peeled reveals a purple surface. Their delicate, mild-onion flavour and fragrance are esteemed in gourmet cooking.

Shallot sections may be set out in the garden as early as February. Fifty small bulbs will supply an average household for one year. Plant the sections 7.5 cm (3 inches) apart, 5 cm (2 inches) deep, in rows 30 cm (1 ft) apart. Harvest mature bulbs in late autumn, before a killing frost. They are mature when the outer skin is papery and red-brown. Dry them like onions and they will keep well for several months.

Shallots may also be grown from seed. They require the same culture as onions, but need a drier soil to reach maximum flavour. Pull the bulbs when they are 6 cm (2$^{1}/_{2}$ inches) in diameter.

- Ambition. Matures in 7–8 months from bulbs. A popular variety that produces a globe-shaped bulb with red-brown skin.

Peas

Peas are an early-seeded crop that tolerates light frosts. For continuous supply of fresh peas, plant sparingly at 2- to 3-week intervals from February through August.

Prepare the seed bed deeply and thoroughly. In the bottom of the planting trench, add a commercial fertilizer high in nitrogen and phosphorus. Use about 450 g (1 lb) to

3 m (10 ft) of row. Sow in rows, 15–23 cm (6–9 inches) wide, spacing the seeds 5 cm (2 inches) apart. Cover with 7.5 cm (3 inches) of fine soil. The space between the rows should be equal to the height of the variety. When the vines are 7.5–10 cm (3–4 inches) tall, side dress the rows with another application of fertilizer. Water the fertilizer well into the soil, then make sure the roots stay moist while the plant is growing. When pea pods form, extra water is necessary to fill them out. Water frequently along the furrows and between the rows during hot, dry weather.

Prolific tall-growing pea varieties require support stakes and wire or string. Dwarf-growing types of peas do not require support. All peas must be picked regularly to maintain maximum production.

Consider the following varieties:

- Maestro. Matures in 57 days. An improved Green Arrow and a tall-growing pea. Produces long, slender pods with 8 to 9 medium-sized peas per pod. The high sugar content of the seed makes it slow to germinate in the spring. Seed in mid-March.

- Early Freezer. 52 days. Produces extra-sweet and early dark green peas. Double set pods contain 6 to 7 peas each. Good for freezing, canning or eating fresh.

- Novella. 65 days. Great yields without the need for supports. Erect plants 60–90 cm (2–3 ft) tall are bountiful with 7.5 cm (3-inch) pods full of peas. Thrives in hot, dry weather that causes other peas to fade.

- Tall Telephone. 77 days. An older variety very suited to the home garden. Vigorous 1.5 m (5-ft) vines produce large pods, each holding 8 to 19 peas.

- Straight Arrow. Very productive main season fresh pea. Long, slender green 10 cm (4-inch) pods show 10–12 medium-sized peas. Plants are disease-resistant and tolerate hot summer conditions without turning bitter or starchy.

- Novella Improved. Top-quality, 7.5 cm (3-inch) dark green pods, which mature mostly at once. Grown for freezer use. Plants are highly disease-resistant and tolerate hot summer conditions.

Peas: Sugar Snap (Edible Pod)

There are a number of names for this group of peas, including Chinese peas, snow peas, sugar peas and eat-all. The pods are cooked and eaten whole. They are easier to grow than garden peas and are picked before the seed swells. Vines often grow to 1.8 m (6 ft) in length.

These peas do well in an alkaline soil, 7.0 pH, that holds moisture yet allows excess water to drain away quickly. Plant and fertilize as you would other peas, in early spring.

Ann MacKay's edible pod peas. Bob Cain photo   *Peas: Oregon Sugar Pod.* West Coast Seeds photo

Popular varieties:

- Mega. Matures in 90 days. Virus-resistant and yields well in either cool or warm weather. Strong vines produce 10 cm (4-inch) light green pods. The peas are crisp, juicy and sweet.

- Sugar Ann. 75 days. An early dwarf variety. Vines do not require support. Pods are plump and sweet.

- Oregon Sugar Pod. 105 days. A heavy producer of double pods 10–12.5 cm (4–5 inches) long. A slow climber, reaching 90 cm (3 ft). May be planted from February through late May.

Potatoes

Digging potatoes at harvest time is a sure marker of changing seasons. Summer is gone and winter approaches; it's time to put the spuds in storage.

Potatoes are a cool-season crop. Plant as soon as the soil can be worked in the early spring.

Potatoes like a slightly acid, low-nitrogen soil that has not been limed for at least two years. Turn the soil deeply and loosen it by working in an abundance of organic material. Avoid using poultry or rabbit manure on the potato patch, as it encourages scab and other diseases.

Dig a trench about 30 cm (1 ft) deep to plant the potato seeds or cuttings. Mound the soil from the trench at one side. Plant small potatoes, 28–56 g (1–2 oz), whole. Cut larger potatoes into pieces with 1 to 2 "eyes" or buds on each piece. Allow the cut sections to dry outdoors for 2 days before planting. To produce about 180 L (5 bushels) of late

Vegetables, Herbs and Fruits

potatoes from tubers, you will need 4.5 kg (10 lbs) of seed sections. For early potatoes, you will need 4.5 kg (10 lbs) of seed sections to produce 36 L (1 bushel) of potatoes.

Set the sections of tubers into the trench about 30 cm (1 ft) deep in rows 60 cm (2 ft) apart. Cover the newly set-out tubers with 10 cm (4 inches) of soil. Sprinkle in the trench a low-nitrogen fertilizer such as a 4-10-10, using about 450 g (1 lb) per 6 m (20 ft) of row. Side dress the planting 3 weeks later with another application of fertilizer. As the tuber tops develop, add more soil until a hill of soil forms over them.

You can also grow potatoes by laying the potato seed on the ground in rows and gently pushing the seed into well-worked soil. Or you can use straw to grow potatoes. Loosen the topsoil, then plant the potato sections and cover with straw to a depth of 20–30 cm (8–12 inches). Try not to let the potatoes become exposed to the light, as they will turn green and bitter. Straw-covered potatoes mature faster than those grown in soil. As soon as the potatoes have developed, lift up the straw and harvest them.

Jim and Pam Gordon's potatoes. Bob Cain photo

Potato plants grow and produce best in full sun, but a bit of morning shade is fine. Keep the planting well watered, especially when the plants are flowering, as this is the time they are forming new tubers. Make certain that excess water drains well from their growing soil.

Early potatoes are ready for harvest about 3 months after planting, when the flowers are fully open. Second early and main crops should be lifted from August onward. Dig them on a dry day and keep them outside for a few hours before storing. You can discourage stored potatoes from sprouting by mixing apples with them. Apples give off ethylene gas, which halts sprouting. One apple placed in a bag of 15 kg (50 lbs) of potatoes will do for the winter. Store in a dark, well-ventilated place kept at about 10°C (50°F).

Proven potatoes include:

- Norland. Matures in 55–60 days. An early maturing red potato with fine taste, good colour and excellent yield. Does not store well.

- AC Ptarmigan. 55–60 days. A high-yielding early potato, round, yellow-fleshed and delicious.

- Epicure. 62 days. An all-purpose potato.

- Superior. 60 days. An early maturing potato that produces well. Stores over winter.

- Yukon Gold. 60 days. A fine early yellow potato, excellent for boiling and baking. Stores well.

- Ranger Russet. 65–70 days. A high-yielding russet that performs well as a baking potato and a French fry spud.

Radicchio

Radicchio has been enjoyed in Italy for centuries and more recently has become popular in Europe and North America, but it is a challenging vegetable to grow. It is important to plant the correct variety in the right season. Early types may be planted outdoors in February with shelter from frosts. Plant seeds 1 cm (1/2 inch) deep and 2.5 cm (1 inch) apart, in rows 10–12.5 cm (4–5 inches) apart. Transplant when the seedlings are 1 month old (and have 3 to 4 leaves each).

Radicchio thrives in soil that has had horse manure added the year prior to planting. During the growing season, provide the soil with fertilizers high in phosphorus and potash and low in nitrogen. (If too much nitrogen is available, the plants will bolt, or go to seed quickly.) Use a 5-10-10 fertilizer at the rate of 1.3 kg (3 lbs) per 30 m (100 ft) of row.

Radicchio varieties that do well on the coast:

- Bianca Di Milano. Matures in 75 days. Sow in early June. Light green leaves cover a white cylindrical head. Plants are frost-hardy and produce well.

- Rubicon Hybrid. 75 days. Large, round head with a firm white centre. Excellent for winter use.

- Vesuvio Hybrid. 80 days. Uniform, deep coloured, 20–23 cm (8–9 inch) cylindrical heads. Resists bolting and tolerates high growing temperatures.

Radishes

There are two kinds of radishes: the summer radish, harvested from late April to November, and the winter radish. For sweet, crisp, mild flavour, grow all radishes quickly, in a sunny site and in soil with an abundance of nutrients and water. Apply well-aged manure over the seed bed in the fall before you seed radishes. When manure is used at planting time, overlush top growth with malformed radishes can result. Also before seeding, work into the soil a 5-10-10 fertilizer, which provides phosphorus and potash to encourage the plant to produce.

Plant spring and summer radishes outdoors in February. Plant the seeds 1 cm ($^1/2$ inch) deep and 2.5 cm (1 inch) apart in rows spaced at 10–12.5 cm (4–5 inches). For a continuous supply of radishes, repeat seeding every 10 days. If the nights are frosty, cover the planting with a sheet of plastic or burlap at night and remove the cover during the day. After the seedlings appear, sprinkle between the rows another application of 5-10-10 fertilizer at the rate of 1.3 kg (3 lbs) to 30 m (100 ft) of row. Water the fertilizer well into the growing soil, or use a liquid fertilizer with the same formula and follow package directions.

Popular summer radish varieties include:

- Early Scarlet Globe. Matures in 22 days. Round, crisp red roots appear quickly. Recommended for very early greenhouse planting.

- Easter Egg. 30 days. Skins are white, red, pink and purple; centre is white. Roots are round, crisp and flavourful.

- Cherry Belle. 22 days. Crisp red and white roots, oval to round in shape, with a mild flavour. Excellent when grown in a cold frame or cool greenhouse.

- French Breakfast. 25–30 days. Long red roots with white blunt bottoms. Great for munching in the garden or slicing for the table.

- Red Silk. 25 days. Uniform, round scarlet 2.5 cm (1-inch) roots on vigorous short tops. Plants resist going pithy or woody.

Fall and winter radishes usually have large roots and grow in rosettes. Some display long, blue-green leaves that are divided into overlapping round scallop-edged leaflets lined up in pairs along each leaf stalk. They look like ferns. Prepare the soil, plant and cultivate as for summer radishes.

Radish seed planted mid-July to August germinates quickly. Cold weather and long days induce radishes to bolt or go to flower at the expense of the roots. The plants need an even supply of water. You can harvest the roots 2 to 3 months after seeding. Unless the soil is stagnant and wet, radish can be stored in the garden under a mulch of leaves or straw during cold winter weather. The tops are killed by severe frosts but the roots remain edible.

Radish: Early Scarlet Globe. West Coast Seeds photo

Winter radishes include:

- Black Spanish Round. Matures in 55 days. This hardy winter radish keeps well. The rough black outside skin covers a tender, milky white interior with a bit of a bite. The root develops up to 10 cm (4 inches) or more in length.

- Japanese Nerima, Long White. 75 days. Long, pointed roots with white flesh.

Radish: French Breakfast. West Coast Seeds photo

- China Rose. 60 days. A fine winter radish with long, 12.5 cm (5-inch) roots. The roots are white, mild and may weigh up to 450 g (1 lb).

Spinach

Spinach is one of the most nutritious green vegetables grown in coastal gardens. Seed in late February and repeat every 2 to 3 weeks until late autumn for a continuous supply. Seed is planted 2 cm (3/4 inch) deep in rows 38 cm (15 inches) apart. Scatter about 25 seeds to each 30 cm (1 ft) of row. Thin the seedlings when they reach 7.5 cm (3 inches); aim for a final spacing of 15 cm (6 inches) between plants.

Spinach is an excellent indicator plant for soil acidity. When the soil is too acid, spinach leaves are sickly yellow and the plant does not thrive. Before seeding, test the soil and apply ground dolomite lime as necessary. Spinach likes a soil with a 6.0–7.0 pH. To raise the pH by one point, apply 4.5 kg (10 lbs) of lime to 9 m² (100 sq ft) of planting. Sprinkle fish meal or a liquid fish fertilizer along the rows when the spinach plants show 3 to 4 leaves.

What is commonly called New Zealand spinach is actually a type of Swiss chard. Some gardeners know it as cut-and-come-again. Maintain the rapid growth of this plant with plenty of moisture and fertilizer. To encourage side shoots, pinch out the growing tips as soon as they develop. Pick the leaves and young shoots of New Zealand spinach frequently to keep the crop producing.

Spinach: Bloomsdale. West Coast Seeds photo   *Spinach: Space.* West Coast Seeds photo

Spinach varieties include:

- Tetragonia Expansa. Matures in 55–60 days. A valuable New Zealand spinach with fleshy green leaves. Plants grow to 90 cm (3 ft). Seed germinates slowly. Soak seed in water overnight before planting.

- Bloomsdale Savoy. 50 days. Thick, dark green leaves are mild and sweet.

- Whitney. 50 days. A new variety that develops quickly yet is slow to bolt. Smooth, oval green leaves decorate the plant. Seed from early spring until fall.

- Space Hybrid. 45 days. Introduced recently from Europe. Produces upright broad leaves. May be successfully grown in greenhouses or cold frames for winter use.

Squash

Squash grows and produces well if its far-venturing roots find fertile soil, enriched with organic humus such as compost, aged manures and ground dolomite limestone. It requires consistently moist soil when at the seedling stage and again later when forming fruit.

Wait to seed squash until late May or early June on the coast. Dig planting pockets and place 125 mL (1/2 cup) of organic fertilizer with a high content of nitrogen and phosphate in the bottom. Cover the fertilizer with a few inches of compost, then seed. Squash seeds require a warm garden soil of 21°C (70°F) to germinate. In 5 to 7 days the seedlings emerge. Keep them growing with adequate moisture and fertilizer.

Cool, cloudy weather will inhibit germination by lowering soil temperature. You can start seeds indoors in March, then transplant to the garden when the weather is more favourable. Out in the garden, make small mounds of soil, water them, and sow 4 to 6 seeds in each hill, 5 cm (2 inches) deep. Avoid watering again until the seedlings emerge.

Plant bush varieties in hills 90 cm–1.2 m (3–4 ft) apart, with rows spaced 1.8 m (6 ft) apart. Full-vined varieties are planted in hills 1.2–1.5 m (4–5 ft) apart and the rows are spaced 3 m (10 ft) apart. When the seedlings are well established, thin to the two most vigorous plants per hill.

Squash plants produce separate male and female flowers on the same plant. Many gardeners hand pollinate the flowering plants, other leave it to the bees. Dropped blossoms or misshapen fruits are a result of poor pollination.

For improved winter squash, remove all little squashes and all new female flowers (the ones with a tiny squash just before the flower). This pruning forces the vine to finish ripening the larger fruit that has already set.

The fruit is ripe when the stem becomes dry and brittle. To harvest squash, cut the stem about 2.5 cm (1 inch) from the fruit. Wipe the squash skins with a solution of 10 parts water to 1 part chlorine bleach to prevent mould while the squash are in storage.

Squash are good growing companions for the cabbage family or they may follow such crops in rotation plantings.

Some popular summer squash:

- Early Golden Crookneck. Matures in 55 days. A vigorous squash that produces meaty fruit 25 cm (10 inches) long and 7.5 cm (3 inches) thick, with a warted golden skin.

- Gold Rush. 55 days. Produces an early, bright yellow zucchini-type squash.

Squash: Gold Rush. West Coast Seeds photo

- Tromboncino. 60 days. A recent introduction from Italy. The light green to
tan vine travels up trellises or over the
ground for several feet. White, tender
fruit is very flavourful in salads or
cooked.

- Hybrid Zucchini Ambassador F1. 50
days. Yields well over the whole summer.
Produces medium green fruit on compact yet open plants for easy picking.

- Peter Pan Hybrid. 55 days. Produces
medium green scallop squash. Fruit
from the bush type plants tastes best
when about 10 cm (4 inches) long.

- Cornell's Bush Delicate. Bushy plants
produce cylindrical fruits about 20 cm
(8 inches) long and 10 cm (4 inches) in
diameter. Creamy white with green
longitudinal striping.

Winter squash:

Squash: Tromboncino. West Coast Seeds photo

- Butternut Waltham. Matures in 85 days.
A pear-shaped squash with orange flesh and tan-yellow skin. A fine winter keeper.

Jim and Pam Gordon's zucchini in flower. Bob Cain photo

- Gold Nugget. 85 days. An All-
American winner with golden
yellow fruits of wonderful flavour.
Each compact bush yields 3 to 5
squash of 450–675 g (1–1 1/2 lbs)
each. Flourishes in cooler coastal
climates.

- Golden Hubbard. 90 days. Reddish
orange, lightly warted skin decorates the fruit. Flesh is deep orange
and very sweet. Squash weighs up
to 5 kg (11 lbs) when ripe. Stores
well.

Squash: Gold Nugget. West Coast Seeds photo

Squash: Table Queen. West Coast Seeds photo

- Uchiki Kuri. 85 days. A recent introduction from Japan. Produces hubbard-like fruit with a bright orange-red outer skin. The skin is smooth in texture with almost no ribbing. Very sweet, creamy yellow flesh with a nutty flavour. A gourmet treat.

- Table Queen. 90 days. A popular acorn variety. Large, dark green fruits with thick orange flesh grow on vigorous vines. The squash store well over winter.

In addition to the above-mentioned squash, there are many fine varieties of spaghetti-type squash. Pick these squash when they are 25 cm (10 inches) long. Cook whole by steaming for 20 minutes. To serve, cut in half, and remove seeds. The pulp resembles spaghetti, ready for butter and salt and pepper.

Tomatoes

Red, ripe, juicy homegrown tomatoes are one of the most sensual of garden-fresh treats. They are eaten as vegetables although technically they are fruits. In proportion to the space they occupy, tomatoes produce more fruit over a longer season than any other garden crop. Two plants for each member of the family will supply a season's worth of tomatoes for eating fresh, cooking and preserving.

Tomato plants produce superior crops if they are grown in a soil that is slightly acid. Do not lime their soil. A sandy loam enriched with organic material is ideal for growing tomatoes.

Locate tomato plants on a bright, sunny balcony, patio or open garden spot. Choose healthy-looking tomato plants at the nursery. Before setting them into the soil, broadcast fertilizer with a 4-12-4 analysis at the rate of 2.3 kg (5 lbs) to 9 m^2 (100 sq ft) of planting area. In hanging baskets or other containers about 25x25 cm (10x10 inches) in size, use 20 mL (1 heaping tbsp) of fertilizer.

Set out the young plants late in the afternoon, or on a cool, cloudy day. Water them immediately after transplanting to settle the soil around the roots and eliminate air spaces. Shade the plants from the direct sun and protect them from wind for a few days.

Set young transplants of tomatoes in a slanting position, roots about 5 cm (2 inches) below ground level and with the lower half of the stem buried. In a few days the upper stem will rise to the light and grow straight up. Additional roots will form on the stem buried in the soil. This type of planting encourages a heavy, sturdy root system.

Plant smaller varieties about 30 cm (1 ft) apart. Before planting large-growing varieties, drive sturdy 2–2.5 m (6–8 ft) stakes into the ground, 1.2–1.5 (4–5 ft) apart. Set out the plants, one at the base of each stake. As the plants develop, tie them loosely to the support stakes with soft twine.

Steady, continuous growth and development is the key to productive tomato plants. Provide them with adequate water and nutrients (look for specially formulated tomato fertilizer at garden supply stores) to keep them in top production. Maintain an even moisture content in the soil. A mulch of old sawdust, ground bark, compost or seaweed moderates rapid moisture changes and supplies other nutrients.

Once a week during dry summer weather, soak the soil around the bases of plants to a depth of 45 cm (18 inches). Tomatoes growing in containers require more frequent watering—as often as every day—during hot weather. Alternating wet and dry spells are one reason tomato plants become stunted and fail to set fruit. A blackening of the lower side of the fruit, known as blossom end rot, is encouraged by inconsistent watering. Avoid watering the leaves of the plants.

If the plants produce lush, soft vegetative growth yet do not set fruit, the problem may be overwatering, insufficient light or over-fertilization with formulas too high in nitrogen.

Prune large-growing plants to a single stem by pinching out shoots or branches ("suckers") that arise at points where the large leaves are joined to the main stem. These suckers are broken out easily. The plant is then restricted to a single main stem from which fruit spurs arise. During the growing period you may have to remove suckers as often as every few days.

In the early part of tomato season West Coast weather is often not conducive to natural pollination from insects or breezes. While the plants are in blossom, give them a gentle shake each day to distribute the pollen. To further encourage pollination, spray the open blossoms with a commercial hormone preparation that induces fruit set, early ripening and seedless tomatoes.

Local garden centres, greenhouses and nurseries have many fine varieties of tomatoes for coast gardens. They may be started indoors from seed in March, or planted from transplants from growers in mid-May.

Ann MacKay's greenhouse tomatoes, 'Cobra.' Bob Cain photo

- Early tomato varieties: Siletz, Oregon Spring, Mountain Fresh Hybrid, Kootenai.

- Main season tomatoes: Better Boy Hybrid, Big Beef Hybrid, Fantastic, Celebrity, Floramerica.

- Cherry tomatoes for the coast: Sweetie, Super Sweet, Early Cherry, Sweet Million.

- Dwarf varieties: Patio tomato, Totem Hybrid, Tiny Tim, Small Fry, Toy Boy.

- Cobra Hybrid, a greenhouse variety that also grows well outdoors in the garden.

- Yellow or golden coloured tomatoes: Lemon Boy, Yellow Pear, Yellow Brandywine.

- Paste or sauce tomatoes: Viva Italia, Roma VF, Persimmon, San Marzano.

Turnips

Turnips are a quick-growing, tasty addition to the home vegetable garden. Many varieties reach a usable size in just 60 days.

Turnip seeds are so small that it is difficult not to seed them too thickly. Pick a sunny location. Press the seed into the soil gently, in rows 45 cm (18 inches) apart. Cover seed with 2 cm (1/2 inch) of sandy soil. Thin the young starts to 15–20 cm (6–8 inches) between plants. Keep the seedlings moist. Sow every 3 weeks from late February until late July for a continuous supply.

Popular varieties include:

- Purple Top White Globe Turnip. Matures in 55 days. Roots are smooth and nearly round, purple at the top and white below. Best harvested when 7.5 cm (3 inches) in diameter, when they are most flavourful and sweet.

- Shogoin. 30 days. Mature roots are 7.5–10 cm (3–4 inches) in diameter. The roots are flattened on top with white skin. Tops make excellent greens.

- Tokyo Cross. 30 days. An improved hybrid turnip with flesh of sparkling white. Leaves make excellent early-season greens.

- Early Italian White Red Top. 30 days. Exceptionally mild in taste.

Turnip: Purple Top White Globe. West Coast Seeds photo

Herbs

Pacific Coast aboriginal people traditionally used herbs for medicine, and in cooking and preserving food. When Europeans arrived on the coast they brought more seeds and cuttings of useful herbs, adding to the indigenous varieties.

Herbs are easygoing. They ask only for a bright, sunny site with a gritty, well-drained, slightly alkaline soil, and some elbow room to grow. Most species will thrive on a hot, dry bank, tucked in a sunny rock pocket or in an open flower or vegetable garden. There is a theory that the aromatic foliage of herbs emits a vapour that hovers above the plants and protects them from harsh afternoon sunshine. Because they are so accommodating of almost all types of soil and other conditions, herbs are often the solution for a problem spot in the garden.

Planting and Cultivating

Plant herbs outdoors in the early spring, from seed or young starts. For convenience, plant annual herbs separately from perennials.

Vegetables, Herbs and Fruits

- **Annuals** include: anise, basil, borage, dill, summer savory, chervil, coriander and fennel, although these herbs often self-seed and new plants spring up each season. You can gather and save their seed for sowing the following spring.

- **Biennials** include: parsley, caraway and angelica. They are started from seed either outdoors in the early spring, or indoors in autumn, to produce the following spring and summer in the garden.

- **Perennials** include: chives, sage, tarragon, rosemary, garden thyme, bergamot, lavender, marjoram, lovage, parsley and mint. Once planted, they return season after season.

While established herb plants will endure extremely impoverished dry soils and other harsh conditions, young seedlings and newly planted divisions require a moist soil and a light application of fertilizer during their growing season. Water them often until their roots are deep and well established. In summer, soak the roots deeply with water once a week. Wash the top growth with a forceful spray from the hose every 10 days to clean the plants of insects and dust.

Kathi Linnman's borage. Bob Cain photo

Herbs will grow without added nutrients; but they perform best with a small amount of fertilizer when they are growing vigorously. Quick-growing annuals such as dill and borage benefit from generous amounts of fertilizer.

Water the plants with a solution of a complete balanced fertilizer just as new growth starts in the spring. Apply organic fertilizers such as bone meal on perennial herb plantings in the late fall, at the rate of 1.3–1.8 kg (3–4 lbs) for each 9 m² (100 sq ft) of planting area. To maintain a sweet (alkaline) soil, apply a sprinkle of ground limestone on their beds every spring.

Keep the herb garden free of weeds. Destroy any plants that are sickly or continually visited by insects.

Drying

You can cut and pick herbs for drying from midsummer until after the first frost. Expediency in cutting and drying is essential, so leave enough time. Harvest herbs on a bright, sunny day, preferably before noon. Once cut, the faster they are processed the better, as precious flavour and oils are lost rapidly.

Leafy herbs such as basil, summer savory and perennial sweet marjoram benefit by being harvested or cut back at the first sign of flower buds. Second and third cuttings in one season are often possible.

Take the cut leafy herbs indoors immediately and wash them with cold water. Shake off excess water and spread them out to dry on a wire screen. Cover with light cheesecloth. If the weather is agreeable, keep the herbs outdoors, but bring them inside by late afternoon.

Lavender. Chuck Heath photo

Harvested leafy herbs may then be tied in small bunches and hung in an airy room out of the sun until dry. Leafy herbs may also be dried in the kitchen oven at a very low temperature. Keep the oven door open and check often. Herbs will dry in less than an hour.

The amount of time it takes to dry herbs naturally depends on the thickness of the leaves and on the heat and ventilation. Test the dryness by crushing a leaf. When it is crisp and falls to pieces easily, it is dry enough for storage.

Flowering herbs, such as camomile, lavender and pot marjoram, should be cut when they are in full bloom. Dry them on mesh racks or hang them in small bunches.

Seeds suitable for drying and storing include coriander, cumin, caraway, dill and fennel. Make certain that they are mature and ripe. The seeds are mature when they can be pulled easily from the heads. Many seeds turn a darker colour when ripe. Leave seeds on the drying mesh for only a few days.

Store dried herbs permanently in airtight jars or other containers over the winter or until needed. You can also freeze fresh herbs. Wash them carefully, drain, put small quantities in plastic bags, seal the bags and place in the freezer immediately.

Some Favourites

A few of the more popular and useful herbs are:

- Basil. Likes full sun, indoors or out. 'Nufar Hybrid' produces the scent of summer; plants are resistant to fusarium blight, a common disease affecting the stems and leaves. 'Red Robin' is an improved dark opal basil with decorative and delectable dark purple leaves.

- Coriander (cilantro). A favourite herb in Latin and Asian cuisine. The leaves are used fresh or dried and the seeds are ground and added to curries. 'Santo' produces flavourful leaves and is slow to bolt in summer.

- Dill. Feathery leaves have a cool, piquant flavour and pleasant fragrance. A mainstay of dill pickles but also an excellent addition to salads, chowders, fish and eggs.

- Fennel. A delicately leafed plant with a strong anise or licorice fragrance and flavour. Use the leaves to garnish salads; and cook with both leaves and seeds.
  The bulbous-stemmed form, called Florence fennel, anise or finocchio, is eaten like celery.

- Marjoram. A hardy winter perennial that is often mistaken for an annual. Grows well as a trailing plant in a hanging basket with good exposure. Plants have purple flowers and tasty, fragrant foliage. Dried and fresh young leaves give delectable flavour to roast lamb, eggs, beans, tomatoes, poultry, fish and soups.

- Mint. A family of vigorous, hardy perennials. Their fast spreading habits can make them a problem in the garden. Restrict them by bordering with large stones, metal edging or other barriers. Use the herb for tea, mint sauce, jelly and juleps.

Herbs: 'Nufar' basil. West Coast Seeds photo

- Oregano. A Greek import. Grow from fine seeds, which are difficult to germinate, or from small plants. The pungent aroma and familiar flavour are mainstays of pizza, pasta, chili, veal and tomato dishes.

- Parsley. Today it crowns roasts and salads; in old Rome it was used to crown victorious athletes. Grows easily in sun or shade from seed, annually, or from small started plants. The flat-leafed Italian variety is richer in flavour and vitamins.

- Rosemary. Grown as an evergreen flowering shrub as well as a herb. Grows to 1.8 m (6 ft) if not cut back. Tiny, bright blue flowers form March through May. Start new plants from cuttings rooted in sand. Harvest the thin, fragrant leaves and use fresh or dried in soups, pasta sauces, pot roasts and stews of beef, venison or moose.

- Sage. A hardy perennial with pebbly grey leaves that are almost evergreen. Seed sown in spring produces usable leaves by summer. In May the plant blooms. Cut back faded flowers and a resurgence of foliage will provide a continuous harvest of leaves. Use fresh or dry (more when dry) in soups, poultry and meat dishes.

- Savory, summer. An annual that may be directly seeded into the garden, thinned, and cut for drying as soon as the flower buds appear.

- Savory, winter. A small perennial shrub that grows no taller than 38 cm (15 inches). Best started as a young plant and placed in a sunny rock garden for life.

Ann MacKay's variegated marjoram. Bob Cain photo

- Tarragon. A hardy perennial that rarely sets seeds. Plants grow to 45 cm (18 inches) high. Propagate by divisions in spring: when old plants die out at the centre, lift and divide them and replant the divisions. Tarragon becomes woody after about July 1. Harvest before then, when the leaves are young and tender. Flavour beef, pork, fish and salads with tarragon. After July, use the woody stems to flavour vinegar.

- Thyme. A small, shrubby perennial, suitable for planting in a rock garden where it can grow undisturbed. Start plants from seed sown in March and April, in a limy soil. Season cheese, fish, sauces, soups and stuffings with thyme.

Fruits

Berries

Hybrid Blackberries

Several blackberry hybrids are available. They are improved forms of the wild blackberry found along the Pacific Northwest coast, in Europe and in parts of Asia.

Brambleberry is gaining in favour with coast gardeners. The culture for this type of berry is similar to that of the red raspberry. Grow these vigorous, productive berry plants in a moist yet perfectly drained soil that is sandy at the base and enriched with organic humus.

A winter mulch of decomposed manure, peat moss or aged sawdust is always beneficial. In spring, give the plants a boost with a 5-10-10 fertilizer, applying 450 g (1 lb) per group of 5 to 6 plants. Water the fertilizer into the soil immediately after application. Give the plants organic nutrients such as cottonseed, blood meal and bone meal in September.

The vertical-growing brambles produce roots that live indefinitely, and the fruiting canes are biennial: they arise one year, fruit the next, then die. Brambleberry tends to be ruthless in growth and if it is not well trained, it soon makes a solid mass of plants, impossible to penetrate. Remove all weak or spindly suckers and starts, and support the fruiting canes (see p. 83). In late fall, cut back the old canes that have fruited, down to within 2.5 cm (1 inch) of soil level, and tie or entwine the new canes on the wires.

Evergreen Brainard and **Himalaya blackberry** vines are so aggressive in their expansion that it is quite difficult to train them into a pattern. Allow them their untamed ways. Give them a heavy post fencing or wild section of the garden to wander in. As an impenetrable barrier or hedge, these vines are superb. Let them grow to cover steep banks and soil will not erode.

Each winter cut back the side growths ("laterals") on the old canes to within 15 cm (6 inches) of their bases and remove extra shoots or overlong growths.

Some gardeners train these wild vines horizontally on permanent trellises. They pinch out the tips of the branches when the desired length is reached, and later head in the laterals. Four canes are sufficient for one large trellis.

Youngberry, Boysenberry, Loganberry, Marion berry, and **Cascade berry** can also be trained on support wires. Their canes produce for 2 years and should be removed promptly after the last fruiting. In the late summer, tip the new young canes to about 1 m (3¹/₂ ft) long. Cut the laterals back the next spring to about 35 cm (14 inches). Some gardeners do not tip the canes but drape them over the wires. To save garden space, they may be wound up and tied to heavy stakes 1.8–2.4 m (6–8 ft) long. Prune the tag ends often.

It usually takes about 3 years from planting time for the canes to produce. Plant the canes early in November or in February. In mid-March of the first year, cut the canes to within 30 cm (1 ft) of the soil level. In mid-March of the second year, cut them back severely to about 45 cm (18 inches).

Some varieties and their characteristics:

- Youngberry. Ripens in July. Large, dark red fruit with excellent flavour. Milder and less acid in taste than boysenberry. Freezes well.

- Boysenberry. July. Vines are vigorous and productive. Berry is dark red and begins to ripen later than Logan or Youngberry. Flavour is a bit acid. Eat the berries fresh or freeze them.

- Loganberry. Produces early; berries are usually ripe by June 15, and production continues through July. Berries are large and dark red with an acid flavour. They are grown to make quality juice and wine.

- Marion berry. Ripens in June. Vigorous long canes support very productive fruiting laterals. Berries are medium to large, bright black and flavourful, highly valued for freezing.

- Cascade berry. Ripens in June and July. A cross of native trailing blackberry with loganberry. Berries are dark red and slightly smaller than loganberry, with a delicious wild blackberry flavour. Berries freeze well.

Blueberries. Chuck Heath photo

Blueberries

Wherever forestland is cut or burned, blueberries and other wild berry plants are sure to spring up. Blueberry is a resourceful plant that thrives in the mild, moist weather conditions of the Pacific Northwest.

For best results, buy young plants at a nursery and transplant them in early spring or fall. Plants produce berries in their third year and a larger crop each season. They mature in 8 to 10 years and produce berries for up to 40 years.

Blueberry roots are fine and fibrous, and form a dense mat several inches thick near the surface, so clay soils are unsuitable for blueberries. They need a sandy peat soil with good aeration. Blueberries are related to heathers and rhododendrons, and need an acid type soil with a pH of 4.5 to 5.0.

Prepare the planting soil thoroughly. Dig a hole 60 cm (2 ft) deep and 45 cm (18 inches) wide. Place in the bottom 50 mL (1/4 cup) of garden sulphur, 1 shovelful of peat moss and 112 g (4 oz) of cottonseed meal. Cover this with 2.5–5 cm (1–2 inches) of sandy soil. Place the roots into the prepared pocket at the same depth as they grew in the nursery, no deeper. Space them 1.5–2.4 m (6–8 ft) apart in rows 2.4 m apart. Plant in blocks of several short rows rather than in long single rows, to encourage cross-pollination. Crops can be grown if only one variety is planted; but the berries are better when you plant more than one variety. When blueberry flowers are pollinated by pollen produced on their own bush, the berries are fewer, smaller and later in maturing. Mulch the planting lightly with aged sawdust or peat moss. The fibrous roots will establish rapidly in the top mulch.

Blueberries require a moist soil with perfect drainage. During the growing season keep the soil around the base of the plants moist but not soggy. Avoid overhead sprinkling while the berries are developing. Dull, yellowish foliage with red speckling usually indicates poor drainage.

Maintain acidity in the soil with the application of ammonium sulphate and an acid reaction fertilizer that is recommended for rhododendrons. The first application is made in early spring, after planting; the second is applied when the berries are first formed. Mature plants (6 to 8 years old) need 170 g (6 oz) of sulphate of ammonia at each application. Dissolve the sulphate of ammonia in water just before applying. Use about 450 g (1 lb) of the rhododendron type fertilizer around the base of each mature bush. Water the fertilizer well into the soil.

The blueberry plant develops short lateral branches, on which most of the fruit grows in the following year. Pruning is necessary when the plants are 3 to 4 years old. During the winter when the plant is dormant, remove old, weak wood and low-spreading branches near the ground. Leave only the erect strong branches.

As blossoms appear on young plants under 3 years old, pinch them off to concentrate the energy of the plant on sturdy development.

Recommended varieties for the coast include:

- Concord. Very productive. Ripens in July or August. Berries are medium-large, with a tart flavour until ripe.

- Stanley. Very vigorous. High-quality and spicy berries ripen during July and early August.

- Pemberton. One of the most productive varieties and well adapted to home gardens. Ripens in July or August. The berry is large and the plant produces heavily.

- Olympic. Ripens in early August. Berries are large and light blue.

- Jersey. Very vigorous and productive. Matures in August or September.

- Pacific. Ripens in July. Likes to spread. Berries are medium-sized.

Raspberries

Raspberries are productive, long-lasting and easily grown. In proportion to the time spent caring for them and the garden space required, they yield more than most other homegrown crops. A properly maintained row of 25 plants yields up to 30 L (30 qts) of fresh fruit a season.

There are three types of raspberries: red, black and purple. **Red raspberries** are the most common type grown on the coast. Grow them by planting or transplanting the full cane, roots and all. Plant at any time of the year, but always with care. To eliminate competition for sunlight, water and soil nutrients, choose a site at least 15 m (50 ft) from large shade trees and 9 m (30 ft) from smaller trees or shrubs. Raspberries succeed in all soils but clay, which is slow to drain. For the best production, plant in fertile soils enriched with humus and sand.

Select plants that have strong canes 6–8 mm ($1/4$–$3/8$ inch) in diameter and well-developed root systems. Do not allow the roots to dry before planting. If the canes cannot be planted immediately, they should be heeled into moist ground.

Prepare raspberry planting soil thoroughly. Spade the area 20–30 cm (8–12 inches) deep. Add 900 g (2 lbs) of complete fertilizer to each 9 m^2 (100 sq ft) of planting area. Generous amounts of sand and humus should also be turned in.

Berries. Chuck Heath photo

Set plants at intervals of 90–120 cm (3–4 ft), in rows 2.4–3 m (8–10 ft) apart. Raspberry plants are shallow rooted, and deep planting is often fatal. Set each plant in the soil with the crown (top) of the roots not more than 2.5 cm (1 inch) below the surface.

At planting time, prune the tops of the canes back to 20 cm (8 inches). Severe pruning strengthens the root system and hastens development of new shoots. Water the raspberry patch at least twice a week in spring and summer. Keep the soil evenly moist during the active growing and producing period.

Each spring after planting, spread a handful of commercial fertilizer that is slightly acid in action around the base of each plant. A handful of cottonseed meal or bone meal may also be added.

To keep the canes from falling over, train them on wire supports. To each of two heavy wood or metal posts, each 1.8–2 m (6–7 ft) long, attach 2 strong crosspieces 50 cm (20 inches) long. One crosspiece should be about 60 cm (2 ft) above ground level, the other about 120 cm (5 ft) above ground level. Place one post at each end of the planting and stretch wires between the ends of the crosspieces. Tie the canes to the wires to keep them vertical as they grow.

Mature red raspberry plants should be pruned back in the spring to 1.3–1.5 m (4^{1}/$_{2}$–5 ft) and tied to the wire supports.

As the plants grow they send out young starts or suckers, which, if left, eventually become new canes that fill in the rows. Thin to 5 to 6 canes per group, and use the shoots for a new planting or give them to a neighbouring gardener. Raspberry canes sprout out and grow one year, produce fruit the next, then die. Cut out all canes that have produced fruit soon after they have finished bearing.

- Some recommended varieties of red raspberries are: Sumner, Meeker, Newburgh, Willamette, Canby. September and Indian Summer are excellent types that bear fruit late in the season.

Black raspberries, commonly known as black caps, are a favourite of many home gardeners. They do not produce suckers. New plants are propagated from layers or divisions of established plants.

Plants are easily increased by pulling down the tips of the canes to the ground and anchoring them so that they take root. Layered tip roots develop well in late summer and fall. Cut the main cane away from the rooted tips in the spring and plant them out on their own. Prune when the new shoots are 90 cm (3 ft) tall. Pinch off the topmost growth bud on each shoot. This forces vigorous fruit-bearing lateral branches to develop.

Black raspberry (*Rubus leucodermis*) is a wild-growing black raspberry found along the Pacific coast. For a cultivated black raspberry, try Munger. Black raspberries are used for colouring in dyes, and are eaten fresh or preserved as canned fruit or jam.

Purple raspberries are a hybrid of red and black varieties. Start, cultivate and prune them as for black caps.

Strawberries

The flavour of these popular berries is best captured when they are picked from the home garden and eaten immediately. Fifty plants yield enough berries for eating fresh and preparing shortcake, ice cream toppings and jams, with some left over for freezing, for a family of four for one season. For a continuous crop, plant 25 June-bearing varieties and 25 everbearing varieties.

Strawberry plants need a site with full sun and excellent drainage. Standing water damages the roots and crowns. Ideally the planting area will be slightly raised.

Avoid planting strawberries in ground in which potatoes, tomatoes, eggplants or peppers have been sown. The soil may be infected with a common virus that can harm strawberry plants.

Set out strawberry plants as soon as the soil is workable in the early spring. Prepare the soil carefully. Strawberries prefer a light, sandy soil with a pH of 5.5–6.0, which can be improved by adding aged manure, kelp, old sawdust, ground bark and peat moss. Cottonseed meal and bone meal are also beneficial. Before planting, rake in a commercial 5-10-10 fertilizer at the rate of 4.5 kg (10 lbs) to 9 m² (100 sq ft).

When planting strawberries, set the crown of the strawberry level with the soil. (The crown is the point where the top growth and root system join.) Spread the roots out naturally in the planting pocket and press the soil firmly around the crowns. Soak the new planting with water to settle the soil around the root.

Plant June-bearing varieties in rows about 90 cm (3 ft) apart, with 40 cm (16 inches) between plants. Everbearing varieties give maximum yields in parallel rows 30 cm (1 ft) apart, with 30 cm between plants.

Newly set out strawberry plants should be kept well watered throughout their first season, and also when the berries first form, and during harvest, and again in August.

Jim and Pam Gordon's strawberries. Bob Cain photo

June-bearing varieties should not be allowed to bear fruit the first year after planting out. The plant will be more vigorous and will eventually produce more and larger berries if all energy is directed into the roots, so remove blossom clusters and runners as soon as they appear. If the stock needs replenishing, transplant runners out in the fall. Everbearing varieties may be permitted to bear fruit in late summer and fall the year of the planting. Keep the planting free of weeds but be careful: strawberries are notoriously shallow-rooted, so deep hoeing does more harm than good!

Each summer, apply fertilizer to the root area near the plants. Prepare a fertilizer furrow 7.5–10 cm (3–4 inches) deep along the side of the row. Use a commercial 5-10-10 fertilizer with added bone meal and cottonseed meal, approximately 450 g (1 lb) to each 3 m (10 ft) of row at each application. Water the fertilizer into the furrow.

Apply fertilizer again each spring after planting, to encourage fruit-bud development for the next season's berries.

After harvest, apply protective mulch to minimize winter kill. Straw, pea vines, shavings, leaves or fine ground bark protect plants nicely. Remove some of the mulch at about the time growth starts in the spring, leaving just a light covering to conserve moisture.

If you are gardening in a smaller space, you can grow strawberries in window boxes, hanging baskets, barrels, jars or pyramids. For planting in pots, baskets or window boxes select young, healthy everbearing varieties. Fill the pot with a light, sandy soil enriched with organic material such as decomposed manure, peat moss or leaf mould.

Place the plants in the container so that the crown is level with the soil. After the plants have begun to show new growth, add liquid 5-10-10 fertilizer to the water every 2 weeks during the summer, following package directions, to encourage sturdy growth and bushels of berries.

Plants growing in containers need water frequently, and soil moisture is particularly important before and during harvest. Water deeply and maintain an evenly moist soil.

To grow 12 to 24 plants in a small space, use larger containers. Several types are available from nurseries, or you can make your own. Wood barrels or steel drums with holes in the sides work well. About 30 cm (1 ft) from ground level, cut rows of holes 2.5 cm (1 inch), spaced 20–25 cm (8–10 inches) apart. Make as many rows as will fit, each 25 cm (10 inches) higher than the last. Stagger the placement of holes in each row so that the holes of alternate rows line up vertically. Down the centre of the barrel or drum, insert a perforated drainpipe and fill it with loose gravel. This is the irrigation system. Fill the barrel or drum to the first row level with prepared soil; over the soil add a few inches of fine gravel or other drainage material. Firm well to prevent settling.

Plant the first row of strawberry starts, then fill with soil to the second row, and continue on to the top. To make certain excess water drains, place the container on concrete blocks or bricks.

Pyramid planters made of metal, concrete or plastic are available, or you can build your own. This type of planter consists of a pyramid-shaped stack of square or round tiers, each usually 7.5–12.5 cm (3–5 inches) deep. To make a pyramid planter, fill the first tier or ring with soil, then place the second tier or ring on top, fill it with soil, and so on. Plant strawberries around the edge of each tier at 25 cm (10-inch) intervals. The plants soon cover the area. Keep all runners cut away.

Strawberry jars are usually made of clay or plastic or ceramic pottery, with openings or pockets along the sides and at the top. Those made of clay have large enough drain holes, but ceramic and plastic containers usually need drainage holes cut in or enlarged.

(To chip out drainage holes in ceramic or pottery, use a hammer and a sharp nail. For plastic jars or containers, use a red-hot ice pick or similar tool.) For drainage, spread several inches of pebbles, broken pieces of pottery or coarse sand in the bottom of the container. If you place pieces of fine screen over the drainage holes, the soil will not be washed away.

- June-bearing varieties for the coast include: Olympus, Northwest, Rainier, Shuksan, Puget Beauty, Marshall.

- Everbearing varieties are: Red Rich, Rockhill, Gem, Streamliner.

Grapes

Grapes are a most rewarding addition to a garden, for their beauty and their produce. Bold, handsome green leaves and bright fruits decorate the vine. And ripe, flavourful grapes from the home garden are far superior to those bought in the supermarket (which are usually picked before they are mature). A fresh grape is a delicacy and a marvel.

Grapes. Adam Gibbs photo

Plant grapes along fences, walls, arbours and trellises, which will support the vines. Grapes require little ground space. And if garden space is severely limited, you can grow grapes in a large container and support the vines with a trellis.

It was grand style in days gone by to decorate an arbour or veranda with grapevines, under whose shade guests were entertained on long summer afternoons. Now, with a renewed interest in outdoor living, grapevines are back in vogue.

Begin with plants 2 years old, purchased from a nursery. Heavily rooted plants of medium size are best. Choose a site with full sun so that they can thrive and ripen each year's fruit. A sloping or raised site will provide adequate drainage.

Grapes need a fertile, well-aerated soil. Heavy clay soils that drain water slowly tend to favour excessive wood growth and to delay the maturing of fruit and wood; this serious drawback can only be compensated for by adding large amounts of organic material and sand to the soil. Grapes must have soil that is friable and slightly acidic.

Grapevine roots reach into the soil 30–45 cm (12–18 inches), so turn and improve the soil to that depth. Plant grapes in early spring. Dig individual planting pockets deep and wide to accommodate the roots without crowding. Spread the roots out naturally, then cover them and tamp the soil lightly. Water well to settle the earth in and around the root system.

Don't use chemical fertilizers at planting time, but you may spray on a transplanting type formula of root-inducing hormones. Just before putting them in, remove all but the strongest shoot and cut it back to 2 growth buds. Leaves and future stems will grow from these buds. Plant the vines at the same depth as they grew in the nursery, or slightly deeper. Allow an area approximately 2.4 x 2.4 m (8 x 8 ft) in size for each vine.

Grapevines are long lived and will endure neglect, yet they respond quickly to attention. Fertilize the vines in winter. (Fertilizers applied in spring or summer encourage excessive growth, which keeps both fruit and wood from maturing.) Apply aged manure in the late fall or winter. A formula high in nitrogen, phosphorus and potash will produce lustrous green leaves, healthy wood and top fruit production. Use a commercial fertilizer with twice as much nitrogen as phosphorus and potash, such as 20-10-10. Apply 250 mL (1 cup) of fertilizer to each mature vine. For vines under 5 years old, use half that amount.

To stimulate the vine in early spring, apply 56 g (2 oz) of ammonium sulphate around the base of each plant. Water into the soil immediately.

Prune mature grapevines during the dormant season, late winter or very early spring before growth starts. The vines bear fruit only on the present season's growth. The green shoots that start to grow in the spring produce grapes in the late summer and fall. These new spring growths are formed on last year's wood.

But don't let the vines bear any fruit until the third growing season, and then only a small crop; by the fifth year the vine should reach full production. During the first two years, train the vine to form a sturdy skeleton on a firm support. Cut all shoots back to 2 or 3 growth buds on the main stems. These produce sturdy shoots, which bear grapes the next spring and summer.

For production of a limited number of large, perfect grapes, leave only 3 to 4 bunches of grapes on each shoot. Pinch out the tips of the extra shoots in summer, when 3 to 4 bunches are evident. Eighty bunches for each established vine can be expected each season. Another benefit of this pruning is to let in as much sunlight as possible on all sides and the centre, and open spaces for air circulation.

Buds within the middle portion of a grapevine produce more fruit than those at either end. Vigorous medium-sized canes produce more fruit than very large ones. When an old, neglected grapevine is cut down almost to the ground level, a new trunk arises. It will be several years before fruit is produced after this drastic treatment, but improved production makes it worthwhile.

- Some good varieties for growing on the coast: Seibel 9110, Beta, Campbell Early, Schuyler, Agawam, Seneca, Fredonia, Pearl of Csaba, Interlaken, Portland, Foch, Cascade, Alden.

- For home wine-making select two or more varieties. For red wine plant Foch, Millot, Chancellor, Chelois, Cascade. For white wine, plant Aurora, Seibel 13047, Seyve-Villard 5276.

Rhubarb

Rhubarb is of ancient lineage. For centuries, the Chinese and Tibetans used the root of one species of rhubarb for medicinal purposes. Today it is popular throughout the world.

The West Coast's cool, moist climate produces tender, succulent stems of rhubarb each season. Just 4 to 5 plants will provide a family with enough rhubarb to eat fresh and to freeze and preserve for a year. Once established in fertile soil, the plants produce bountiful crops for many years.

Start with healthy divisions from a friend's rhubarb planting, or from a nursery. Plant them in early spring, in deeply cultivated soil. Spade the ground 35–45 cm (14–18 inches) deep and turn into the soil liberal amounts of decomposed manure and compost. Dig planting pockets 25 cm (10 inches) deep. Place a handful of commercial 5-10-10 fertilizer in the bottom of each pocket.

Cover the fertilizer with 7.5–10 cm (3–4 inches) of sandy soil. Place the base of the tuberous root in the prepared planting pocket and work sandy soil in around the roots. The crown should remain uncovered, 7.5–10 cm below ground level. Water the new planting deeply.

Rhubarb may also be started from seed but it requires patience. Sow the seed in a cold frame in March or April. Protect the seedlings from frost. In midsummer, set the seedlings in the garden. Space them about 30 cm (12 inches) apart in rows 75 cm (2^{1}/2 ft) wide. The following spring the young plants will be ready to be set in a permanent place in the garden.

Rhubarb roots should not want for water when they are growing and producing. Maintain an evenly moist soil in spring and summer.

Rhubarb should not have a single stalk removed during the first season after it is transplanted. Take only a few stalks in the second season: remove the largest, most vigorous stalks as soon as the plant is mature. Leave a few on the plant to nourish the rootstock. Seed stalks should be removed as soon as they appear, unless you need seed for a new planting; then let the seed ripen before harvesting.

When harvesting rhubarb, pull the stalks; do not cut. Bend the stalk sideways, then pull firmly and quickly. Only the stalks are edible. Rhubarb leaves contain oxalic acid, a harmful substance if eaten.

In late fall, apply a top dressing of organic fertilizer such as tankage (a fertilizer made from refuse bones), blood meal, bone meal or old manure. In early spring, as new

Rhubarb. Chuck Heath photo

shoots appear, sprinkle 250 mL (1 cup) of 5-10-10 fertilizer in a wide circle around the base of each mature plant. Water the fertilizer in immediately.

Rhubarb may be forced in a cool basement or garage or under the greenhouse benches in winter. Dig a few roots from the soil in the late fall, place them in a tub or other container and cover the crowns with 2.5–5 cm (1–2 inches) of sand, soil or fine wood ash. Keep the plants moist and in a dark, frost-free place. The roots will produce fresh rhubarb all winter and early spring.

About the first of November, cut all stalks growing outside down to the ground. Mulch with old leaves or compost over the crowns. Evergreen fir boughs placed over the plantings provide extra winter protection.

When the clumps begin to throw small, spindly stalks, it is time to lift, divide and replant the sections. This is best done in the early spring. Split old, overcrowded crowns into sections ("divisions") with a sharp shovel. Cut down between the eyes, or growth buds, leaving as large a piece of storage root as possible, with at least one large growth bud on each section. Plant the new divisions immediately. A 6- to 7-year-old plant may provide as many as 10 new plant divisions.

- Valentine is a hybrid rhubarb with deep, bright red stalks. Strawberry and MacDonald are also superior varieties and grow well on the coast.

Tomatoes
See Vegetables, p. 71.

Tree Fruits
See Fruit Trees, p. 143.

Sex, Violence and Gardening

The paper in my old Underwood typewriter was blank, and so was I. My thoughts were on the weedy garden on our little island, not on the "Guides to Gardening" I was supposed to write. I pushed back my chair, got up from the desk and went out into the garden.

Chickweed was my nemesis. I bent down on all fours and began pulling up a vigorous-growing patch. A few minutes later, as I reached for a hand trowel, my eyes found two pairs of gumboots. I looked up to see a shy, lithe young girl and a striking Viking-type youth with carrot-coloured hair and a full beard.

The bearded one said, "Hope you don't mind if we visit your island?"

I answered, "You are both welcome. Walk about and enjoy."

"Who does all the gardening?" he asked

"My husband Al and I," was my answer. "We need to be self-sufficient."

The shy one spoke quietly. "How do you make a living way off here?"

"We earn a bit by selling produce and animals," I offered. "Also I write garden articles and books on gardening."

The rusty Viking threw back his head and roared. "You can't make any money writing books about gardening! There is no sex or violence in that kind of book."

"Oh, hold on a minute," I interrupted. "You think gardening isn't filled with sex and violence? Did you ever hear of the Venus fly trap, a plant that eats its prey in a snap? How about grafting, and I don't mean the kind that some politicians practise. Garden grafting is done by bringing together the inner bark of the stock and the scion, so a strong union can take place— now, you can't get any sexier or more violent than that. And, while we're on the subject, how about hybridization, when the pollen from one flower is placed on the stigma of another flower?"

By now I was pulling violently at the chickweed roots.

He persisted. "We do all right in our garden," he said. "A fine cash crop that affords us trips in winter to the Caribbean."

The shy one's dreamy blue eyes were cast down and her cheeks were bright crimson.

"We don't need any garden book to tell us how to grow our weed," he added.

I didn't say a thing. I just kept on weeding and thinking, some's got it all.

CHAPTER 3

Flowers and Such

ONE OF THE GREAT ADVANTAGES OF GARDENING ON THE WEST COAST is that by selecting annuals, perennials, biennials and bulbs carefully, you can have blooms all year round, and a garden of abundant colour from May through October. Plants should be placed and combined with others according to their colour, ultimate height, season of bloom, and texture and hue of leaves. An evergreen background of trees and shrubs sets off the brilliant colours of flowers to the best advantage.

To attain a continual parade of colour, group early flowering plants behind later flowering ones, and select plants that follow one another into bloom over as long a period of time as possible.

Leucojum, or snowflake. Adam Gibbs photo

Annual Flowering Plants

Annuals are satisfying to grow for all gardeners. Rookies and veterans alike can enjoy a bright, blooming summer with annuals. They come in every colour of the rainbow, along with a few not found in the rainbow. They sparkle in window boxes, hanging baskets, in beds under trees and shrubs, or in rows for cutting. Young flowering annuals planted among the fading tulips and daffodils gracefully conceal the dying bulb tops, and around a new home, annuals cover the bare ground while new trees and shrubs develop.

The garden annual usually lasts one growing season. Between spring and fall, the seed is sown and the plant flowers, drops its seeds and dies. To enjoy constant colour, plant seeds or starts of some annuals that flower early in the season, others that are showy in midsummer, and a few that will ring down the fall curtain. Begin with viola, pansy, and early cosmos, phlox and sweet alyssum. Midsummer is the time for nasturtium, lobelia, zinnia, verbena, carnation and mignonette. Late summer and autumn are woven in the orange and golden tapestry of sunflower, Unwin dahlia, late cosmos, poppy and marigold.

Nasturtium. Deb McVittie photo

Many hardy flowering annuals may be seeded directly into the open ground; others are started indoors. A useful general rule is that annual seeds may be sown outdoors after the apple blossoms fall, or in early June.

Consider the plants' preference for sun or shade. Full sun lovers include petunia, snapdragon, portulaca, poppy, daisy, marigold, cosmos, larkspur and zinnia. Annuals that grow well in partial shade include clarkia, coreopsis, godetia, iberis, lobelia, nicotiana, verbena, viola, salpiglossis, coleus, schianthus, impatiens and balsam.

Prepare the seed bed thoroughly. Spade the area to a depth of at least 30 cm (1 ft). Work into the soil organic material such as leaf mould, peat moss and aged manure. Rake the seed bed level and spread on a complete 5-10-10 commercial fertilizer at the rate of 1.3 kg (3 lbs) to 9 m² (100 sq ft) of planting. Water the fertilizer in. Keep the germinating seed bed moist at all times.

Cover the seeds with fine soil to a depth of about 3 times their diameter. Fine seed such as petunia, lobelia and snapdragon is barely covered: just press it into the topsoil.

Thin the young seedlings as they appear. Every extra plant in a garden is a weed, competing for food, water and light, and overcrowded seedlings develop into weak and

Godetia. Adam Gibbs photo

spindly plants. Encourage rapid growth by keeping the plants well nurtured. Every 2 weeks during their early growth add a booster-type liquid fertilizer to the soil, following package directions.

The more tender annuals such as balsam, petunia and lobelia require a long season of growth. Start them indoors in March or April, or select starts from greenhouse, nursery or garden centre. If the starts are already in bloom, you will be able to select colour and size more easily than by guessing from pictures in a seed catalogue.

Dig a planting pocket for each annual. Lift the plant from its starting container with care. Avoid disturbing the roots. If the plant was started in a fibre or peat pot, leave the plant in the pot when you put it in the planting pocket. The container will break down and improve the surrounding soil.

Soak the soil around the roots with a transplanting hormone solution to overcome transplant shock and start the plants into renewed growth. Keep your newly planted annuals well watered until they take hold. Well-established annuals should be watered 2 to 3 times a week. Water early in the morning to allow the foliage to dry by evening.

Encourage compact, well-formed plants by pinching out the centre of many annuals such as snapdragon, pansy and heliotrope. This will encourage branching. Maintain vigorous growth by removing old flowers and seed pods from the plants.

Strawflower, larkspur, geranium, statice, marigold, bells of Ireland, Chinese lantern, dianthus, cockscomb and zinnia are ideal for dried winter bouquets.

Aster

Asters are prized annuals. They bloom in a complete palette of even colours and they produce a variety of flower forms, from single to formal doubles. There are two distinct types: branching, which grow into large, productive plants and have strong, straight stems that work well in cut flower arrangements; and upright, which make lovely flower borders or container plants.

'Matsumoto' is a new variety of aster, grown for its early summer flowering, and cut-flower possibilities. The plants are uniform in size and upright in bearing, with a wide colour range. 'Powderpuff' asters also offer a wide spectrum of colours, with fully double blossoms on the 90 cm (36-inch) tall stems. They bloom from early summer until the first frost. Early 'Ostrich Plume' asters are spectacular with large, twirled flower petals in all shades. 'Dwarf Queen' is an early summer double aster with colourful chrysanthemum-like blossoms atop 30 cm (1-ft) tall stems.

Larkspur. Adam Gibbs photo

'Duchesse Formula Mix' produces bold, elegant peony-like blooms on strong, straight stems. The flowers come in 8 colours, including new bi-colours, silvery rose and silvery blue.

Avoid planting asters in the same area each season: rotate them to prevent disease. Keep their growing soil slightly moist, but water only in the early morning. This prevents powdery mildew, which appears as a whitish-grey growth on the leaves. If powdery mildew does infect the plants, spray with a solution of 15 mL (1 tbsp) of baking soda, 5 mL (1 tsp) of vegetable oil and 3 drops of dishwashing liquid in 4 litres (1 gal) of water. Spray the plants with the solution every week until the disease disappears.

Lobelia

Lobelia, another first-rate flower, is available as dwarf border plants or trailing varieties that work well in hanging baskets and other containers. 'Cambridge Blue' is a common edging plant with light blue flowers. 'Crystal Palace' is a dwarf with dark blue blossoms. 'Compact Rosamond' is a low grower with deep carmine red flowers and a white eye. 'White Lady' is a dwarf with glossy green leaves and white flowers. 'Sapphire' is a trailing plant covered with deep blue flowers and a white centre.

Newer lobelia varieties include: 'Riviera Blue Splash,' white with a picotee blue edge; 'Mrs. Clibran,' showy with deep blue, white-eyed blooms; 'Copelia,' a bright blue flowering lobelia; and 'Regatta Lilac,' a vivid lilac show-stopper.

Lobelia needs partial shade for best performance, and the plants can endure a windy seashore setting.

Marigold

Marigolds are among the most popular annual plants in North America. Giant varieties bloom with flowers 10–12.5 cm (4–5 inches) across on plants 90–120 cm (3–4 ft) tall. Miniature types grow to 20 cm (8 inches) high. Among the most spectacular marigolds are the tall-growing African varieties. Blooms reach 7.5–10 cm (3–4 inches) across in lemon yellow or orange hues. Stems are tall and sturdy. A spectacular example is 'Cracker Jack,' with its giant double carnation-type blooms in gold, orange and yellow hues. Inca F-1 hybrids have sturdy dark green foliage capped with large, bright yellow and orange blossoms. The more recently introduced Antigua F-1 hybrid marigolds are short and bushy, with dwarf flowers, and they bloom earlier in the season and more profusely than African marigolds.

African marigold. Les Dickason photo

'Snowdrift' is the new almost-white marigold. The blooms start with a cream hue and gradually turn white with a hint of cream in the centre. Stems reach 30–37.5 cm (12–15 inches) in height. 'Yellow Galore' is a tall grower with stems stretching to 45 cm (18 inches). This new variety is recommended by the Royal Horticultural Society. 'Harlequin' is topped with brilliant blossoms having red petals distinctly divided by a yellow stripe and a small bushy centre at the top.

Dwarf (French) marigolds are exquisite for borders and edgings. 'Naughty Marietta' has bright gold- and maroon-splashed petals and shows well in a border. 'Red Head' is mahogany with a crested centre of orange tipped with maroon. French doubles include Spry hybrids, 'Yellow Pygmy' and 'Butterball.'

'Bonanza Bolero,' a new All-American Selections winner, is an improved dwarf marigold. Its bright yellow flowers are 6 cm (2^{1}/$_{2}$ inches) wide, with red tips. The plant reaches 20–30 cm (8–12 inches) in height and flowers early.

Petunia

A neophyte gardener bewildered by the great variety of flowers cannot go wrong with petunias. They are brilliant in boxes, hanging baskets and planters, or tumbling over walls, banks and rocks. Full sun coaxes more blooms from petunia plants. Keep their growing soil well watered and fertilized with a plant food high in phosphorus and potash for sturdy growth and abundance of blossoms.

Super petunias. Adam Gibbs photo

Plants of the hybrid bedding or **multiflora** class grow to 30–35 cm (12–14 inches) high, and are covered with bright blossoms. Colourama Mixture multifloras show off in shades of pink, white and purple.

Grandiflora petunias are giddy with ruffles and frills. Low, compact plants grow about 30 cm (1 ft) high, with huge and vivid flowers. 'Bouquet' is one of the finest grandiflora petunias, with early fully double-fringed blooms in a wide range of colours. Ultra mixtures have been bred to produce large flowers on a compact, spreading plant. The newly introduced 'Prism Sunshine' is a bushy grandiflora adorned with creamy yellow flowers.

Cascade (**balcony**) petunias spill from hanging baskets, containers or window boxes with floral abandon. 'Super Lilac Cascade' and 'Hulahoop Red' are excellent new choices as well.

Dwarf petunias make beautiful borders and ground covers. Consider 'Red Carpet,' 'Chiffon Morn,' 'Falcon Pink Morn' and 'Carpet Lilac.' 'Purple Wave' and 'Pink Wave' represent a new breed of ground-cover petunias. A single plant will cover 90–120 cm (3–4 ft) of space and grow about 15 cm (6 inches) high.

Snapdragon

Snapdragons are flowering annuals, but they thrive in the mild West Coast climate and often they are grown as biennials or perennials. Give them a place in the sun, and be sure of the size in choosing a location: some snaps grow stately, most are medium in height and a few are dwarf in stature.

Rocket hybrids were improved to resist midsummer heat. Their 90 cm (3-ft) stems are set with large, evenly spread flowers. Rockets soar in shades of bronze, flame, gold, pink, red and white.

'Floral Carpet' snapdragons are compact and are available in a full range of colours. Grow them as edging or border plants.

'Redstone,' 'Gold Coin,' 'Pink,' 'White Goddess,' 'Cherry Improved' and 'Bronze' are new snapdragon introductions developed especially for cut flower enthusiasts. These plants produce long spikes on sturdy stems that reach 90 cm (3 ft).

Tetra snapdragons have particularly heavy stems and large, ruffled flowers. They grow to 75 cm (30 inches). 'Giant Tetra' shows mixed colours; 'Crimson Tetra' snaps are a deep velvety red.

Snapdragons. Adam Gibbs photo

Dwarf snaps include the 'Floral Carpet' and 'Floral Shower' series, which grow 15 cm (6 inches) high in red, bronze, lilac, white and yellow.

Sweet Pea

Franciscus Cupani, a monk with an interest in botany, observed the wild sweet pea (*Lathyrus odoratus*) in Sicily in 1700. He sent some seeds to a schoolmaster in Middlesex, England, with whom he corresponded regularly and exchanged seeds. The schoolmaster was a hybridizer. From these first seeds of the wild sweet pea he developed plants with stems bearing 1, 2 or 3 small, blue-purple blooms and a sweet scent. A pink and white bicolour sweet pea named 'Painted Lady' followed, and hybridizers soon developed new colour tones, improved forms and sturdy stems on vigorous vines. Frills and ruffles were introduced. Today, sweet peas come in shades of white and cream, pastel colours and lively tones of red, maroon and purple, and the vines reach soaring heights. Through all of this the sweet pea has kept its beloved fragrance.

It is a good idea to prepare the planting soil in the fall, or 1 to 2 months prior to seeding. Choose a site that is out in the open, where the vines will be exposed to full sun. Sweet peas must start in cool, moist early spring weather. Seed most types of sweet peas outdoors anytime from late February to late March. (Plant wintering or overwintering varieties in autumn.)

Sweet pea seed can be unpredictable in germinating. Soak the seeds in water for 24 hours before planting to hasten germination. Some gardeners chip the outer shell of the seed, or rub the shell with sandpaper to speed the process.

Prepare a planting trench at least 45 cm (18 inches) deep and 30 cm (1 ft) wide, in a south orientation if possible. In the bottom of the trench, place a few inches of fine gravel, sand or wood ash as drainage material. (The wood ash is also a fine source of potash for the plants.) A layer of seaweed in the bottom of the planting is a plus. Sprinkle 450 g (1 lb) of a 15-10-10 fertilizer to each 3 m (10 ft) of planting row or trench. Top this with 5–7.5 cm (2–3 inches) of light, sandy soil.

Kathi Linnman's sweet peas. Bob Cain photo

In the planting trench, which is now 10–12.5 cm (4–5 inches) deep, sow the seeds in a double row 7.5–10 cm (3–4 inches) apart and 5–7.5 cm (2–3 inches) deep. After the seedlings appear, thin the plants to 7.5 cm (3 inches) apart in the double row. As the plants grow, fill in around the base with more soil, and provide support for the vining types. String or wire netting, twiggy branches or a trellis will provide adequate support to the tendrils.

Sweet peas languish if neglected. Keep them growing vigorously with additions of fertilizer and lots of water. As the young starts leaf out, apply a complete fertilizer high in nitrogen. Two to three weeks later, sprinkle a complete fertilizer along the bases of the plants but about 7.5–10 cm (3–4 inches) away, at the rate of about 900 g (2 lbs) to each 4.5 m (15 ft) of double row. Liquid "bloom boosters" and liquid fish fertilizers are beneficial. Apply as directed.

Keep the roots moist by soaking the soil along the rows at least twice a week during dry summer weather. Avoid overhead sprinkling, as this encourages mildews and other plant diseases. Sweet peas will cease to bloom if allowed to go to seed. To prolong the blooming season, gather flowers frequently. Cut the stems with a sharp knife; never pull them from the plant. Cut some of the foliage along with the flowers: this causes the plant to branch into more flower stems.

A variety introduced recently by Cornell University is called 'Winter Flowering.' Sow the seeds before October 15 and provide the plants with a trellis. When fall temperatures average 13°C (55°F) they germinate rapidly and bloom in late November and through the Christmas holidays. If outdoor temperatures are below 13°C (55°F) seed the sweet peas in a cool greenhouse. The plants grow straight to 60–120 cm (2–4 ft) and bloom quickly.

'Winter Elegance' is an overwintering variety that blooms 2 to 3 weeks earlier than many other types. Sow the seed in early fall for colour in April. Ruffled petals in soft pastel shades of pink, salmon, lavender and white make this a gorgeous spring addition.

The 'Mammoth' series flowers in early spring on the coast. It produces large, bold blooms in shades of crimson, lavender, deep rose, navy blue, rose pink and salmon. Seed it outdoors in autumn or very early spring.

The 'Spencers,' or summer flowering main-crop varieties, produce large ruffled and frilled blossoms. Vines stretch skyward.

From early summer on, the flowers of 'Galaxy' sweet peas are stacked closely on long, sturdy stems, as many as 8 blossoms per stem.

'Novelty' sweet peas show fair-sized flowers on dwarf plants. Each plant develops into a compact bush 10–30 cm (4–12 inches) high, with as many as 5 to 8 ruffled flowers on each stem. Supports are unnecessary. 'Little Sweetheart,' 'Knee-Hi,' 'San Francisco,' 'Bijou' and 'Butterfly' hybrids are exquisite miniatures when planted in borders, window boxes, rock gardens, hanging baskets or patio containers.

'Old Spice Mix,' first developed between 1702 and 1907, then hybridized further, is a twenty-first-century winner. Highly scented flowers in a wide range of colours, including bi-colours and stripes, decorate this climber.

Zinnia

Zinnias are grouped by height, bloom size and character of flower. Colours of blossoms vary from vivid to muted. Zinnia flowers range in shape from the long, skinny petals of cactus types like Zenith Hybrids to the daisy-like flowers of the Pinwheel series.

'Envy' zinnia is startling with apple-green double blooms 7.5–10 cm (3–4 inches) across. Stems stretch to 60–75 cm (2–2$^{1}/_{2}$ ft). 'Old Mexico' flowers are splashed with red, yellow or mahogany tones. 'Sunbow' is especially suited to short summers. Semi-double flowers are small and come in many colours. 'Dreamland Rose' is a winner for indoor flower arranging: the blossoms remain fresh for a week or more. Dahlia-formed flowers are 10 cm (4 inches) across and grow on stems 25–30 cm (10–12 inches) tall. 'Dreamland Scarlet' is a companion of 'Dreamland Rose,' with bright red blossoms. 'Tropical Snow' is adorned with sparkling white flowers

The tiny 'Thumbelina' zinnia, an old Gold Medal winner, has small 15 cm (6-inch) stems covered with white, yellow, pink, lavender, orange or scarlet flowers. 'Lilliput,' 'Tom Thumb' and 'Red Buttons' are also charmers.

Two new All-American Selections in the zinnia field are 'Profusion Orange' and 'Profusion Cherry.' They produce sensational flowers and show tolerance to powdery mildew and leaf spot. Cherry rose or bright orange blossoms top stems 30–45 cm (12–18 inches) tall.

Zinnias thrive in bright, sunny locations. Select healthy young nursery transplants. The roots dislike disturbance, so take care in transplanting seedlings to their permanent place.

Other Annuals

Agrostemma 'Pale Pink' shows pale pink blooms on the ends of long, light stems. It is attractive in cut flower arrangements or in mass garden plantings.

Chaenorrhinum 'Summer Skies' is a winner with a massive show of true blue colours. In sun or shade, this plant will shine in hanging baskets or borders.

Cheiranthus 'Charity Mix' produces compact-growing plants with golden and rusty shades of wallflowers. Cut back in summer for fall colour.

Flowering kale and cabbage are modern favourites. 'Sunrise' is green with a white centre; 'Sunset' comes in shades of green with a rose centre. Both have compact heads on long stems, and are excellent for winter flower arrangements.

Geranium 'Black Magic Rose' is a new and original plant: bright pink blossoms set off dramatic black foliage edged with lime green.

Helianthus 'Earthwalker' is a new sunflower, with terra cotta-shaded flowers atop tall plants.

Malva 'Mystic Merlin' produces hollyhock-type flowers in shades of magenta, mauve and deep blue. Blooms are 5 cm (2 inches) across and cover the 1.5 m (5 ft) tall plant.

Nasturtium 'Empress of India' has dark leaves and deep scarlet flowers, which add beauty and a tangy taste to salads.

Oenothera 'Sunset Boulevard' is a new evening primrose that blooms during the day. Frilly apricot-orange flowers grow on upright stems. The plant may return year after year.

Pansy 'Nature Hybrid Mix' is bred to combine the free-flowering nature of violas and the size of pansy blossoms. These plants tolerate both hot and cold weather.

Pepper 'Chilly Chili' is grown as an ornamental pepper, and may also be eaten (it has medium to mild heat). Clusters of short chili peppers grow in shades of orange, red and cream among contrasting dark green leaves.

Petunia 'Primetime Series (Crystal Mix)' plants are more weather- and disease-resistant than less recent varieties. They also have larger flowers that bloom earlier. The mix includes all veined colours, including pink, plum and dark red.

Portulaca 'Margarita Rosita' gives the garden hot pink flowers on a compact, low-growing plant. Flowers shine in hot or cool weather.

Rudbeckia 'Cherokee Sunset' has large double flowers in sunset shades, quite striking in the annual garden. Plants develop a strong basal branching pattern.

Verbena 'Serenity Mix' is a balanced mixture of early-blooming flowers. The trailing blooms, in shades of pastel lavender to white, pink and carmine red, are decorated with lacy foliage. 'Calypso F-2 Watercolour Mix' blooms are a designer blend of blue and lavender shades. The plant's semi-spreading growth pattern and long flowering period makes it a winner.

Perennials

Perennials were originally collected as wild plants from Switzerland, India, Mexico, China, Japan, South Africa and other countries. Then they were hybridized because of their hardiness, beauty and dependability.

Perennials usually die to the ground in winter and start growing again each spring. They are rugged and enduring, and they grow prolifically on the Pacific coast.

Prepare the soil well for perennials. Deep digging encourages sturdy roots and productive plants. For each hardy perennial plant, prepare a planting pocket approximately 45 cm (18 inches) deep and at least 30 cm (1 ft) wide to allow the roots of the plant to spread out naturally. Place 12.5 cm (5 inches) of sand or fine gravel in the bottom, and over this drainage material layer 7.5–10 cm (3–4 inches) of composted manure. Cover the manure with several inches of a soil filled with humus. Make a small mound of earth in the centre of the planting hole and place the plant on it, spreading the roots over the mound. Fill in around the roots carefully. Firm the soil well around the crown (the point where the roots and top growth join). Leave no air spaces. Water the new planting deeply and thoroughly.

Note: Exceptions to this are peonies, Oriental poppies and other plants with large, fleshy roots. They are planted shallow. The crowns of delphiniums are not covered.

Keep the area moist until the plants are reestablished. In midsummer sprinkle a 5-10-10 fertilizer around the plants and water thoroughly.

Alternatively, many perennials may be directly seeded in the garden. Germination and growth are rapid in midsummer. Columbine, pyrethrum, coreopsis, gaillardia, delphinium and primrose seeds are started outside in the garden during June, July and August.

Remove faded blossoms and withered foliage from the plants whenever you see them. Cutting the old flower heads as soon as they fade often stimulates side buds. Trim back creeping and trailing plants such as arabis and alyssum after flowering to keep them compact. Remove seed heads unless they are needed for propagation. After a late fall frost cut the stalks to the ground.

Perennials go underground after the first fall killing frost. Their roots need protection from the action of the ground alternately freezing and thawing, which can thrust the crowns and roots out of the soil. Lay several inches of peat moss, aged sawdust, bark or compost material over the planting.

Propagate your perennials by taking cuttings or slips in the summer. Make a cutting about 5–7.5 cm (2–3 inches) long by cutting the stem just below a node. Remove the bottom leaves, leaving only 2 to 3 top leaves. Place the cuttings in a rooting mixture of sand and peat moss and keep them moist and in the shade.

Trailing or creeping perennials such as ajuga, phlox or pinks may be increased by layering. Bend a long branch or stem to the ground and peg it down under 2.5–5 cm (1–2 inches) of soil. Leave 2.5–5 cm of the stem or branch tip out of the soil. When roots form on the layering, cut the new plant from the older one and transplant it.

When your perennials reappear in early spring, give their soil a boost with a plant food containing a high percentage of phosphorus and potash to stimulate growth and development. Apply the fertilizer around the base of each plant, using 900 g (2 lbs) for each 3 m (10 ft) of row. Reinvigorate perennials by lifting and dividing them every few years. If a plant is not divided, the crown that produces flowers will bear fewer flowering stocks and over years may die out completely. Divide them every third year, *except* peony, Christmas rose, bleeding heart, lupine and geum, which must be well established in one location to bloom profusely. These plants should be disturbed only after 5 to 6 years.

Phlox. Adam Gibbs photo

Separate and replant perennials after they have flowered. To dislodge the plants, dig a trench around the root area 20–30 cm (8–12 inches) deep and 15–20 cm (6–8 inches) away from the crown. Push a garden fork straight down into the trench and work the fork gently back and forth on all sides until the clump lifts out of the ground.

Holding it in your hands, shake it gently until all the soil falls from the roots. Some perennials will pull apart easily; others must be cut into sections with a sharp knife. Each part that you pull or cut from the mature clump should have both roots and new shoots attached. Discard the woody centres and retain the young, vigorous outer growth. Then transplant as for young plants (see above).

Chrysanthemum 'Crazy Daisy' produces double, quilled white flowers with yellow centres. They are wonderful in borders and cut flower arrangements.

Erigeron 'Azure Fairy' are striking with double mauve flowers on strong stems. This flower blooms the first year when planted from seed.

Dianthus 'Ipswich' grows in drifts of pink, fragrant, spicy blooms. The grey foliage is lovely in all seasons.

Helianthemum 'Rock Rose' is covered in glossy green leaves with small, poppy-like blooms in early spring. The

*Bleeding heart (*Dicentra spectabilis*). Adam Gibbs photo*

plants bloom in the second year after seeding, in shades of red, cream and pink.

Hollyhock 'Peaches and Dreams' flower the second year after planting from seed. Huge double blooms in creamy peach, often tinged with pink, grow on tall, stately stems.

Lychnis 'Blushing Bride' is a free-flowering plant. In early summer, pink and white blossoms top numerous silver stems and generous foliage.

*Bleeding heart (*Dicentra spectabilis alba*). Adam Gibbs photo*

Yucca. Adam Gibbs photo

*Tickseed (*Coreopsis verticillata*).* Adam Gibbs photo

*Primrose (*Primula *'Garryarde guinevere').* Sandra Evelyn photo

Red yarrow in foreground. Sandra Evelyn photo

*Black-eyed Susan (*Rudbeckia*) and* Salvia.
Adam Gibbs photo

Hosta. Chuck Heath photo

Flowers and Such

Pink tree peony. Sandra Evelyn photo   *Sedum.* Adam Gibbs photo

Perennials suitable for growing in sunny drought conditions include thistle, gaillardia, lavender, sedum, yucca, yarrow, artemisia, achillea, rudbeckia, perennial helianthus, coreopsis.

Perennials that thrive in the shade include columbine, anemone, campanula, doronicum, candytuft, phlox, veronica, astilbe, hosta, viola, lily-of-the-valley, primrose.

Perennials that attract butterflies include salvia, lobelia, phlox, goldenrod, bleeding heart, clematis, astilbe, buddleia, anemone, gaillardia, sunflower, day lily, stokesia, sedum, thistle, Michaelmas daisy, monkshood.

Particularly fragrant perennials include lily, monarda, peony, phlox, lavender, dianthus, clematis.

Biennials

Flowering biennials are at their colourful best just after the exuberance of spring. They require 2 years from seed to bloom. In the first year, vegetative growth and roots are developed. In the second year, the plant flowers, scatters seeds and dies. Occasionally a biennial endures several winters.

Start biennials from seed in May, June, July or early August in a seed bed with fine, sandy soil, and separate from other plantings. Turn the seed bed and work the soil to a depth of 45 cm (18 inches). Rake the surface smooth, then soak with water. Place the seeds carefully, 5–10 cm (2–4 inches) apart in rows that are about 60 cm (2 ft) apart. Fine seed needs only to be pressed into the soil with a board, or placed on the soil and sprinkled with sand. Cover larger seed with a fine layer of soil or sand, to a depth twice the diameter of the seed. Keep the newly seeded area evenly moist. Use a fine mist of water to penetrate the topsoil.

Seedlings are ready to be transplanted to their permanent position in the garden when they develop 2 sets of leaves. To ensure good growth and continuous bloom, prepare the permanent location thoroughly. Turn the soil deeply and work in a compost or fertile humus and commercial plant food. Use 1.3 kg (3 lbs) of 5-10-10 fertilizer for each 9 m² (100 sq ft) of area. Biennials fail over winter if they are poorly drained, so provide for adequate soil drainage by planting on a slightly raised area, or place generous amounts of coarse sand or small gravel at the bottom of each planting pocket.

Transplanting is best done on a cloudy or rainy day, or in the late afternoon. Prepare a generous-size planting pocket for each specimen. The roots of biennials should be spread out as far as possible to absorb nutrients and moisture. Fill around the roots and crown with fine soil and press down firmly.

Canterbury Bells

Canterbury Bells, or the Campanula family, are a large and versatile group. They are the last biennials in the year to bloom. The variety calycanthema is the cup and saucer form, named for its petal-like outer parts, which may be deeply divided or just a little lobed. Sturdy, erect stems 75–120 cm (2¹/2–4 ft) high support white, blue, lilac, pink and deep purple fluorescent blooms from May through July.

Canterbury Bells grown from seed seldom flower the first year unless sown early indoors and transplanted outdoors in the spring. Give these plants a place in the light shade with a nutrient-rich, well-drained soil. They do not tolerate soggy conditions around their crowns. The seed is tiny in size: plant it in fine sand or vermiculite for good germination. On the West Coast, these plants often return year after year from natural seeding. Extend flowering by removing faded blossoms so that second buds can develop behind the spent cup and saucer.

Canterbury Bells. Adam Gibbs photo

Forget-Me-Not

Forget-me-nots are often grown as a carpet among spring-flowering bulbs. Sometimes they flower in the fall. Seed them outdoors in May for flowering in the following early spring, and keep them moist. Tiny white, blue and pink blossoms smother the plant. 'Pinkie' is covered with bright pink blossoms all summer. 'Myosotis' and 'Sapphire' develop brilliant blue flowers. 'Alpestris White Ball' is a low, compact grower with groups of white blossoms.

Foxglove

Foxglove (*Digitalis*), known during medieval times as "Folks' Gloves," is a beloved biennial that grows well on the West Coast.

Spikes of huge bell-shaped blossoms rise dramatically above other plants, and they often flower in the same season they were seeded. Sparkling foxgloves are found in white, cream, apricot, yellow, rose, pink, red and purple. Many have interesting markings or spots inside the florets. In the garden, group 3 to 5 foxgloves against a backdrop of dark evergreens for an effective woodland scene.

Foxglove and Oriental poppy. Deb McVittie photo

Foxgloves prefer partial shade but will thrive in full sun. Provide them with a soil generous in humus. Care for them as you would any biennial, but you don't have to worry about them: foxgloves tolerate neglect.

Cut down the parent stalk after the plant has flowered to make room for the young rosettes that cluster around the base of the old parent plant. These tiny plants will flower the following season.

'Foxy Mix' blooms the year it is seeded. The dwarf plants are crowded with bell-shaped blossoms.

Purpurea alba is an unspotted, pure white form. 'Glittering Prizes' is a mixture heavily spotted and blotched with chocolate or maroon. 'Sensation' is an old but beautiful variety. 'Dwarf Temple Bells' is adorned with dainty primrose-like bells that hold up during heavy summer rains. 'Excelsior' types have flowers all around the stem instead of only on one side, as is the case with some older strains.

Hollyhock

Hollyhocks are cultivated as biennials, but if their spent flowering stocks are cut back after blooming, the plants often thrive and bloom for many seasons. Give hollyhocks a place in full sun. Sow the seed outdoors in May. Single and double blooms come in a full palette of colours, ranging from almost black through rust grey to pure white. Blackcurrants whirl with double blossoms. Deep purple flowers are swirled over with white. 'Double Appleblossom' produces papery pink double flowers. 'Summer Carnival Mixture,' a native of China, has deep crimson, light pink, rose, red, yellow and white double flowers. 'Arabian Nights' produces an almost black flower. 'Pioneer Mixture' is an old-fashioned hollyhock with large single flowers in shades of white, red, pink and rose.

Honesty

Honesty (money plant) is a biennial planted primarily for its decorative fall seed pods. Translucent silvery circles about 3 cm (1 1/4 inches) across grow on sturdy stems 60–90 cm (2–3 ft) high. Flowers appear in early summer. They resemble wild mustard bloom, except they are purple or white.

Honesty plants flourish in sun or shade. They are persistent; usually they self-seed and can even become a nuisance. Plant them out of the way, where they won't impede other plants, and cut them for dried arrangements.

Iceland Poppy

Iceland poppies, with their fragrant, 7.5 cm (3-inch) flowers swaying on slender stalks about 30 cm (1 ft) tall, often flower along with the daffodils and tulips. They are true perennials in their native habitat, but when they are grown in the garden, they assume all the characteristics of biennials. They bloom the first year from seed and often self-sow freely.

Iceland poppies show colours from white through lemon and orange to red. Grow them in a light, sandy soil with excellent drainage: they fail if water collects around their crowns.

'Nudicaule Sea Shanty' produces stems like tall masts, which bear red blossoms. 'Gartford Giant,' a recent hybrid, develops crepe-paper-like flowers in hues of white, yellow, orange and gold-apricot. 'Pizzicato' produces colourful flowers at the expense of leaves. The stems are short and stocky and well able to endure strong West Coast winds.

Sweet William

Sweet Williams, with their big, bright heads of scarlet, wine, pink, coral and white, explode in the hot summer sun. Plant them in a sandy, well-drained soil that has been generously limed. If allowed to self-sow, the flower becomes dull and drab. Start them with new seed every second year to keep them bright. Sow seed in July or August for the following season and press the seeds into the soil to make sure they germinate.

'Barbatus Super Duplex' produces blooms on tall, sturdy stems, in a magical range of colours. Florists find this variety a long keeper for cut-flower use. 'Hybrid Rainbow Loveliness,' with fancy fringed flowers in hues of carmine, lilac, pink and white, a few of them beclouded, is remarkable.

Wallflower

If only for their fragrance, wallflowers are welcome in the garden. They are also the earliest of the biennials to show colour: in sheltered areas they begin flowering in late January, in tawny tones of gold, dark red, bronze, orange and yellow.

Sow wallflower seed outdoors in May. A well-limed, sandy loam is ideal, but they will survive in amended clay (clay to which lime and sand have been added). Wallflowers are more productive in a bright, sunny site. They are ideal in rock gardens, as they need a sloping root run. Poorly drained winter-wet soil will destroy them.

Siberian wallflower. Deb McVittie photo

'Fair Lady Mixed' is a tall English wallflower with sweet-scented flowers in shades of purple, red, yellow and orange.

The Siberian wallflower is a free-blooming, low-growing plant. From early spring to fall a smattering of flowers in shades of orange or yellow cluster on the stems.

Alpine wallflower is an erect miniature plant with grey-white foliage and lilac or mauve flowers.

Dwarf scarlet bedder is a good choice for border or rock garden plantings. Single red flowers grow on short, sturdy stems.

'Double Dream Mixed' produces double flowers in a great range of colours, on plants that grow to 30 cm (12 inches) tall.

Spring-Flowering Bulbs

Early spring-flowering bulbs play a major role in the wintry landscape. Snowdrop, squill, iris, aconite, narcissus (daffodil), crocus, puschkinia, anemone and chionodoxa push up through the cold earth, breaking the spell of winter with goblets of blossoms that spill over with gold, orange, vermilion, and shades of blue, apple green, rose and sparkling white.

Bulbs may be planted in drifts (groups), among rocks and evergreens, or naturalized (adapted to the wild) in woodlands. They are small but hardy, and multiply rapidly.

Encourage early colour by planting the bulbs in sheltered but open places where the first spring sunlight warms the ground. Select a planting area with thorough water drainage. Plant small bulbs (the size of peas or smaller) approximately 7.5 cm (3 inches) deep and 2.5–5 cm (1–2 inches) apart in groups of 3 or more. For each bulb, dig a small pocket with a hand trowel and place 2.5–5 cm (1–2 inches) of sand in the bottom, then set the base of the bulb on the sand. Fill in around the bulb and over the top lightly with fine, sandy soil.

Miniature iris. Deb McVittie photo

Each fall provide bulbs with generous amounts of organic material such as bone meal, fish meal or decomposed manure. Miniature bulbs are best left on their own for several years. If a plant begins to deteriorate, bearing fewer and less attractive flowers, rejuvenate it. In late July, after all the foliage dies down, lift, separate or divide the bulbs and replant them immediately.

Galanthus, or **snowdrop**, blooms in late winter with white nodding flowers tipped in green. Plant the small, truncated bulbs 5–7.5 cm (2–3 inches) deep, in clusters. Give them a cool, moist, shady spot where their leaves make a dark, shining foil for the flowers. They colonize well under a canopy of large fir trees.

Starry **Chionodoxa**, or **glory-of-the-snow**, bloom bright in March and April. They are sky blue with white centres, but some varieties have intense pink or pure white flowers. Each dwarf flower spike bears 11 to 12 blossoms. Plant 5 to 6 bulbs in a space no larger than the palm of your hand. Cover the tiny bulbs with 5 cm (2 inches) of soil at the most.

Snowdrop. Chuck Heath photo

Squills, or **Scilla**, are rose pink, blue and white. These Siberian immigrants brave the hardships of winter to appear in the early spring landscape. They open into flaring bells, 1 to 3 to a stalk, which droop gracefully from stems 12.5–15 cm (5–6 inches) high. The 'Spring Beauty' variety has a touch of violet in its blue. Squills thrive on neglect. Plant the bulbs in groups, about 7.5 cm (3 inches) deep and 5–7.5 cm (2–3 inches) apart. They are especially effective when planted in rock gardens or in a woodland.

Leucojum (snowflake) is a member of the amaryllis family. It is a noble flower despite its diminutive size. Crystalline bells hang in bunches of 6 to 7 from dull green stems, which reach upward to 17.5–20 cm (7–8 inches). If you like unusual plants, this one belongs in your garden. They grow equally well in sun and shade. Set them at least 10 cm (4 inches) into the ground. The species *Leucojum vernum*, the most commonly grown on the coast, has bell-shaped flowers edged in green. They bloom with the snowdrops in spring.

Winter flowering **miniature iris** usually have 4 leaves growing at angles, and flowers are produced singly on short, stout stems. *Iris danfordiae*, which blooms at the same time as squills, is a charming addition to the garden. Bright golden blossoms top 7.5–10 cm (3–4 inch) stems on this early dwarf iris. Tiny *I. reticulata* bursts into bloom before the first crocus. Each deep violet flower has a bright orange marking or "beard." *I. histriodes major* produces a bright purple flower. Plant dwarf iris 7.5 cm (3 inches) deep and 7.5 cm apart in groups of 5 or more. With full summer sun and perfect drainage, iris will multiply rapidly in the garden or woodland.

Blooms of **winter aconite** (*Eranthis*) appear as buttercup-golden blooms resting on emerald green cushions of leaves. In dull weather the flowers close, but when the spring sun breaks through they throw open their golden cups. Winter aconites bloom bravely for

Winter aconite. Adam Gibbs photo

about 6 weeks. After the blooms have faded, the beauty of this plant's foliage remains until May. And once established, winter aconite stays in the garden for life. It does not always appear above the ground the first winter, but if you obtain fresh tubers or soak dried ones in water overnight, you should have success. Plant small tubers 5 cm (2 inches) deep and in groups. They naturalize well under the protection of deciduous shrubs or trees. *Eranthis hyemalis* has deep yellow blooms foiled with finely cut foliage. It is the earliest of the winter aconites to flower, and it will tolerate wet, poorly drained locations. *Eranthis cilicica*, a species from Asia Minor, has finely cut bronze foliage. *Eranthis tubergenii* is a hybrid with large, golden yellow flowers, which are long-lasting because they are sterile.

The **miniature daffodils**, all of which belong to the genus *Narcissus*, are welcome visitors in spring. Like little clowns, they poke through cold ground to rebel happily against the bleak clouds above. With flower petals pulled back like rabbit ears, the tiny daffodil stands a full 15 cm (6 inches) tall.

Hoop-petticoat (*Narcissus bulbocodium*) is a fine flower with unpredictable flowering habits. A few rise and shine right after the Christmas season, others wait until February or March. Bright yellow hoop-petticoat-shaped blossoms come out on stems 10–20 cm (4–8 inches) tall. The leaves are fine and rush-like in appearance. *N. minimus* is a miniature imitation of the golden 'King Alfred' (see p. 115). The tiny trumpet flowers are supported by straight 7.5 cm (3-inch) stems. *N. cyclamineus* are tiny treasures for their January and February flowering. Dwarf in stature, they have drooping orange yellow cups that are bent sharply backward, and lemon yellow petals. *N. juncifolius* is another miniature daffodil with fine foliage. Each 10 cm (4 inch) stem holds 1 or 2 tiny yellow flowers, which are appreciated for their fragrance and early arrival.

Give miniature daffodils a place in full sun to approximate their natural Mediterranean habitats. Plant them 7.5–10 cm (3–4 inches) deep in the early fall.

In early spring, the blooms of **species (wild) crocus** open flat and starry in sunshine, and close up tightly in wind, rain and snow. The outer petals are deep yellow or orange with brown or purple; the flower is lilac, blue or pearly white. *Crocus chrysanthus*, a newer strain, has unusual flowers in delightful colours and a fragrance like a touch of honey. *C. balansae* is orange with dark brown feathering; *C. korolkowii* is violet with yellow and purple stripes; *C. imperati* is violet and buff inside, lined in purple. Plant them in large colonies, and don't make the common mistake of planting species crocus corms too deeply. Cover them with 5 cm (2 inches) of fine soil at the most.

Anemone, or **windflower**, belongs to the buttercup family. Anemones bloom bright and early in shades of soft blue, deep rose, scarlet and white. Plant anemones under Japanese maple, azalea and other feathery shrubs for a striking effect. *Anemone blanda*, with small, starry flowers, grows 15–20 cm (6–8 inches) tall and is the earliest blooming of all the hardy anemones. Newer selections produce larger flowers and foliage. 'Blue Star,' 'Pink Star' and 'White Splendour' are aptly named for their flower colour; 'Radar' produces purplish red blooms.

Crocus

Spring crocus is usually the first flower to break winter's hold on the garden. The plants push up through the earth with grassy leaves and blooms of white, yellow, blue and lavender. Some species are striped and variegated in combinations of colours.

Crocuses produce new corms on top of the old ones. The crocus that flowers so bravely in early spring withers away and is replaced by many young ones. Leave them undisturbed year after year, and they will reproduce. New seedlings appear like grass at the base of the parent plant to form a corm and flower. Scatter groups of crocus corms under trees and shrubs in woodland settings, and tuck them in rock pockets.

Plant the corms in early autumn to encourage strong root growth.

Choose sunny spots so the first spring sun will open the crocuses wide. Prepare a sandy, well-drained bed deep enough for the roots to find nourishment and moisture when needed.

Crocus. Deb McVittie photo

For each corm, dig a planting pocket 12.5–15 cm (5–6 inches). Sprinkle bone meal in the bottom, then a handful of sand. Set in the corm, add 5 cm (2 inches) of soil, firm the planting and water well.

In the late spring, apply a commercial 5-10-10 fertilizer to the planting, using 1.3 kg (3 lbs) per 9 m² (100 sq ft) of planting. The fertilizer feeds the old corms and thus stimulates the development of next year's crop.

Daffodil

Fall planting is as seasonal as raking leaves and the first frost on the pumpkin. Daffodils bring the first big splash of spring colour, and under the right conditions they even blossom in snow. They are reliable and hardy, and they have a bitter taste that repels deer and rodents. Daffodils are a large group of narcissus plants, usually those with long, trumpet-shaped flowers, but most gardeners use the names *daffodil* and *narcissus* interchangeably.

Daffodil plantings are permanent, so choose a site carefully. Sites with full sun or semi-sun are best. Turn the soil to a depth of 45–50 cm (18–20 inches). Spade in generous amounts of aged manure, bone meal and superphosphate. A well-drained, sandy soil with organic humus added is an ideal growing medium.

A mother daffodil bulb is composed of a number of old and young portions, and will yield 3 to 4 blooms. A round bulb has no offsets and produces 1 to 2 flowers. Double-nosed or triple-nosed daffodils produce 3 or more flowers.

Spacing and depth of planting are governed by the area available, the size of the bulbs and the texture of the soil. Generally, the correct planting depth is 10–12.5 cm (4–5 inches) from the nose, or point, of the bulb. Small species are set in the soil to a depth about twice their diameter. Space miniatures a few inches apart; larger plants need 20–25 cm (8–10 inches). Whatever type you are using, make a planting pocket for each bulb and put in a handful of coarse sand for drainage, then put in the bulb, "nose" up.

Daffodils do not benefit by yearly lifting. Leave the bulbs undisturbed in the ground until the planting becomes too crowded. But do lift and separate them every 5 to 6 years, or the size and number of flowers will diminish every year. When it is time to lift them, do so as soon as the foliage has yellowed and before the new roots have had a chance to grow. In separating the bulbs, remove only the divisions that pull away easily. Bulbs that are firmly attached to the parent bulb should be left. Clean the bulbs and store them in a well-ventilated place until they are replanted.

In the late spring, as the flowers fade, apply to the planting soil fertilizers high in phosphorus and potash. Use 1.3 kg (3 lbs) granular fertilizer per 9 m^2 (100 sq ft), or use liquid fertilizer according to package directions.

After the petals fall, cut off the flower heads to prevent seeds from forming and to redirect the plant's energy to the bulb. Do not cut flower stems or leaves, and don't braid the foliage. Let the plant mature (cure): this provides nourishment to rebuild the bulb for next season's flowers.

Daffodils come in a range of forms, sizes and colours, and cover a long season of bloom. Trumpet daffodils are the best known. They produce one large flower to each stem. The trumpet, or corona, is the same length or longer than the perianth, the row of flower petals at the back. Varieties include 'Mount Hood,' a pure white; 'Unsurpassable,' deep golden yellow; and 'King Alfred,' the old favourite golden.

Large-cupped daffodils also have one flower to each stem. The corona is shorter and broader than that of the trumpet type: it may be as small as a third the length of the perianth, yet it is still long in relation to the perianth petals. Examples are 'Dunkeld,' a yellow with an orange crowned cup; 'Mrs. R.O. Backhouse,' with a pinkish cup set off against a white background; and 'Semper Avanti,' with a cream perianth and orange cup.

Small-cupped daffodils are true to their name. Cups or small trumpets may not exceed a third the length of the perianth. Well-known kinds include 'La Riante,' with a white perianth and a flat crown marked with a reddish star; 'Firetail,' with a cream outer perianth and an orange-scarlet cup; and 'Polar Ice,' all white.

Double daffodils often produce a single flower on each stem. The flower is double or multi-formed. 'Daphne' has small, fragrant white flowers resembling gardenias; 'Texas' is chrome yellow and orange; 'Twink' has alternating petals of primrose and clear orange.

Triandrus daffodils, with slender, graceful stems, bear several bell-like flowers. They are forced easily for early winter colour indoors (see p. 228). 'Geranium' is white with an orange cup; 'L'Innocence' is white with a deep yellow eye or cup; 'Cheerfulness' has cream coloured petals intermingled with short orange-yellow petals.

Jonquilla daffodils are characterized by narrow, rushlike leaves and fragrant flowers in clusters on long stems. Three favourites are 'Cherie,' with a white perianth and small pink cup; 'Trevithian,' with pale yellow flowers; and 'Helios,' with light yellow perianth and dark yellow cups.

Tazetta daffodils (*N. tazetta* and *N. poeticus ornatus* crossed) produce flowers in clusters of 4 to 8 to each flower stem. 'Chinese Sacred-Lily,' 'Grand d'O' and paper-white narcissus are the hybrids of this group. They are admired for their fragrance and the fact that they can be forced to flower indoors.

Division *Poeticus* members are recognized by their white petals or perianths and large, dark red centres, as 'Pheasant's Eye.' *Narcissus poeticus* is intensely fragrant. 'Comus' has a white perianth and lemon yellow eye, edged with deep red; 'Snowking' has broad overlapping white petals and a flat cup with a wide orange margin.

The *Barri* narcissus is named for Peter Barr, who introduced to England narcissus with small, brilliantly coloured cups that are less than a third as long as the petals. 'Raity,' 'Cordovan' and 'Mountain Pride' are fine examples.

Hyacinth

Hyacinths are fragrant and bright with flowers in April, when most daffodils and other narcissus have fled and before the tall, late-flowering tulips bloom. Plant hyacinth near pathways, doorways or driveways where the fragrance can be enjoyed most often. They are also elegant when forced to bloom indoors in late winter (see p. 228).

Hyacinths are available in exciting deep reds, purples, yellows and oranges, as well as soft pastel shades.

Select firm, plump bulbs with an average diameter of 17.5 cm (7 inches). Choose a sunny place that has quick winter water drainage and plant them outdoors in the late autumn, along with tulips and daffodils. Prepare the planting soil as for tulips (see p. 118). Plant the bulbs 15–17.5 cm (6–7 inches) deep, as measured from the base of the bulb. Space them 15–20 cm (6–8 inches) apart, in groups rather than rows. Handle the bulbs carefully, as they bruise easily.

Hyacinth bulbs may remain in one site for 3 to 4 years. When the flowers become smaller, remove the bulbs and select new ones. Some gardeners propagate hyacinth plantings by "scooping" or "scoring." After the foliage of the plant dies down in the late spring, cut a scoop out of the base of the bulb so that all layers of bulb scale are cut through. Alternatively, score the bulb by making 2 deep cuts across the bottom or base of the bulb in the form of an X. After scooping or scoring, replant the bulb. Place the base on 2.5–5 cm (1–2 inches) of sharp sand, then cover it with soil 3 times as deep as the diameter of the bulb. Several small bulblets will grow from the cut areas. After they form, remove them from the mature bulb and plant them out individually. Flowers come in 3 to 4 years.

Mulch over the planting with light material in late October. When green shoots appear in early spring, remove the mulch.

Fertilize a hyacinth planting generously after it flowers. Fertilize in late summer with a complete 4-12-8 commercial fertilizer, applying 1.3 kg (3 lbs) per 9 m^2 (100 sq ft). In the fall, spread wood ash (19 L/5 gal per 9 m^2/100 sq ft) over the planting, as well as blood meal and bone meal (2.3 kg/5 lbs per 9 m^2/100 sq ft).

Snip off the heads when the flowers fade. Allow the leaves and stems to mature without damaging them. When the foliage pulls away easily it is ripened.

Tulip

The "Red Lilies" discovered in 1554 growing in the fields of the Turkish Empire were actually tulips. At that time the flowers were the love symbols of Persia. From the Turkish and Persian gardens they were taken to Holland and auctioned from counting houses like stocks. At the peak of the tulip-import frenzy, in 1634, nobles, citizens, farmers, seamen and servants all speculated in the tulip market—driving prices to insane levels. One tulip of the variety Admiral Liefkens (crimson, on white) sold for $750. A Rotgans (white stripe with rose) fetched $1,500. A Viceroy tulip bulb was exchanged for possessions valued at $1,825. Today's coast gardener may purchase a top-quality tulip bulb for a dollar and select from scores of different classes of tulips and more than 2,000 varieties. Tulip colours range from sparkling white to almost black as night. True black tulips are difficult to hybridize and they are rare. Some flowers are ovals; others are almost square; and flower petals may be round, pointed, twisted, convoluted or laciniated (fringed).

Tulips. Mary Palmer photo

Plant tulip bulbs from September to November, to give the roots time to make sturdy growth before winter's cold sets in. Locate your tulip plantings in light, sunny sections of the garden. Cultivate the planting soil to a depth of 60 cm (2 ft). Spade in generous amounts of sand to allow excess water to drain quickly. Tulip bulbs will deteriorate if the soil holds stagnant water. Spread wood ash (19 L/5 gal per 9 m²/100 sq ft) and blood meal and bone meal (1.3 kg/3 lbs per 9 m²/100 sq ft) and rake lightly into the topsoil.

Plant tulips in colonies of at least a dozen, and make other plantings in several sections of the garden for an outstanding effect. A concentration of one colour in each group is most effective. Avoid planting in a single, long line; plant them in groups for a more natural effect. Work with high-quality bulbs (bargain bulbs are no bargain) and plant only those that are clean, firm, heavy and healthy, with smooth, dark brown skin. Discard any bulbs that are discoloured, mouldy and/or soft.

Depth of planting varies with the type of bulb. Plant small species (wild botanical) tulips 7.5–10 cm (3–4 inches) deep, and larger types, 20–25 cm (8–10 inches) deep. Deep planting makes for superior flowers and a more permanent planting. Make a planting pocket for each bulb and put a handful of sand on the bottom, which will keep the base of the bulb dry but allow the roots to reach down for moisture. Plant the bulb

pointed end up. The rounded side of the bulb contains the first big leaf. Plant the bulb with that side toward the direction from which the flowers are to be admired.

In early spring, as green shoots appear, apply a commercial 5-10-10 fertilizer at the rate of 225 g (1/2 lb) to 9 m² (100 sq ft). Water it into the soil.

Do not tie or braid the leaves for a neater appearance. If the planting is unattractive, lift the entire plant, roots, bulb and top and replant in a sunny, well-drained, out-of-the-way place to cure (mature). Many gardeners scatter seeds of flowering annuals among the tulips to camouflage the leaves during the maturing time.

Yellow tulip. Bill Waldron photo

In late spring, as the flowers fade, give the planting soil—and foliage—soluble fertilizers high in phosphorus and potash, according to directions on the label.

Remove the flower heads as they fade to prevent seed pods from forming and redirect the plant's energy into bulb production. Allow the foliage to remain until it matures. If you cut off the leaves before the tulip matures, there may not be any new bulbs to replace the one that shrivelled. Bulbs develop after the flower heads are removed. Continue to water and cultivate until the foliage is withered.

Tulips are usually not long-lived. The first year after planting, they produce quality flowers of uniform size and height. They should also produce well in the second and third years, but they must be lifted and stored after the fourth or fifth year. Let the plant mature fully. When the foliage shrivels, lift each bulb carefully. Wash the soil from the roots and pull away the dead top growth. Spread the bulbs in a shady, well-ventilated area to dry, then store them over the summer in wire-mesh-bottomed boxes or mesh bags.

Species (wild) tulips are the first to push up and burst with colour in early spring. They include Kaufmanniana, Fosteriana, Greigii and Eichleri. Kaufmanniana is one of the most remarkable groups of hybrids; many have mottled or spotted foliage. They are well suited to rock gardens. They are low-growing and look like stars when they are wide open.

Fosteriana tulips, including the well-known 'Red Emperor,' are a brilliant scarlet. A black patch at the base of the flower, powdered with yellow, resembles a black crouching beetle. The 15–25 cm (6–10 inch) stems seem too fragile to support the huge flower.

Greigii tulips are low-growing, enormous flowering species tulips that come in vivid yellows, oranges and reds. Brown or purple blotches or spots decorate the leaves. Give them a sunny site.

Eichleri tulips are rare. A large flower, which grows atop a short stem, is often crimson with a patch of grey, and shows pink and yellow on the outside of the petal. The flower has a distinctive black base. Before the earliest species tulips are finished flowering, Fusilier tulips break through in bright orange and scarlet; 3 to 5 flowers the size of large acorns appear on each stem.

On the coast, the main tulip season starts in April and May with the early singles and doubles. Early singles attain a height of 38 cm (15 inches). They are excellent for forcing into flower indoors (see p. 228). 'Keizerskroon,' 'Diane' and 'Sunburst' are favourites.

Early double-flower tulips resemble peonies in their flower form. They are full-petalled in shades and combinations of red, violet, white and yellow. Early doubles show colour a little later than the early singles. They are also several inches shorter. 'Peach Blossom,' 'Schoonoord,' 'El Toreador' and 'Vuurbaak' are noteworthy doubles.

Bridging the season between early and late varieties are the Triumph tulips, a cross between the late-flowering Darwins and the single earlies. Triumph tulips have stems about 40 cm (16 inches) tall. Large flowers are often edged with another colour. Plant 'Blizzard,' 'Edith Eddy,' or 'Sunmaid' for an early April showing.

Darwins are giant tulips. Huge, globular blooms in a brilliant range of colours are supported on tall, slender stems. Darwins can be counted on for at least 3 weeks of display, and when cut and taken indoors will last more than 2 weeks in arrangements. 'Glacier,' 'Charles Needham' and 'Aristocrate' are fine examples of Darwin tulips.

Breeder tulips are the descendants of the old Dutch tulips. The blossoms open in the warmth of day and close as evening approaches. They flower in tawny shades of old gold, bronze, terra cotta and brown. Breeder tulips are almost as large as Darwin types.

Cottage tulips were collected from the cottage gardens of the British Isles in the sixteenth century. A commercial trade in these tulips never developed, but they carried on in individuals' gardens, where they were rediscovered. The flowers grow in clear colours, predominately shades of yellow and orange, and are often flushed with another tint. There are no purples, lavenders or bronzes in this group. Cottage tulips bloom in May, with tall, stiff stems and magnificent flower cups whose petals are sometimes pointed.

Lily-flowered tulips, with graceful, reflexed and pointed petals, bloom along with the Darwins and soar to 60–75 cm (2–2^{1}/$_{2}$ ft) tall. 'White Triumphator,' 'West Point,' 'Captain Fryatt' and 'China Pink' are interesting varieties.

Parrot tulips are exotic, with deeply laciniated (fringed), twisted petals, which often have green markings. They are the latest tulips to flower, in shades of deep maroon to red, pink, yellow, orange, blue and multicolour. The 30–38 cm (12–15 inch) stems are weak and slender for the size of the flowers. Hybridizers are striving for taller and stronger.

Rembrandt tulips, or broken tulips, are variegated in shades of different colours. They are often grouped with the Darwins. Stripes and flames of colour appear on backgrounds of yellow, red, violet, brown or white. This colour variegation is due to an introduced virus, so avoid planting Rembrandts near solid-colour tulips.

Summer-Flowering Bulbs and Tubers

Begonia

Tuberous begonias are summer show-offs. Cascading from hanging baskets, bursting from containers or thriving in sheltered garden corners, they splash colour around the yard. Colours range from crystal white to delicate pastels and vibrant scarlet, crimson and copper. The flower petals may resemble carnations, roses, camellias or hollyhocks. Begonias prefer shade, but not abysmal darkness. In densely shaded areas the plants will grow spindly and fail to flower. A light area beneath the shelter of high branching trees or under a porch roof is ideal. They like the early morning or late evening sun.

Tubers vary from 1–15 cm (^{1}/$_{2}$–6 inches) in diameter. The size of the tuber does not affect the quality of the blossom; however, the larger the tuber, the larger and greater the number of flowers.

Flowers and Such

Begonia. Chuck Heath photo

Start tubers indoors in late March or early April, in time to set the plants outdoors around the first of May, when all danger of frost is past. Plant them in a warm, moist atmosphere, about 16°C (60°F). When light pinkish sprouts appear, plant the tubers in flats, or individual containers. Fill the containers three-quarters full with peat moss and sand. Soak this rooting mixture thoroughly with water before planting. Press the tubers into the rooting mixture concave side up until the top is covered by at least 1 cm (1/2 inch). Space the tubers 5–7.5 cm (2–3 inches) apart. Keep the planting in a bright location out of direct sun, and keep the rooting mixture moist at all times but not saturated. When the first 2 leaves are well developed and the stems are 7.5–15 cm (3–6 inches) high, they are ready to be transplanted in 12.5 cm (5-inch) pots. If the weather is warm they may be planted directly outdoors.

When it is time to move them outside, prepare the soil by spading and turning in several inches of peat moss, leaf mould, compost and dried manure. Healthy, productive plants are grown in soil rich in fibrous humus, well drained but retentive of moisture. Tuberous begonias have a front and back: the point of the leaves faces frontward. Plant them so the flowers all face in one direction. When tuberous begonias are planted in a fertile, porous soil enriched with organic materials, additional nutrients need not be given until flower buds appear. At this point apply a bloom-inducing liquid fertilizer with an analysis of 0-10-10, according to directions on the label.

If the leaves are pale or a soft light green and cupped upward, the plant needs fertilizer. If buds and partly developed flowers fall from the plants, it usually means there is too much water and/or nitrogen in the soil. If the foliage curls, apply a 2-10-10 fertilizer using 15 mL (1 tbsp) per plant.

Keep the soil around the plants moist but not soggy. Do not allow water to remain on the foliage in the late afternoon or evening.

Disbudding enhances the beauty and size of begonia flowers. Each stem usually bears 3 flower buds. The centre bud (male) is larger and the petals are circular; the 2 side buds (female) are small and somewhat elongated and each has a small, bulbous structure at the base of its petals. This bulbous structure is an immature seed pod. Remove the 2 female side buds as soon as they appear, leaving only the male or middle flower to develop into a large exhibition blossom.

Harvest the tubers for winter storage after the first light frost damages the foliage in October. Before storing tubers for the winter, cure them by keeping the entire plant, along with any adhering soil, in a ventilated room, 13–16°C (55–60°F). Gradually withhold water. When the stems separate easily from the tuber, clean the tubers by gently removing the soil and any top growth. After the tubers have been cured for 10 days in shallow, well-ventilated flats, they are callous and firm. Store them in fine, almost-dry peat moss in a cool, frost-free place.

Caladium

Caladiums, with their exotic paperlike blossoms, are dramatic in a shady garden or patio. Marbleized leaves are veined and striped in crimson, rose pink, white and green. The plants are available to home gardeners in full leaf in late spring and summer, or as semi-dormant tubers in early spring.

Start semi-dormant bulbs, which are tender and slow to sprout, indoors in a warm place: at least 24°C (75°F). Use a starting medium of sphagnum or peat moss. Since this is a crown-rooting bulb (the roots form around the top or centre eye), place the bulb upside down in the starting medium. Press it halfway in, and moisten with warm water. Water sparingly until root growth is well started.

When sprouts appear and roots are 10–12.5 cm (4–5 inches) long and thick, plant each bulb in a container 15–20 cm (6–8 inches) in diameter and depth. Use a growing mixture of one part each sharp sand, leaf mould or compost, and charcoal. Add a sprinkling of dried cow manure, blood meal or bone meal. Transplant them to the garden when they have produced 4 sets of leaves.

During summer keep the plant luxuriant with liquid plant fertilizers (follow package directions) and a moist soil. Caladium leaves lose moisture quickly and failure of the plant is usually due to insufficient water. Mature plants produce odd blooms: in the centre, a spathe-like bloom forms, similar to the flower on a mature philodendron, but white or cream in colour. Remove this bloom, as it drains strength from the plant.

In the early fall, the plant produces a few new leaves and the older ones drop away. Withhold water and prepare the tuber for dormancy. After the foliage dies down, take the tuber from the soil, clean it, dry it and store it in a warm, dry place for the winter months.

Canna

Evocative of Gauguin paintings, the bright flowers and bold leaves of cannas add a tropical note to the landscape as they thrust their brilliant flower spikes toward the summer sun. Canna foliage is dark green, bronze or variegated green and white. Several stately unbranched stalks grow from a single rootstock. Flowers are brilliant in blazing burnt orange, rose pink, yellow, scarlet and a few pastels. Wilhelm Pfitzer of Germany introduced a dwarf group of canna that bears his name. 'Pfitzer's Cherry Red' or 'Shell Pink' is striking when planted in containers on a deck or patio.

Canna tubers are available at garden centres and nurseries in early spring; plants are usually ready for outdoor gardens in late April and May. You can start divisions of the tuberous roots indoors in March, or in a cold frame or greenhouse. Plant them individually in 12.5–15 cm (5 to 6-inch) containers. Fill the bottom of each container with several inches of light, sandy soil. Cannas are semitropical; they need constant warmth. Keep them at an indoor temperature of 18–21°C (65–70°F). When the sprouts are 7.5 cm (3 inches) high, transplant the starts into larger containers and keep them in a greenhouse or cold frame until all danger of frost is over.

Cannas may be increased by lifting the started divisions and carefully cutting each into as many sections as there are shoots. Leave as much of the fleshy division with each shoot as possible and take care not to damage the small roots. Replant these small divisions individually.

You can also plant canna tubers directly outdoors once the soil has warmed. Generally these plants bloom by midsummer, a few weeks later than those started indoors in March.

Prepare the planting areas for cannas early in the spring. Give them an open, sunny site. Cannas are heavy feeders, so cultivate the soil deeply, with generous amounts of moisture-retentive material such as peat moss or fine bark turned into the ground. The plant's massive root system reaches down several feet. Dolomite lime, decomposed manure and commercial 5-10-10 fertilizers are beneficial.

Dig an adequate planting pocket for each division. Take a firm ball of earth with the roots of each division and set it in the hole. Space the plants in groups about 45 cm (18 inches) apart for an effective showing. Water the new planting thoroughly and deeply. Cannas are rapid growers and need moisture at their roots constantly. Dry soil retards their growth and deforms the flower spikes. A light mulch of ground bark or peat moss maintains a moist soil and discourages weeds.

When the plants are setting flower buds, apply a liquid fertilizer such as a fish emulsion, or a liquid plant food high in phosphorus and potash. Follow the directions on the label.

On the coast, cannas should be lifted and stored over the winter. As soon as the fall frosts have blackened the foliage, cut it off the plant. With a sharp knife, cut the stalks back to 15 cm (6 inches) from the ground. Turn the clumps upside down, wash off the soil and leave them to dry for a day. Take the tuberous roots indoors before night. To prepare for winter storage cut off the feeder roots and remove the remainder of the stumps by making a V-shaped cut close to but not into the roots.

After the divisions are made, label them for colour and variety. Place them in open trays in a warm, dry place for a few days until the cuts have healed and the skin dried. Then place them in a wooden box buried in dampened peat moss. Store them at 7–10°C (45–50°F). Examine the divisions occasionally during the winter for signs of drying or decay. Discard any that appear soft or withered.

Some cannas to select are 'La Traviata,' deep rose pink; 'Madame Butterfly,' pink with creamy borders; 'Primrose Yellow'; 'Rosalinda,' pink and cream; and 'The President,' scarlet.

Colchicum

Any late summer garden is enhanced immeasurably with colchicums, commonly known as meadow saffron or autumn crocus. Goblets of wine, purple, pink and pure white flowers stretch forth and meet the misty mornings of September. The blooms of some species are marvelously tessellated or checkered in two tones.

Colchicums belong to the lily family. They resemble autumn-flowering crocus (a species of crocus) but have 6 centre stamens instead of 3. Individual flowers do not last long, but they follow one another in quick succession.

Colchicums are available for planting in August. Choose a sunny location, which encourages more flowers. Plant the corms among ground covers such as thyme, arabis,

Colchicum (C. autumnale). Sandra Evelyn photo

iberis or dwarf phlox, which protect them from soil splashed up by heavy rains. Thick, glossy green leaves appear in spring and grow as tall as 60 cm (2 ft). In June they begin to turn yellow and lie about in a deathbed scene. Remove the leaves when they pull away easily, usually in late June. Colchicum flowers appear in late summer and endure poor weather with amazing fortitude, flowering through frost, wind and rain and staying colourful when most flowers are losing their beauty.

Colchicums are simple to grow and increase rapidly. Give them a fertile soil that is enriched with organic humus. A top dressing of bone meal and dried manure should be made in early spring. Colchicums suffer if the soil becomes too dry. Water the planting frequently and thoroughly in the summer.

Once planted, corms are best left undisturbed for several years. If the plants show signs of deterioration, reset them after the foliage dies down and before blooms appear, usually in July and August. Plant so that the top of the corm is covered with 10 cm (4 inches) of soil. Space the corms 15 cm (6 inches) apart in groups. (If left unplanted, they will flower without benefit of soil, as the flower is built in the corm, but the corm will eventually wither and die.)

Colchicum autumnale (autumn crocus) is the most common species planted on the coast, with star-shaped blooms about 5 cm (2 inches) in length, in hues of lilac. *C. alpinum*, a lovely and rarely grown plant of the greatest delicacy, is the smallest of the species and the first to bloom in August. Charming pink-lilac goblets 2.5 cm (1 inch) high bubble through the warm summer earth. Foliage consists of 2 narrow, inconspicuous sheaths. *C. speciosum* and its varieties, which bear larger flowers, are considered the finest of the group.

Winter- and spring-blooming colchicums are rare and little known. The variegated *C. luteum*, bright yellow, blooms in late winter. *C. montanum* blooms with spring snowdrops. *C. decaisnie* sparkles in a rock garden.

Dahlia

Dahlias are truly international. Spanish conquistadors discovered dahlias growing in the gardens of the Aztecs, and Andre Dahl, the Swedish botanist, devoted a lifetime to improving them. Abbe Cavanillis, director of the Royal Gardens of Madrid, named the plant in honour of Andre Dahl. They are now known throughout the world.

On the coast, dahlias fill summer gardens with luminous, iridescent colours: smouldering reds, yellows, browns, bronzes, clear lavender, white and combinations in all shades. The flowers resemble marigolds, chrysanthemums, carnations or zinnias. Some produce gargantuan flowers while others are the size of buttons. Plants vary from a few inches to yards high.

Dahlias are grown to perfection when given full sun, adequate summer moisture and a sandy soil enriched with humus and fertilizers. Flower colour is intensified by the amount of sun the plant receives. Sunlight also determines the size of the blossoms and the condition of the foliage. Four hours of full sun a day during the growing season is ideal. Keep dahlias away from tree roots, hedges, weeds or other plants.

Dahlias may be planted as full-grown clumps of tubers, single tubers or growing green plants, which are obtained from cuttings or seeds. Divide clumps before planting, by separating the old rootstock into individual sections, each with a growth eye or bud attached. Plant only a single tuber for each bush. If you plant the entire clump, only leaves and a few flowers will grow. Green plants or cuttings are made by placing the rootstock in moist sand or peat moss in early spring and keeping it in a light, warm place. When the shoots are about 5 cm (2 inches) high, cut them from the tuber and root in moist sand. When the plants are rooted well, move them outside when the weather warms.

Dahlia. Deb McVittie photo

Dahlias may also be grown from seeds. Start them indoors 6 to 8 weeks ahead of the last frost. Plants grown from seed usually become single or semi-double forms that are quite different from the seed parents and the flowers are often disappointing, though occasionally a winner does emerge.

Plant dahlia tubers in a warm soil in early May. Prepare the planting site ahead of time, in the autumn or early spring. Dig deeply into the soil generous amounts of wood ash (19 litres/5 gal per 9 m^2), seaweed (19 litres/5 gal) and bone meal (900 g/2 lbs), and spread 5 cm (2 inches) of decomposed manure over the planting area.

Large-growing dahlias should be spaced 90–120 cm (3–4 ft) apart. Small ones should be planted about 60 cm (2 ft) apart. When planting divisions of rootstock, dig a pocket 30 cm deep and 30 cm wide (1 x 1 ft) for each plant. Drive a tall, sturdy stake into the bottom of the planting hole as a support. In the bottom of the pocket, layer on several inches of sand or fine gravel. Cover the drainage material with an enriched sandy soil. Add a handful of fish meal, and 60 mL (1/4 cup) each of bone meal and blood meal; or add a handful of granular commercial 5-10-10 fertilizer. If kelp or seaweed is available, add a layer 7.5 cm (3 inches) deep and cover it with 2.5 cm (1 inch) of soil.

Place the tuber in the pocket horizontally, with the growth bud pointing upward, and cover with 5 cm (2 inches) of soil. As growth proceeds, gradually fill in more soil around the plant until it is level with the surrounding ground. When setting out green plants or cuttings, bury the root ball 2.5 cm (1 inch) deeper than the surrounding ground, down to the level of the first leaf.

As natives of the tropics, dahlias are accustomed to sudden midday downpours. Water the plants, leaves and all, during sunny summer mornings. Avoid watering late in the day: wet foliage in the evening or overnight encourages plant diseases.

Apply 5-10-10 or soluble fish fertilizer when the top growth reaches several inches, and again as flower buds appear. At each application, spread about 250 mL (1 cup) around a large plant and 60–125 mL (1/4–1/2 cup) at the base of miniatures. Water the fertilizer into the soil after each application.

For exhibition-type flowers, wait for the first cluster of 3 buds to appear, then pinch out the 2 side buds. A succession of huge long-stemmed flowers will result. Cut dahlia flowers for indoor arrangements when they are fully open. Make a clean cut so the stem ends won't be crushed. Many flower arrangers sear the cut ends immediately in a flame, or plunge the stems into boiling water for about 30 seconds. After searing, immerse the stems in deep cold water, up to the flower heads, and leave them for several hours before arranging.

On the coast, dahlia tubers will survive when left in the ground over winter. However, if they stay in the soil year after year, they will slowly deteriorate, producing inferior foliage and blossoms. In the late fall, after frost has blackened the leaves and stalks, take the dahlia roots from the ground and store them. Take great care in digging up the tubers, which may be 60 cm (2 ft) long. Work down gently with a spading fork to loosen the soil without injuring the tuber. Dig deep and lift the entire clump of roots out of the ground. Turn them upside down and allow the moisture to drain from any stems that were previously cut. Wash the soil from the roots and dry them in the sun or in a well-ventilated shelter.

Tubers store best if not cut into sections. Keep them in damp sand, sawdust or peat moss. Examine the tubers occasionally during the winter. If they have shrivelled, sprinkle them lightly with water, and discard any that show signs of deterioration.

Unwin hybrid dahlias are available from nurseries in early May. They produce short, stocky plants with semi-double or double flowers, and a few singles. Blossoms completely cover the small plants until frost cuts them down in the fall.

Gladiolus

Coast gardeners grow "glads" (members of the iris family) for their beauty of colour and variety of forms. Flowers range from miniatures, doubles, dragons and exotics to novelties and innumerable standard and giant types. Plain, ruffled, laciniated (fringed), grotesquely horned and spurred florets are available in most colour combinations. The range of colours is being extended constantly by hybridizers.

Plant gladiolus successively from March to July, for flowers from early July until November. Depending on the variety, gladiolus will flower in 70 to 120 days from planting. Select 2-year-old corms that are clean, vigorous, plump and high-crowned, 3.5 cm (1 1/2 inches) or more in diameter and 2 cm (3/4 inches) thick. These measurements are important: the diameter indicates the size and number of flower spikes that will grow, and the thickness indicates the bulb is young and vigorous.

Gladiolus thrives in a sandy loam soil enriched with organic material. Break up the subsoil carefully and add coarse sand. Fork in organic material such as leaf mould, compost, ground bark, peat moss and wood ash.

The nature of the soil and the variety of gladiolus govern depth of planting. In a heavy clay, plant large-growing kinds 10 cm (4 inches) deep. In light, sandy soil plant large glads 15 cm (6 inches) deep. Plant miniatures 5–7 cm (2–3 inches) deep. Large-growing glads are spaced 7.5–12.5 cm (3–5 inches) apart; tiny ones can be closer together.

Dig a planting pocket for each corm. Place 15 mL (1 tbsp) of a complete commercial fertilizer, low in nitrogen 2.5–5 cm (1–2 inches) below the corm and cover with 2.5–5 cm of sand. (A fertilizer too high in nitrogen produces soft leaves and stems.) Phosphorus develops the root system, which in turn produces firmer buds and hastens flowering. The chief effect of potash is to increase the size and vigour of the corm. As the flower buds swell on the plants, apply a light ribbon of fertilizer along the row, at a rate of 250 mL (1 cup) to 3 m (10 ft). Continue to fertilize the soil lightly every 2 weeks during the growing season.

Glad roots grow deeply. Soak the soil to a depth of at least 45 cm (18 inches) twice a week during summer droughts. You should stake tall gladiolus, as wind, rain and the weight of the flowers will bend or break the growing spikes.

Remove the plants from the ground in late October, even if the foliage is still green. If you leave them any later than that, the corms are vulnerable to insects and diseases.

Lift the corms and remove the top growth. Corms that were planted in the spring will be shrivelled, and a new corm will be growing above the wrinkled remains of the old corm. Save the mature corm. A number of small offshoots will be attached to its base. Keep these tiny cormlets for future stock: they will flower in 2 years. Store the cormlets indoors over the winter in moist sand or peat moss. They should remain in a moist, plump condition, but should not start to show sprouts. Plant the cormlets as soon as the ground can be worked in spring. Space them 10 cm (4 inches) apart in rows 45 cm (18 inches) apart and follow planting directions above.

To keep corms fresh, soak them for 6 hours in a solution of 20 mL (4 tsps) of Lysol and 4 litres (1 gal) of water, then store them in a mesh bag at 4–10°C (40–50°F).

Lily

The West Coast landscape is breathtaking with mountains and valleys carpeted in native lilies such as *Lilium columbianum*, avalanche lily, *L. washingtonianum* and the western trillium.

Lilies range from miniatures 2.5 cm (1 inch) or so in diameter, to immense blossoms on stems 2.4–3 m (8–10 ft) tall. All colours are to be found among the many lily hybrids and species. Forms vary from chiselled trumpets to bowls and reflexed flower petals.

Lilies have definite preferences. Because their roots stay active through the winter, they will not tolerate excess groundwater. They need good drainage, so plant them on a slight slope.

Select a planting site where the plants will be protected from strong winds and afternoon sun. Morning sun is desirable. Lilies like to keep their feet cool, and they enjoy the companionship of dwarf rhododendron, azalea and low-growing ground covers. Avoid planting lilies near tulips, squash, cucumbers, melons or other members of the cucurbit family (gourds), to prevent plant diseases.

To plant, dig down approximately 45 cm (18 inches) and remove the existing soil. Place several inches of coarse sand or fine gravel in the bottom of the planting area. To retain moisture in spring and summer, use a humus-type soil over the drainage material.

Prepare a planting pocket for each lily. Spread a handful of bone meal or blood meal in each pocket. Cover this with coarse sand and place the base of the bulb on the sand. Fill around the bulb with light, sandy soil. Depth of planting varies according to the type of lily. *L. candidium*, or Madonna lily, and *L.*

Asiatic lily 'Yellow Kiss.' Bob Cain photo

excelsum (or *testaceum*) are covered with only 2.5 cm (1 inch) of soil. Other lily bulbs are planted 12.5–15 cm (5–6 inches) deep.

Maintain a moist growing soil for lilies during spring and summer. Water the planting deeply twice a week during dry spells. A soil soaker hose will service several clumps at a time. Let the water seep slowly to a depth of at least 15 cm (6 inches). Conserve moisture, reduce weed growth and prevent root injury by mulching over the soil with ground bark, compost, peat moss or old sawdust.

Lilies are heavy feeders. They need two applications a year of a commercial 5-10-10 fertilizer: one in early spring and the other in the middle of summer. Use 1.3 kg (3 lbs) to 9 m² (100 sq ft) of planting.

When cutting lily blossoms for floral arrangements, don't take more than half of the stem with the flower. The bulb is dependent upon the leaves and the other stems for its growth.

Treat lily bulbs like live plants, for they never are completely dormant. Lily plantings should not be disturbed if they are producing well. Lift, divide and replant the bulbs only when they become overcrowded and the flowers are few and inferior. Transplanting is best done in the early fall. To increase your lily planting, remove the offsets, or small bulbs, that form around the mother bulb. Wait until flowering is finished. Dig carefully around the stem of the plant to expose the bulb, but leave the basal roots intact. Discard any shrivelled outside scales and break off a few firm ones. Replant these 5 cm (2 inches) deep in a sandy soil. In 2 to 3 years they will be blooming.

Lilies can also be grown from seed, and although they seldom grow true to type, they do produce some interesting results.

Asiatic hybrids have upright flowers that grow singly or in clusters. They include 'Enchantment', red; 'Golden Chalice'; and the Rainbow hybrids. Other Asiatic hybrids, derived from the same parents, have flowers that are selected for their outward-facing characteristics. Members of this group are 'Prosperity', yellow; 'Paprika', crimson; and 'Corsage', pink and yellow. Asiatic hybrids with pendant flowering characteristics, noted for hardiness and vigour, include 'Citronella', yellow with black spots; 'Harlequin', pastel shades; and 'Bittersweet', orange.

Martagon hybrids are derived from forms of the European *Lilium martagon* and the Asian *L. hansonii*. A wide range of colours and graceful forms are represented in this group: 'Bellingham', red, yellow, orange; 'Shuksan', light orange, maroon spots; and 'Afterglow', red, spotted maroon.

Aurelian hybrid trumpet lilies contain true funnel-formed cultivars and hybrids. This group covers a wide range of colours: 'Black Dragon', white, reverse maroon; 'Copper King', orange, reverse maroon; 'Green Magic', white, tinted green; and the most widely grown trumpet lily of all, the 'Regale', white, yellow throat and dark reverse.

Aurelian hybrids are extremely hardy and vigorous and well suited to coast climates. Those with bowl-shaped, outward-facing flowers include 'First Love', pink and gold; and 'Heart's Desire', white with orange throat, which have the bonus of being very fragrant. The Aurelian hybrids with star-shaped, flat-opening flowers include 'Golden Sunburst', yellow; and 'Orange Sunburst', bright orange.

Oriental hybrids come in many forms. *Auratum*, variety *platyphyllum*, is a bowl-shaped lily with open flowers and fragrance. It has vigour and a strong urge to grow. White blooms with gold-spotted bands cover the plant in August and early September. 'Little Rascal', a unique miniature strain, has pure white outward-facing flowers. A dwarf habit of growth makes it suitable for growing in containers. 'Crimson Beauty' features breathtaking pure white flowers with a deep cherry red band in the centre of each petal.

Oriental hybrids with flat-faced flowers are derived from native species. Examples include the famous Imperial selections. 'Cover Girl,' with outward-facing shell-pink flowers almost 30 cm (12 inches) in diameter, is always popular. 'Imperial Crimson' is exotic with crimson flowers carried on stems 2 m (7 ft) tall. 'Imperial Pink' is an aristocratic addition with large pink blossoms on sturdy stems. The plants are hardy and vigorous.

Oriental hybrids with recurved flowers originated from natives found in Japan, China and Taiwan. 'Allegra' produces pure white flowers with light green centres that are especially desirable as cut flowers. The spectacular 'Enterprise' has crimson flowers with silver margins. 'Grand Commander' is a hardy grower outdoors or in a greenhouse. The flowers are warm red with pure white edges and dark spots at the base.

Day Lily

Day lilies, or *hemerocallis*, are tough, interesting plants. They were cultivated in ancient China before the development of a written language. The earliest recorded use of the plant was as food during famine. Day lilies are palatable, digestible and nutritious. Today, petals of day lilies are used in soups, various meat dishes and noodles. They are sold under the Oriental names *gum-tsoy* and *gum-jum*.

Day lilies travelled to western Europe from the Orient by way of the Mediterranean region, then they journeyed across the Atlantic to the New World.

Day lilies differ from other flowers known generally as lilies in that each blossom lasts but a day. They are grown from tuberous roots instead of the scaly bulbs that produce the other lilies. Day lilies are permanent and practical, and they produce a riot of

Day lilies. Adam Gibbs photo

colour in summer. The blossoms of vivid red, orange, yellow, purple, lavender and subtle melon tones may live only a day each, but many follow on the same plant, so the show goes on.

In day lilies, the pale flowers are the most fragrant. Many open their petals at night. Some boast big flowers on tall stems; others are miniatures with exquisite tiny blossoms. A few may be flat, bowl-like or spidery in form. Newer introductions have bars or marks on the petals in contrasting colours. Giant day lilies stretch skyward 1.2–1.5 m (4–5 ft). Dwarf varieties are scarcely more than 30 cm (1 ft) high. A few tropical varieties have evergreen leaves. The leaves of coast day lilies are strap-like, bold and bright green. They die down in winter.

Day lilies are tough, but plant and tend them carefully. Plant the roots in spring or fall, or in containers, in a spot that gets at least 4 to 5 hours of sunlight each day during their growing and flowering time.

Day lily roots are numerous, dividing into many fibrous branches that penetrate deeply into the ground. A soil amended with organic humus often produces a soil acidity near neutral—and that is ideal for day lilies. Prepare each planting hole by digging deeply (about 5 cm/2 inches) and filling in with humus, peat moss, old sawdust, compost or leaf mould. Form a cone of soil in the middle of the planting hole. Place the crown of the plant over the cone and lay the roots down along the sloping sides. The crown (where roots and stems meet) should be 3.5 cm (1½ inches) below the surface of the surrounding soil. Mulch over the new planting with 5 cm (2 inches) of peat moss or other humus. Water deeply.

In spring and summer, when flowers are being produced, keep the soil evenly moist deep down. Water about twice a week during dry periods.

After 5 to 6 years in one location, day lilies become overcrowded and require lifting, dividing and replanting. Do this in late autumn, immediately after the plant finishes flowering. To divide, lift the entire plant, wash the soil from the roots, and cut off the top leaves within 15 cm (6 inches) of the crown. Use a sharp knife or sharp spade to make the divisions. Each new division should have several strong roots and 3 to 4 top cut leaves attached. Set each division back into the soil immediately after cutting. Space large-growing plants 90 cm (3 ft) apart in all directions. Space dwarf or miniature types 30 cm (1 ft) apart. Each spring apply a commercial fertilizer higher in phosphorus and potash than nitrogen around the base of each plant. Use 225 g (½ lb) of fertilizer around each mature plant. Water into the soil immediately after application. Blood meal stimulates growth and improves the colour of the flowers and leaves. Give each of the developing plants 124 mL (½ cup).

In late fall, cut the leaves to the ground and cover the crowns with a protective mulch. This prevents the roots from being thrust out of the ground by alternate freezing and thawing of the soil.

Fall-Flowering Bulbs

Fall-flowering bulbs and corms endure late autumn weather conditions with amazing fortitude, showing no concern for wind, rain or biting frosts. Select and plant many of these bulbs and corms in late August.

Acidanthera

Acidanthera, or iridacea, is an autumn-flowering plant gaining favour on the coast. The blooms appear as small replicas of gladiolus and miniature iris. Six or more tiny flowers are suspended on gracefully arching stems all through late summer and fall. Blooms begin at the base of the flower stalk and continue until the last bud at the top of the stem opens. If you remove faded blooms, side shoots soon appear to produce more flowers.

Acidanthera blooms are striking in colour. Some are whitish with chocolate brown or crimson markings, others are bicoloured white and crimson or white and purple. There is also a pure white variety.

A growing site in full sun is required. The corms prefer a gritty, well-drained soil enriched with organic leaf mould, peat moss and aged manure.

Plant corms about 7.5 cm (3 inches) deep and 10–12.5 cm (4–5 inches) apart. Water well when the plant shows green leaves, and continue to keep the soil moist until the flowers fade and the foliage begins to cure. Then allow the ground to become dry by late fall. At that time, lift and store the corms as for gladiolus.

Autumn-Flowering Crocus

Autumn-flowering crocus (as distinct from *Colchicum autumnale*, commonly known as autumn crocus) bloom bravely from September until early spring. They produce flowers after their thin, grassy green foliage has ripened and disappeared. Flowers are sparkling white, with golden throats and scarlet stigmas, or they may be blue, violet or pale lilac with a feathered darker lilac outside. Most are sweet-scented. With a selection of corms, you can have blossoms from late September right through winter into early spring.

Plant them in groups among evergreen ground cover to conceal their fading spring foliage. Sunny rock gardens are ideal. Set the corms in the ground in late summer, spaced 5–12.5 cm (2–5 inches) apart, in colonies, and cover with 5–7.5 cm (2–3 inches) of sandy soil. Leave autumn crocus in one site to form a thick covering along with other ground-hugging plants. Lift, separate and replant the corms only when they become overcrowded. Divide and replant in late September.

Cyclamen

Hardy cyclamen are the butterflies of the flower kingdom. Tiny, elfin flowers, charming miniatures of the florist's cyclamen, carpet the forest land of the coast. Blooms rise in great profusion from flat corms that do not divide but only increase in size with age. A

Cyclamen (C. hederifolium). Sandra Evelyn photo

mature corm will eject great numbers of seeds into the surrounding area from coil-spring seed stalks.

Plant corms in late summer in an area protected from cutting ground winds and early morning sun. Use a well-drained soil filled with organic humus. Space the corms 12.5–15 cm (5–6 inches) apart in clumps of at least 3, and cover with 2.5 cm (1 inch) of soil. If mulched over lightly with peat moss or fine ground bark, cyclamen plants will establish and increase, creating a hardy carpet.

Gayfeathers

Liatris, or gayfeathers, are striking with tall, gold spires of fluffy flowers in shades of rosy purple, sometimes white. They produce colour from mid-July until the late fall frosts, and they are outstanding in the fall landscape. Individual liatris flowers have many thready petals, which provide butterflies, bees and praying mantis with easy landing platforms.

Give the plants a dry, sunny location. They will endure almost any soil and they resent fertilizers. Start seed or plant tubers in March, with a sterile seed starter mixture (available at nurseries). Cover the seeds lightly and press down to firm them into the soil. Water well and keep them in a warm place. Plant the tubers under 2.5 cm (1 inch) of soil and space them 15–20 cm (6–8 inches) apart. Seed will likely bloom the second year. Mature plants produce numerous offset corms that you can transplant most successfully in early spring.

Lily of the Field

Sternbergia lutea, a native of Palestine and noted as the "lily of the field," is among the most colourful autumn-flowering plants. Flower stems stretch upward 12.5–15 cm (5–6 inches), and sunny, golden chalice-like blossoms open wide in autumn at about the same time as dogwood and Virginia creeper leaves turn a burning red. Sometimes the plant is listed as *Amaryllis lutea*, or winter daffodil. Unlike many of the other hardy autumn bulbs, it produces neat foliage at the same time it flowers.

S. *lutea* demands perfect soil drainage. Prepare the planting site in a raised area, or provide several inches of drainage material at the base of the root zone. Plant the bulbs early in September to a depth of 12.5 cm (5 inches) and space them 7.5 cm (3 inches) apart. When the plantings become overcrowded, wait until after they finish blooming, then lift and replant them.

Resurrection Lily

Lycoris squamigera, or the resurrection lily, is so named because of its unusual growth cycle. Its leaves shoot out of the ground in spring, develop, ripen and disappear by late June. Then the flower stalks appear—entirely without leaves. Eventually a crown of pink-ish buds appears; a day or so later, the flowers open fully: 6 to 8 florets, each about 10 cm (4 inches) long, decorate the flower spike. The sweet-scented blossoms are pink with lavender shadings, and resemble small spidery amaryllis flowers.

A site with light shade is best. As the plants do not have foliage when they flower, mix them in with ferns and other foliage-producing plants that enjoy shade. Plant the bulbs in the fall, in a gritty, well-drained soil with added compost, peat moss and manure. Leave the bulbs undisturbed for many years, or until flowering is reduced. Lift and divide the bulbs in late summer; replant them immediately.

Heather and Heath

Heathered hills are as much a part of Scottish tradition as bagpipes and haggis, and once seen, the heath-covered moors of England are not to be forgotten. In their native areas, which range from Ireland to the Mediterranean and parts of South Africa, heaths and heathers grow with seeming indifference to soil, climate or temperature.

This group of plants is not native to the Pacific Northwest. Drifts of them have been introduced to our gardens and have adapted well, making brilliant displays across the local landscape.

Heath (*erica*) and heather (*calluna*) are related closely, but are distinguished by flower as well as foliage. *Calluna* bears flowers in dense terminal spikes, and the tiny leaves are opposite one another. Its coloured calyx is longer than the flower petals. *Erica* has needle-like leaves arranged in whorls spread far apart on the stem.

Mixed heather. Adam Gibbs photo

The term heath is also used to refer to the entire family of mountain laurel, rhododendron, azalea, blueberry, cranberry, trailing arbutus and wintergreen. They all demand similar growing conditions, except for exposure to the sun. Heaths and heathers enjoy an open sunny position; the others need only morning sun to thrive.

Heathers and heaths are ideal ground covers for sunny slopes. They flower in variations of white, pink, purple, rose, red and orange. Many have bright golden and bronze foliage. Some are low-growing and spreading; others are tall, almost like miniature conifers. They vary in height from 10 cm (4 inches) to 2.4 m (8 ft) tall.

Most heathers and heaths are available in containers for planting out. Transplant them at any season of the year (but not during hard frosts). Arrange the plants in drifts or groups, using one variety in a group. Once established they will spread into dense mats that need a minimum of maintenance.

These plants are native to moors and peat bogs and they like a soil that is light, slightly acid and generous in fibrous humus. Give them several inches of growing soil enriched with organic humus such as peat moss, woodsy leaf mould, ground bark and aged sawdust. Before removing each plant from its container, water the roots thoroughly. If the plant is so well established in its container that there is a tight, matted ball of roots, loosen the roots gently with a strong pointed stick. Roots bound in a pot tend to stay bound when transplanted.

Sink the plant about 2.5 cm (1 inch) deeper in the garden than it was in the pot. (The surrounding soil inevitably settles.) But avoid planting too deeply; otherwise fine new roots may develop on the buried portion of the stems, with a corresponding lack of new root action beneath. In times of drought these delicate new roots will suffer. Firm the planting, and water it thoroughly.

Keep the soil moist in dry summers. In early spring give heathers a rhododendron fertilizer, about 45 mL (3 tbsp) for each mature plant. Water the fertilizer well into the soil after application.

Evergreen heath and heather are pruned for form and compactness. The more severe the pruning the more compact the plant and the more brilliant the flowers. Prune after flowering, to within 2.5–5 cm (1–2 inches) of the current season's growth. In some sections of Europe, heather fields are burned over each year to renew the plants.

Heath and heather are easily propagated. Cuttings and layerings are most successful. Take cuttings in July, when the new growth is half-ripened. With a sharp knife, cut cleanly and make a 3.5 cm (1 1/2 inch) cutting. Strip the foliage from it. Dip the cut end in a root-inducing hormone powder and insert into a half-and-half mixture of sharp sand and peat moss. Keep the rooting mixture moist. Rooting will usually occur in 4 to 6 months.

Stem layering may done at any season, though spring is best. Pull a long branch down to the ground, scratch the underside lightly and mound soil over it, holding it down with a forked stick or rock. Keep the parent plant moist. Roots should form in several months. Then cut the layer from the parent plant and move it to a permanent spot.

Spring heath is low-growing and attains a height of 15–20 cm (6–8 inches). It blooms from November through May with bell-shaped flowers. Three well-known varieties of spring heath are 'Springwood White,' 'King George' and 'Ruby Glow.'

Erica mediterranea, the Biscay heath, grows to 1.2–3 m (4–10 ft). The flowers are often lilac-pink, white or dark red. Some varieties are lightly scented. *E. Alba* is a compact plant. It produces pure white blooms from January to May. *E. melanthera*, the black-eyed heath, is a South African native that is extremely prolific of bloom. The flowers are rosy with black anthers, and it often grows to 60 cm (2 ft). It is also popular on the coast.

E. vagans, the Cornish heath, is 20–25 cm (8–10 inches) tall with a spreading growth. Purple, pink or white flowers appear from July to October. It is a fine edging or border plant. 'Mrs. Maxwell,' a robust-growing Cornish heath, has 45 cm (18-inch) stems covered with rosy red flowers.

The common heather, often called Scotch heather, is *Calluna vulgaris*. It is variable in colour, form and growth. Garden varieties begin to bloom in July, in colours from white to pale pink to cream. Many have coloured foliage. 'H.E. Beale' has double heather-pink flowers crowded on tall, erect stems. Flowers of this variety last exceptionally well. *Alba plena* produces double white flowers on 20–30 cm (8–12 inch) spikes above brilliant green foliage. The plant is full and bushy when mature.

Calluna searlei exhibits a feathery growth and white flowers. It blooms in late summer. *C. nana* is a low-growing, moss-like heather with bright green foliage and clusters of lavender-pink flowers that appear in August.

Ferns

Pacific Northwest forests are often bordered and blanketed with hardy ferns, which gracefully unfurl their fronds in a variety of forms, textures and shades of green, brown and gold. They are nature's ground cover and they come in sizes ranging from miniatures to magnificent giants.

In the garden, planted among rhododendron, azalea and other broad-leafed evergreens, ferns maintain a cool, moist soil and enhance the appearance of the landscape. Growing among spring bulb flowers, ferns spring up at just the appropriate time to conceal the yellowing foliage of daffodils and tulips.

Plant ferns in early spring or late autumn. It used to be that gardeners simply lifted ferns from nearby woods; but so many woodlands are being denuded by the practice that it is wiser to purchase ferns from a nursery.

Avoid planting ferns where they will get lots of afternoon sun. Bring in soil from a woodsy area where leaves have fallen each autumn. Rotting logs make a natural rooting material for ferns. Space large-growing ferns 90–120 cm (3–4 ft) apart in all directions; space smaller ones proportionately closer. Avoid crowding. Setting ferns too deeply in the soil is a common mistake. The crown (intersection of roots and stem) should not be buried, and any underground roots should be covered with 2.5–5 cm (1–2 inches) of light soil that is slightly acid in reaction. Ferns do not like to be cultivated. Their roots (rhizomes) lie almost on the surface of the soil. Instead of cultivating, use mulching material to protect the plants from weeds and conserve moisture. A mulch of sand, ground bark, peat moss or a leafy compost conserves moisture and keeps the planting weed-free. Water every 10 days.

An established fern requires little attention. An annual top dressing of sand and humus, with a light sprinkling of bone meal and an acid type fertilizer, is advisable. The crown-forming ferns tend to grow out of the ground and expose their roots. Replant them at the correct depth.

Ferns increase by creeping, enlarging their crowns or releasing spores, which appear in brownish sacs either on the undersides of the fronds or on separate stems. The gardener can also divide ferns. Those of a tufted habit, such as spleenwort and woodsia, are easily divided. Separate the dense mat of wiry rootlets with a gentle pull. The polyglots form carpets of tangled, creeping rootstocks and surface stems: large sections of them are cut up like sod and replanted.

To grow ferns from spores, take a mature frond that has spore cases on the underside and place it on a sheet of heavy paper, spore side down. The spores will soon shed,

*Maidenhair fern (*Adiantum pedatum*). Bob Cain photo*

appearing as a dark dust on the paper. You can keep the spores for several weeks before planting, or plant them immediately. Clear plastic dishes with lids are ideal. Fill them about half full with vermiculite and cover the vermiculite to within 1 cm (1/2 inch) of the top with finely sieved and sterilized woodsy soil or peat moss. Sterilize the soil by baking it for 1 hour at 120°C (250°F). This reduces the chances of damping-off. Add the sterilized soil to the containers while it is still hot, and wet down with boiling water until the whole is just damp, with no film of water on the surface. Put lids on the containers and let them cool. Then dust the surface lightly with the spores, replace the lids, store the containers at room temperature and ignore them until the surface looks green. This indicates that the spores have germinated.

After the spores have germinated, stimulate them by exposure to increased hours of light, either natural or fluorescent. Keep the planting wet but not flooded. Water with an atomizer. The film of water will permit the movement of sperm to fertilize the eggs. After an egg has been fertilized, a tiny fern appears. Except for the occasional watering, leave the plant undisturbed until the tiny plants are large enough to be handled by tweezers, as long as 6 months. Then transplant them to individual containers filled with a sterilized mixture of one part leaf mould, one part topsoil, and one part sand or vermiculite. Move the plants out to the garden when they are well established.

Adiantum pedatum, or maidenhair fern, produces lacy parasols tilted on polished mahogany stems. A native of coastal woodlands, it thrives in a moist, humus-filled soil. Maidenhair ferns are at home in heavily shaded gardens.

Dryopteris austriaca, or spiny wood fern, grows in a vase shape. Erect stems grow to 90 cm (3 ft), sometimes branching, and drooping to produce secondary crowns. This fern is often found in wet woodlands in a humus-filled soil. It likes shade and moisture.

Blechnum spicant, also known as the deer fern, develops narrow evergreen fronds that reach 90 cm (3 ft). The yellowish green fronds are pleasing among garden shade plants such as hydrangea and fuchsia.

Blechnum penna marina is a dwarf that looks like a small native deer fern. It forms a tiny rosette of leaves close to the ground, and spreads by forming new rosettes as it creeps. It is especially pleasing when grown beneath rhododendron.

Athyrium filix-foemina, the so-called lady fern, is deciduous. Its lacy fronds grow in dense tufts, as tall as 90–120 cm (3–4 ft). This fern tolerates more sun and drier soils than most.

Dryopteris goldiana, Goldie's shield, is a giant golden-green wood fern that is often planted as a single. It grows to 1.2 m (4 ft).

Phyllitis scolopendrium, hart's tongue fern, is a most striking shade plant. It endures wet or dry garden conditions. The thick, ribbon-like fronds have a golden-green touch of colour. The plant combines well with spring bulbs such as galanthus and hostas.

Polystichum acrosticoides, the Christmas fern, is the earliest fern to emerge in spring. It forms a dense clump of graceful 60 cm (2-ft) evergreen fronds. Clumps stay evergreen through much of the winter. This fern is superb in a shady garden site with trillium and primrose.

Grasses

With their exotic textures and colours and their grand flowering plumes, grasses often add a bold flourish to the garden landscape. They provide year-round interest with fresh new growth in spring, feathery flowers in summer and dried materials for home and garden in winter.

Plant grasses near pools, use them as screens or grow them in containers as accent plants.

Arundo donax

Tall, stout *Arundo donax*, the giant reed, forms huge clumps of grass with flower stalks that may stretch upward to as high as 12 m (40 ft). Giant leaves of the plant grow out alternately along the stalks at regular intervals. The flowers are drooping plumes. They are reddish when they first open.

Arundo donax can be a nuisance with its creeping rootstocks. Keep the planting confined in a container sunk in the ground. Cut the canes as they become less attractive. New growth replaces them rapidly.

Blue fescue grass. Adam Gibbs photo

Protect this grass from severe winter weather by covering with burlap or cardboard. Do not use plastic. Propagate it by taking underground stem cuttings in the early spring.

Pampas Grass

Pampas grass (*Cortaderia*) is a curious giant grass variety. Give it a sheltered site in the background along a fence or wall. It is particularly handsome growing along a stream.

Pampas grass forms large clumps with long, narrow leaves. Plume-like flowers rise above the clumps on tall stalks in late summer and fall. Mature clumps can reach 3.6 m (12 ft) in width, and some flower stems reach skyward to as high as 6 m (20 ft). Plumes are creamy white or pinkish when mature. The plumes of male plants are coarse and heavy as oats; female plumes are soft and fluffy as cotton candy.

Pampas grass is hungry and thirsty. Give it generous amounts of bone meal in the early fall. In spring add 450 g (1 lb) of commercial 5-10-10 fertilizer to the soil of each mature plant. Maintain an evenly moist soil around the base of the plant during the growing season.

Divisions of mature clumps may be made in the early spring to increase the planting. Take divisions from the outside of the clump, as they are more vigorous. Cut away or thin old leaves that pack up around the base of the plant: eventually they will suppress new growth. In April, cut back the previous year's foliage and stalks.

Other Grasses

Tiger grass (*Thysanolaena maxima*) is a tall grower, evocative of bamboo. Broad, lance-shaped leaves bring variation to the landscape. Flower heads appear as fine, hair-like green tufts. Give this grass a fertile, damp soil to grow well in summer. Divide the roots to propagate.

Festuca ovina glauca, or **blue fescue grass**, forms rounded tufts from which spires of insignificant flower and seed heads appear in spring and summer. The plant will not tolerate poorly drained soil. It benefits from cutting back in late fall. To increase *Festuca*, divide mature clumps into several sections in the early spring. It makes a great ground cover under conifers like Koster blue spruce.

Miscanthus sinensis, or **morning light**, is a silver-edged foliage grass with feathery flower stalks that grow 1.8–2.4 m (6–8 ft) tall in the fall. The variety ***Purpurascens***, or **purple maidengrass**, produces green foliage in spring that becomes purple-red in fall, and beige flowers on stems 1.5 m (5 ft) tall. Another *Miscanthus sinensis* variety, ***strictus***, or **zebra grass**, is distinctive in a garden. Horizontal bands of yellow cross the leaf blades.

Phalaris arundinacea picta, or **ribbon grass**, develops green and white striped leaves that reach 60–90 cm (2–3 ft) in height. This fast spreader with its strong runners can be a nuisance, but it makes a good soil stabilizer on steep banks.

CHAPTER 4

Trees and Shrubs

LIVING ON AN ISLAND forested in giant fir, spruce, yew, juniper, cedar, hemlock and pine trees, Al and I were well aware of the many benefits of trees and shrubs. They give shade, they offer food and protection to animals and other plants, they help clean the air we breathe, and the foliage, branches and twigs they shed replenish the soil. In the yard or garden, trees and shrubs give shape to a landscape, and colour, fragrance and texture all year round. They screen a less-than-perfect view, accent the lines of homes and garden structures and absorb noise and dust. Birds build their nests there, children find hide-aways, and a swing or hammock tied to a tree is a warm-weather pleasure like no other.

Saucer magnolia. Adam Gibbs photo

Planting Trees and Shrubs

Birch, dogwood, hawthorn, magnolia, scarlet oak, sweet gum, tulip and walnut are best planted in the spring, when root damage heals readily. Most other fruit, flowering, ornamental, deciduous and evergreen trees and shrubs are planted in autumn. Container grown trees and shrubs may be transplanted in any season.

Allow enough room for the plantings. Generally, flowering shrubs such as forsythia and hydrangea need 3.2 m² (36 sq ft) of area. Lilacs need 3 m (10 ft) on all sides. Oaks should be planted approximately 12 m (40 ft) apart, and flowering and standard fruit trees require 6 m (20 ft) all around.

If roots stand in water for long, especially in winter, the tree will fail, so before planting trees and shrubs, check for adequate soil drainage. Dig a hole 90 cm deep and 45 cm wide (36 x 18 inches). Fill it with water and note how long it takes for the water to disappear. If it takes more than 12 hours, drainage is inadequate. To correct poor drainage, add generous amounts of coarse sand or fine gravel below the root zone. Plant specimens on ground with a gentle slope to encourage excess water to drain.

For each tree, prepare a planting pocket at least twice the size of the root system. Remember the nurseryman's saying: dig a $50 hole for a $5 plant. Dig out the topsoil and lay it at the side. Place liberal quantities of fine gravel and sand in the pocket. Add several inches of composted manure mixed with sand and humus. Place the roots of the tree in the hole, without crowding or twisting, at the same depth as it was grown in the nursery. Make sure the tree or shrub is erect, backfill about three-quarters of the topsoil, and tamp down the soil to remove air pockets.

Then fill the planting pocket with water and add the remaining original topsoil. Sprinkle water on the needles or leaves of evergreens after planting, and water all transplants regularly until they are reestablished. Lack of moisture is one of the main reasons new transplants fail.

Plant grafted shrubs like roses, with the bud union (where the top and rootstock are joined) level with the ground or 2.5–5 cm (1–2 inches) above. To avoid soil suckers developing from the rootstock, plant grafted lilac and viburnum with the bud union 5 cm (2 inches) below soil level, to encourage the grafted-on tops to form their own roots. These roots ensure a longer life: the grafted-on roots are usually short-lived, intended only to provide the shrub with a fast start.

Transplanting is a shock to any tree, shrub or other plant. Relocating is a struggle, partly because the root system has been disturbed and its capacity to absorb water and nutrients is reduced until feeder roots rejuvenate. As well, portions of roots or branches are often injured or broken.

Prune any damaged parts to clean, live wood and dust the cuts with fungicide. Top and side pruning may be in order for deciduous fruit or shade trees. Cut back approximately a third of their terminal and side growths to compensate for root loss. Trees and shrubs having many diffused branches and twiggy growths should be trimmed lightly on top and all sides. Cut out any crisscrossing branches for a free flow of air and sun to the centre of the specimen.

Evergreen trees and shrubs require less pruning than deciduous types. Do not cut the leader (the long, vertical branch at the top) of a single-stemmed deciduous tree, unless a low-headed tree is required. Avoid the use of chemical fertilizers when planting. A slow-release organic fertilizer is better. Root-inducing hormone transplanting formulas are also beneficial. Don't add fertilizers in the planting area until the tree is well established and ready for the "flush" of spring growth.

Wind is a fact of life on the coast, and newly planted trees and shrubs may be compromised by gusts in any season. Protect transplants by driving sturdy stakes into the ground before planting, to avoid damaging roots, and attach support wires. Where support wire may touch the tree, pass it through a piece of garden hose to prevent it from cutting into the bark and stem of the tree. Remove any labels attached by wire, heavy twine or plastic, or loosen them as the tree expands with age.

Conifers

Conifers are the great individuals of the coastal landscape. They blanket mountains and valleys and perfume the air. Strong and resilient, bold and dramatic in size, colour and texture, they define the region as much as the ocean.

Arborvitae

Arborvitae are conifers that grow very slowly: they stay small for years, sometimes decades, so they make good plants to use for borders, rock gardens and containers. They come in many varieties. Holmstrup cedar, *Thuja occidentalis* 'Holmstrup,' is one of many excellent choices for rock gardens or low hedges. It is compact with a natural pyramid shape and tight, bunchy bright green foliage. It grows slowly and reaches 2.4–3 m (8–10 ft) on maturity.

Mixed conifers. Adam Gibbs photo

Cedar

Cedars have beautiful horizontal branches, which make them very decorative trees in the garden. The needles are spirally arranged and scattered on long shoots. The bark of the tree is dark grey. Oval cones grow upright.

Cedars prefer a well-drained soil. When pruning them, do not remove the leaders. The fine pyramidal shape of the tree will be destroyed and the tree will lose its character.

Cedars. Adam Gibbs photo

Several species of cedar are unique for their form and colour:

- Atlas cedar (*C. atlantica*). Blue-green needles. Tree has an upright leading shoot and can grow to 18 m high and 9 m wide (60 x 30 ft). The variety *Pendula* has informal weeping branches.

- *C. a. glauca.* Striking with silver-blue needles on graceful spreading branches.

- *C. deodara* (deodar cedar). A fine choice for an accent tree and an eager grower reaching 24 m (80 ft) in maturity. Lower branches sweep the ground, then turn upward. Foliage has a softer texture than most conifers. Needles are dark bluish green, 2.5–5 cm (1–2 inches) long.

- *C. d. aurea.* A smaller version with golden new needles that turn green in summer.

- *C. d. kashmir.* An outstanding specimen with blue-green needles and a more weeping shape.

- *Cedrus libani* (cedar of Lebanon). Similar to *C. deodara* but needles are green and shorter. A slow grower, attaining less than 30 cm (1 ft) per year; but eventually grows to 30 m high and 18 m wide (100 x 60 ft). A variety, *Pendula sargentii*, is a slow grower with a weeping habit.

Fir

Abies, or fir species, are tall, straight, symmetrical trees with uniformly spaced branches. They produce seed cones in shades of purple, violet, blue, red-brown and green, and hold them erect on the tree. Fir needles are not sharp and stiff like spruce, but soft and fragrant.

Firs lose their lower branches and become scrawny if they do not have full exposure to the sun. For successful cultivation, plant firs on a well-drained north slope with surrounding conifers set near enough to break strong winds yet not so near that they hinder air circulation or block sunlight.

Firs demand fertile, humus-rich soil. Fertility may be improved by spreading decomposed manure around the base of the tree every spring. An application of a 5-10-10 fertilizer in the spring is also beneficial. Use 2.3 kg (5 lbs) of fertilizer for each mature 6 m (20-ft) tree, scattering it around the drip line (the circle that follows the outer edge of the upper branches).

Firs are attractive in the garden while young but they can become intrusive in later years, so place them carefully if you don't plan to move or cut them down in maturity. They are more suitable for grouping in the background, or as specimens in open areas. Grafted, low-growing types are designed for smaller gardens.

- Douglas fir (*Pseudotsuga menziesii*). A handsome pyramidal tree with dense, soft foliage and dark green or bluish green needles, which spread all around the branch. Adaptable to any soil condition except swampland, and popular in shoreline gardens for its ability to withstand high winds.

- Balsam fir (*Abies balsamea*). A hardy species with shiny needles, green on top and whitish underneath. Foliage is very fragrant. Grows to 30 m (100 ft) or more when mature. The cultivated dwarf variety, *Nana*, is a low, slow-growing plant suitable for the rock garden.

- Korean fir (*A. koreana*). A slow-growing tree that reaches 9–12 m (30–40 ft) after many years. Short, shiny green needles. The smaller variety *Aurea* produces gold-green needles. Prostrate form suitable for growing on steep banks or rock gardens.

- Noble fir (*A. procera*). Grows to 60 m (200 ft). Stiff blue-green needles cover short, stiff branches. Decorative cones cover the tree.

- Nordmann fir (*A. nordmanniana*). A graceful garden tree and a vigorous grower that will reach 15 m (50 ft) in cultivation. Dense, glossy green foliage, with silver beneath, covers the branches.

4

Hemlock

Hemlock (*Tsuga*) is a graceful tree with scattered horizontal branches clothed with small, flat, rather soft needles. The tree bears quantities of tiny cones. Hemlock attains an air of dignity in age. It tolerates severe pruning, so is a popular choice for hedges. This tree requires an acid type soil and an abundance of moisture at its roots. It is one of the few evergreens that will thrive in shade or sun.

- Canadian hemlock (*Tsuga canadensis*). Grows to 24–27 m (80–90 ft). Branches droop slightly at the ends. Green needles with white bands beneath grow symmetrically on branchlets. Sargent weeping hemlock forms a broad-growing shrub 60–90 cm and 1.8 m wide (2–3 x 6 ft).

- Mountain hemlock (*T. mertensiana*). Foliage is blue-green with a tint of silver. Cones are 5–7.5 cm (2–3 inches) long. Grows to 27 m (90 ft) in nature; to 6–9 m (20–30 ft) in a home garden.

Juniper

Various types of juniper (*Juniperus*) have been developed to suit almost every landscape need. Low-growing varieties grow to 60–90 cm (2–3 ft). Spreading types creep along the ground. Shrubby growers reach 1.8–2.4 m (6–8 ft) in height. Upright growers stretch to 9 m (30 ft).

Junipers develop two kinds of needles. One is scale-like, with tiny, triangular, closely overlapping scales that make the branches look like braided cord. The other is needle-like, with short, stiff needles that give the branches a fine-textured appearance. Many of the most popular junipers have both types of needles.

Junipers endure poor soil, drought, and heat, although they appreciate a moist soil in dry summers.

Creeping junipers (*J. horizontalis*) include Bar Harbour, a moderately fast-growing prostrate plant 30 cm (12 inches) high with a spread of 15–20 cm (6–8 inches). Its steel-blue foliage turns to an attractive wine colour in winter. It is fine for rock garden planting. Blue Rug Juniper (*J. horizontalis wiltoni*), a creeper with soft, bunchy, frosty blue foliage, reaches 10–12.5 cm (4–5 inches) high and 15 cm (6 inches) across. Blue Pacific juniper, *Juniperus communis* 'Repanda', forms a low ground cover of evergreen foliage, deep bluish green in colour.

J. chinensis are medium-sized plants with strong, spreading branches:

- Gold Coast juniper (*J. chinensis aurea*). A gracefully branching, compact shrub with gold foliage, whose gold tones deepen in cold weather.

- *J. c.* Mint Julep, or Sea Green. Develops brilliant mint green foliage. Compact in growth with arching branches that create a fountain-like form.

- *J. c.* Mountbatten. A medium-sized shrub or small tree with a columnar shape and greyish-green leaves.

- Compact Gold Tipped Juniper *(J. c. pfitzerana aurea compacta)*. A dwarf grower with graceful, dense-growing branches.

J. sabina are dense, wide-spreading shrubs, variable in height but usually under 1.8 m (6 ft), and spreading to 6 m (20 ft) wide with age. They are great as fillers on large, open banks. Foliage is grey-green and scale-like.

- *J. sabina* Broadmoor. A neat, low, wide-branching spreader with an extremely dense mounding and soft, graceful, bright green needles. An excellent ground cover.

- *J. s.* Calgary Carpet. An improved selection from the Arcadia juniper with a much lower and wider-spreading habit and soft green needles.

- Juniper tam *(J. s. tamariscifolia)*. A well-known spreader with a mounding form, growing to 75 cm (30 inches) high and 1.2–1.5 m (4–5 ft) wide. Foliage is blue-green in youth and matures to a dark green.

Some varieties of *J. squamata* are:

- *J. squamata Meyeri.* A silver blue-needled shrub with an irregular outline and unique in colour and form. Upward-growing limbs reach to 2.4 m (8 ft). Used as a specimen, and usually planted alone.

- *J. s.* Blue Carpet. A spreading low-grower with silver blue foliage.

- *J. s.* Blue Star. An attractive dwarf form of irregular growth. Spreading and mounding branches display steel-blue needles. Grows to 1.2 m tall and 1.5 m wide (3 x 5 ft).

Rocky Mountain juniper *(J. scopulorum)* varieties include:

- *J. scopulorum* Moonglow. A medium-sized shrub of 1.8 m (6 ft) with a dense, com-pact branching habit and intense silver-blue needles.

- *J. s.* Wichita Blue. A bright silver-blue foliage densely arranged on a wide pyramidal shrub. Striking in the landscape.

Pine

Pine *(Pinus)* differs from other evergreens not only in appearance but also in the way it responds to sun, wind and soil type. A pine that is awkward and gawky in its early years may become graceful as it matures. The naturalist John Muir wrote of pines: "Finest music in the wind."

Pines like light, sandy soil with a pH of 5.5–6.0. They respond well to direction or pruning: widen, heighten, thin or thicken by pinching or pruning them.

- Scotch pine (*Pinus sylvestris*). Thrives in coast gardens, where the sea spray seems to drench it with life. Grows straight and regularly branched in youth and over time becomes picturesque, with spreading, slightly drooping branches and an irregular crown. Grows to 21–30 m (70–100 ft). Needles occur in bundles of two, blue-green, stiff, twisted and 5–7.5 cm (2–3 inches) long. Dull brown to grey cones are 5 cm (2 inches) long. Yellow-red bark on the upper trunk is decorative.

- Japanese black pine (*P. thunbergii*). Thrives by the seashore. Spreading, often drooping branches form a broad conical crown that becomes irregular with age. A moderate grower that reaches 30 m (100 ft). Needles in twos are bright green, stiff, and 7.5–10 cm (3–4 inches) long. Cones are grey-brown and 5–7.5 cm (2–3 inches) long.

- White pine (*P. strobus*). A native of Newfoundland and Manitoba. Branches of young tree are horizontal in regular whorls, forming a symmetrical, open tree; form becomes broader and more open with age. Needles in bundles of five are soft, blue-green and 5–10 cm (2–4 inches) long. Light brown cones are 5–10 cm long. Variety *nana* is a compact, rounded shrub.

- Dwarf mugho pine (*P. mugo mughus*). A fine container or rock garden plant and one of the most widely used pines in landscape design. Shrubby and symmetrical; grows slowly to 1.2 m (4 ft). Needles are dark green.

- Black pine, Austrian pine (*P. nigra*). A sturdy, handsome, symmetrical tree that becomes broad and flat-topped with age. Grows slowly but reaches 18 m (60 ft). Dark green needles occur in twos. Cones are solitary or in clusters, 7.5 cm (3 inches) long.

- Shore pine (*P. contorta*). A picturesque tree with uneven branches that are contorted by coastal winds. Grows rapidly to 10.5 m (35 ft). Dense, dark green needles occur in twos. Glossy brown cones 3.5 cm (1 1/2 inches) long appear on older trees. An ideal tree for the seacoast, growing wild from the northern coast of California to Alaska.

Spruce

Spruce, or *Picea*, can be identified by examining a twig: when the needles break off, they leave jagged projections on the twig. Also, spruce needles are sharp, pointed and stiff, and spruce cones hang down whereas fir cones stand up. The large spruce species are especially valuable as background and windbreaks. Low-growing forms are useful for hedges, foundation plantings and rock gardens.

Prune spruce plants only to shape. If a branch grows too long, cut it back to a side branch. To slow growth and encourage a more dense plant, remove part of each year's growth to force side shoots.

Spruce. Bob Cain photo

- Norway spruce (*Picea abies*). Grows taller than 30 m (100 ft). It develops rapidly into a stiff, deep green pyramid when young; later tends to grow horizontally with branches drooping. *P. abies engelmannii* (Engelmann spruce), a small- to medium-sized tree, is an attractive and hardy variety. Needles are grey-green.

- Dwarf Alberta or dwarf white spruce (*P. glauca conica*). The most popular garden conifer because of its bright green foliage, dense growing habit and perfectly shaped cone.

- Colorado spruce (*P. pungens*). A medium- to large-sized conical tree with stout, glabrous green shoots. Foliage varies from green to grey and spreads all around the branchlets.

- *P. iseli fastigiate*. A true blue, compact, columnar tree with straight ascending branches. Full exposure to sun brings out the blue tones of the needles.

- Dwarf blue spruce (*P. pungens globosa*). A dwarf, flat-topped, globular bush of dense growth with grey-blue leaves.

- Blue spruce (*P. p. glauca*). Grows to a medium height and is variable in form. Blue colour of needles becomes less intense with age.

Other varieties of spruce include nest spruce (*P. abies nidiformis*), a dwarf, dense, flat-topped bush of spreading habit, whose branches form a series of tight horizontal layers; *P. a. ohlendorffii* is a small, conical bush of dense habit, with yellowish green foliage; *P. a. pendula* is an unusual form of shrub with pendulous branches, the leader of which can be staked to any height, leaving the side branches to droop to the ground.

Yew

Taxus, or yew, is a top choice for landscaping. Yews have richly coloured needles summer and winter, and they thrive equally well in sun and shade. The shrubs are more shade- and moisture-tolerant than other conifers. Yews will even endure drought after they are established. Shearing and pruning are necessary to keep the yew shaped. Red and some-times fleshy yellow seed cups appear (they are poisonous if eaten).

- Western yew (*Taxus brevifolia*) grows in coastal areas of BC and the north-west US, in a loose, open shape to a height of 15–18 m (50–60 ft). Dark, yellowish needles. In nature it prefers moist, shaded areas.

- English yew (*T. baccata*). Slow to reach a height of 6–9 m (20–30 ft). Dark green needles cover wide-spreading branches. Poisonous red berries form on mature trees. The variety *T. b. repandens* is a low-growing ground-hugger of a shrub. Branches droop at the ends.

- Japanese yew (*T. cuspidata*). Reaches 15 m (50 ft). Garden varieties include *T. c. densiformis*, a low, dense, compact shrub. Foliage is dark green above and yellowish beneath.

Western yew. Peter A. Robson photo

- *T. media*. A few hybrids of Japanese and English yew. *T. m. hicksii* is a narrow, upright tree, slightly broader at the centre than top or bottom; *T. m. eddie* forms a compact, pyramidal, seedless tree with dark green needles; *T. cuspidata nana*, a dwarf Japanese yew, grows in bush form, suitable for hedges.

- Irish yew (*T. baccata stricta*). An erect column tree with stiff green needles. It grows to 4.5 m (15 ft). A variety, *aurea*, similar in growth and habit, has gold needles.

Flowering Trees for All Seasons

Spring

Spring is wonderful everywhere, but West Coast springs are particularly spectacular because they are long, with subtle variations of form and colour. The first blossoms, often

Indian plum, emerge in February, when much of the rest of Canada and the northern US are still under snow. Then come the maples, alders and dogwoods, until the coastal forests are cloaked in rich, glorious colour.

Gardeners choose flowering trees based on space limitations, scale proportions and landscape characteristics, together with cultural and maintenance requirements. Trees with sparkling flowers, interesting foliage, attractive bark or unusual fruit are chosen for visual effect, and they also contribute to privacy and balance the landscape. As shade trees in summer, they are more than welcome.

Crabapple

Ornamental crabapple trees are rightly popular. In branch structure and silhouette, the crabapple resembles a small fruit-producing apple tree.

Like other members of the rose family, these trees require a bright, sunny site. Their growing soil should be fertile, enriched with organic material and well drained. Flowering crabs are drought-resistant: they can survive on 30–38 cm (12–15 inches) of water during the growing season. When summer watering is necessary, soak the root zone deeply once a week.

Severe pruning of the crabapple will encourage a lot of soft shoots and destroy the natural gracefulness of the tree. In winter, prune only shoots that arise from the base of the tree and below the graft union (see p. 144), and prune long, ungainly top growths and parts that are dead or damaged.

- Siberian crab (*Malus baccata*). The first spring flowering crabapple to show colour, grown for its bright yellow and scarlet fruits. Fragrant white flowers appear by the end of March. Tree is vase-shaped with dense growth, reaching heights of 6–9 m (20–30 ft).

- Pink weeping crabapple (*M. echtermeyer*). Produces pendulous branches; grows 3–4.5 m (10–15 ft) tall and about as wide. Spring blossoms are single and purplish red. Foliage is reddish or bronze, then turns green. Striking purple cherry-like fruits in late summer and fall.

- Japanese flowering crabapple (*M. floribunda*). An exquisite tree. Slender, arching branches smothered with single blossoms in spring. Flower petals are deep rose red on the outside, and snow white inside, with a light fragrance. Yellow or reddish edible fruits. Sturdy in growth, reaching to about 5.5 m (18 ft) at maturity.

- *M. sylvestris eleyi*. Produces a storm of magenta rose blossoms in early April. Tree is upright and spreading, growing to 6–7.5 m (20–25 ft). Spring leaves unfold reddish to purplish bronze, then turn green with reddish veins in late summer. Large cherry red fruits are produced well after flowering.

- *M. almey.* Magnificent fiery orange to crimson flowers. White markings at the base of each flower petal create a star shape. Scarlet apples hang on the branches long after the leaves have dropped.

Flowering Dogwood

Flowering dogwood (*Cornus nuttallii*) is a native of the Pacific Northwest. It is BC's official floral emblem. The tree matures to a height of 15 m (50 ft) with a spread of 4.5 m (15 ft). Opening spring flowers give a creamy yellow effect, which changes to snowy white after a few days. Bright green leaves turn orange and scarlet in autumn. Native dogwoods are further ornamented in fall with sparkling red berries.

*Dogwood (*Cornus*): 'Eddie's White Wonder.'* Adam Gibbs photo

- 'White Wonder' (*Cornus nuttallii*). Huge, long-lasting white flowers cover slightly weeping branches in spring. Fall foliage is striking in brilliant red.

- Pink flowering dogwood (*C. florida rubra*). A small-growing tree with deep rose or red blossoms or bracts. Young leaves are reddish. 'Apple Blossom' and 'Spring Song,' both bright pink in bract colouring, are excellent cultivars. Another is 'Cherokee Chief,' with deep pink bracts.

- 'Cloud 9' (*C. florida*). A vigorous tree that flowers at an early age. Huge, brilliant red bracts and orange and red fall foliage.

Flowering dogwood. Adam Gibbs photo

Pink dogwood. Adam Gibbs photo

- Japanese flowering dogwood (*C. kousa*). Flowers when in full leaf, followed by pinkish red berries like hanging raspberries. Berries are edible, with the flavour of strawberries.

- *C. kousa satomi.* A recent introduction, with magnificent red bracts in early June. Green leaves soon follow the flowers.

- *C. alba* 'Bailhalo', or ivory halo dogwood. A dense, compact form of silverleaf dogwood. Finely textured variegated foliage with a wide band of white against the green. Dark red twigs appear in winter.

Pruning of dogwoods is necessary only to improve the shape of the tree. Early spring, before growth begins, is the ideal time to prune dogwoods.

Magnolia

Flowering deciduous magnolias open the gates of spring on the coast, when sparkling goblets of blossoms fill the uplifting branches in March and April.

Magnolias require space for their far-reaching limbs—at least 3.6 m (12 ft) all around. Plant them on a north slope that is shaded in late summer and fall. They thrive under the canopy of high-branching trees. (An open, sunny situation is recommended for summer-blooming varieties.) Magnolias are native to moist, fertile, well-drained woodland soils of the coast. They require a slightly acid soil, like rhododendrons and azaleas. Grafted forms of magnolias should be planted with the graft union about 5 cm (2 inches) below the soil.

Signs of fertilizer deficiency are small, sparse, pale leaves and short twig growth. Established magnolias benefit from a spring feeding of a fertilizer formulated especially for rhododendrons. Apply 1.3 kg (3 lbs) to each mature tree. Cottonseed and blood meal are appreciated in autumn. Use 450 g (1 lb) of each around the base of a tree 4 to 5 years old.

Magnolia soulangeana *'Lennei' with* Rhododendron *'Blue Diamond.'* Sandra Evelyn photo

Magnolias resent pruning. Cut the plant lightly, when necessary, in late spring to give the wounds time to heal during the growing season. Any cut larger than the diameter of a pencil should be coated with a sealing pruning paint. When pruning deciduous magnolias, cut the branches out, not back.

Magnolia stellata, the star magnolia, is magnificent in February. Downy unopened flower buds decorate the leafless shrub until the spring sun welcomes them open. A star shape is formed by 12 to 18 single petals. Spring leaves are long, narrow, thick and dark green. Sparkling white, pink or purplish red flowering stellatas grow well in coastal gardens. Seeds with vivid colours slowly descend from the blossoms on threads and are quickly devoured by birds.

Magnolia 'Elizabeth.' Sandra Evelyn photo

The star magnolia stretches to 3.6–5.4 m (12–18 ft). Plant it in the open to greet the first warm glow of the February sun. When grown near the ocean, early-flowering magnolias should be planted on the lee side of a house or trees, to protect them from salt air and prevailing winds.

M. soulangeana is the most common deciduous magnolia. On bare, grey branches, white, rose or purple goblet-shaped flowers form from April through May. Knobby seed pods appear in late summer. The tree is characteristically low-forking or - branching and wide-spreading in growth and can reach a height of 7.5 m (25 ft) and a spread of 4.5 m (15 ft).

Varieties include 'Alexandrina,' rose pink outside, white inside; 'Rustic Rubra,' rosy red outside, white inside; 'Leonard Messel,' purple-pink; and 'Ballerina,' pale pink; uniquely new is 'Butterflies,' with yellow blossoms.

Prunus

Prunus trees, a large genus of deciduous trees that includes peaches, plums, cherries, apricots and almonds, offer many choices.

- *Prunus blireiana.* A flowering plum and one of the first to show colour. Deep pink double blossoms crowd on twiggy limbs and branches as early as February and March, followed by bright coppery leaves that remain until autumn.

- *P. pissardii Nigra.* Noted for its dark red foliage. Pink flowers appear in March and April.

- *P. cerasifera* 'Thundercloud.' Deep purple leaves and mountains of light pink single flowers in early spring. Fruits are almost the colour of the leaves.

- 'Kwanzan' (*P. serrulata*). A rather stiff upright tree that thrives on the coast. Double rose pink flowers cluster in groups during April and May. Foliage unfolds at the same time as flowers.

- 'Mount Fuji' (*P. serrulata*). One of the earliest of the cherries to bloom. White semi-double blossoms in pendulous clusters, and bright green leaves.

- 'Shirofugen' (*P. serrulata*). Double white flowers begin as pink buds. Branching outline is horizontal.

- 'Amanogawa' (*P. serrulata*). A thin, narrow-growing tree suitable for crowded quarters. Semi-double pink flowers decorate upright branches in spring.

In Japan, flowering **apricots** (*Prunus mume*) are honoured in February with a special celebration. The fruits are quite sour. The tree has a tendency to become bush-like if not thinned frequently. In autumn, after its first year in the garden, prune all shoots to 15 cm (6-inch) stubs. The next year, cut back half the young growth to 15 cm stubs; cut back the other half the following year, and continue the alternating pruning routine in succeeding years. The flowers are exquisite and fragrant.

- *Prunus mume* 'Dawn.' Early to flower with large, ruffled double pink blossoms.

- *P. mume* 'Bonita.' Double crimson red blossoms.

Almonds are among the first of the flowering *Prunus* trees to give the garden colour. They are small in size and twiggy if not pruned frequently. Some types grow to 4.5 m (15 ft) tall with an equal spread. A few are dwarf or semi-dwarf in stature. In autumn, hard-shelled nuts form.

- *Prunus triloba* forms a shrub reaching 3 m (10 ft) in height, with double rose coloured flowers in early spring.

- Dwarf Russian Almond (*P. tenella*). Diminutive in size, growing to 1.2 m (4 ft) and producing white, pink or rose-red blooms.

- *P. glandulosa*. Small tree from China and Japan. Grows to 1.5 m (5 ft), with white or pink flowers.

Flowering **peach** trees produce flowers on the new wood of the previous year's growth. After the tree has flowered, prune the branches that bear flowers, cutting them back to 15 cm (6-inch) stubs.

In summer, multi-branched new growth develops from the stubs. These branches will be covered with blooms the following spring.

- *Prunus persica atrosancvines*. Perhaps the most distinctive flowering peach, with deep rose-coloured blooms.

- *P. persica* 'Peppermint Stick.' Striking, with striped red and white flowers.

- *P. p. cardinal*. A bright rose-crimson, double-flowering variety.

Weeping Redbud
The weeping redbud, or lavender twist (*Cercis canadensis*) 'Covey' is a unique recent introduction that grows a profusion of lavender-pink flowers in spring, preceding dark green heart-shaped foliage. The trunk has a distinct zigzagging growth pattern.

Summer
Once the spectacular spring-flowering trees have dropped their blossoms, the summer-flowering trees show their colours.

Franklin Tree
The Franklin tree (*Franklinia alatamaha*), named for Ben Franklin, is an exceptionally choice specimen for an open lawn. It grows to 6 m (20 ft) and usually grows shrubby on the coast. The leaves are deciduous and glossy green. Large, white saucer-like flowers appear in late summer, and the tree is spectacular with flaming red foliage and the white flowers, which persist through autumn. The Franklin tree needs fertile, acid soil, and may die to the ground each year and come up to bloom on spring shoots. It grows easily from

seed and blooms in 6 years. It is especially spectacular growing among rhododendron and azalea.

Golden Rain Tree

The golden rain tree (*Koelreuteria*) is a deciduous tree from northern China. It is slow growing but eventually reaches 9 m tall and 7.5 m wide (30 x 25 ft). This tree takes on great character with age, as its branches become gnarled, tortuous and thorny. Luminous yellow flowers in large panicles (loose, branching clusters) open in July and August through September. Pink triangular seed pods develop from the fading flowers. The tree's attractive fern-like leaves lend a light, airy touch to the summer garden. The golden rain tree will endure heat, drought, strong winds and alkaline soils.

- *Koelreuteria paniculata* 'September.' Bears small, bright yellow flowers with a touch of scarlet in the centre. Flowers are followed by ornamental pods, papery in texture and pale green in colour. Pods turn brown in the fall and shed small, dark seeds that germinate readily.

- *K. p. fastigiata.* A sharply upright form.

- *K. p. formosana* (Chinese flame tree). Showy red and orange seed pods appear in autumn resembling tiny Japanese lanterns.

Japanese Pagoda Tree

The Japanese pagoda tree (*Sophora japonica*), also called the Chinese scholar tree, is impressive in size, form, colouring and time of flowering. The leaves are delicate, long and dark green in summer. In July, August and September, clusters of yellowish white pea-like flowers hang from the tree. These are followed by shiny green seed pods that dry and turn yellow in autumn. The pods remain on the tree through the winter and become quite ornamental. Insects such as Japanese beetles cannot resist the blossoms, but as soon as they eat the flowers they fall to the ground in a stupor, which makes it easy to gather and remove them.

- *Sophora japonica columnaris.* A narrowly upright form commonly planted.

- *S. j. pendula.* A handsome weeping form.

- 'Regent.' A select cultivar with exceptionally striking foliage. It blooms while quite young.

Katsura

The katsura tree (*Cercidphyllum japonicum*) is a wide-spreading tree valued for shade. It grows to 9 m (30 ft) tall with a spread of 2.4 m (18 ft). The fine-textured, heart-shaped leaves turn brilliant red in autumn. Its most distinguishing feature is its flowers, which grow all along the old wood of the branches and even on the trunk. Blossoms are rosy purple and pea-like in form. New growth is tinted red throughout the season. Tiny dry fruit capsules remain on the tree in winter.

- *Cercidphyllum japonicum pendulum.* A rare form of the katsura tree, with long pendulous branches.

- Chinese katsura tree (*C. j. sinense*). Delicate and ornate. Produces darker red foliage and is more upright than *C. japonicum.*

Chinese katsura tree. Sandra Evelyn photo

Magnolia

Summer-flowering magnolias are totally different in appearance from the spring-flowering types. The blooms, which appear among the green leaves, are saucer-shaped and pendant, each with a conspicuous central group of crimson stamens. They are delightfully fragrant. To fully enjoy the flowers, plant summer magnolias on a slope or at the top of a wall. By autumn, small cones with red seeds have replaced the blossoms.

- *Magnolia grandiflora.* A huge, vigorous evergreen tree with handsome leaves and large, fragrant, creamy white blossoms in summer.

Saucer magnolia. Adam Gibbs photo

- *M. g.* St. Mary's. An early-flowering tree with intriguing leaves that glisten on top and are fuzzy brown beneath.

- *M. g.* Victoria. A native of Victoria, BC that will withstand -23° (-10°F) cold, yet will not tolerate freezing winds. Broad leaves are green in all seasons. Fragrant flowers, similar to other *M.g.* blooms, are white and as wide as 25 cm (10 inches) across. Tree will grow to 6 m in height and 4.5 m in spread (20 x 15 ft).

Pseudo-Camellia

Stewartia, the pseudo-camellia, is a Japanese import. It greets the summer with sparkling white flowers resembling single camellias. Golden stamens stand proudly in the centre of the flower. The tree is small, growing to 4.5 m tall and 6 m wide (15 x 20 ft). The bark peels and shreds in intricate patterns, and fall foliage is a blaze of colour. Permanent planting of the tree is necessary: it will not tolerate root disturbance when it is mature.

- Korean stewartia (*Stewartia koreana*). Showy, with shallow cupped white flowers 7.5 cm (3 inches) across in late June and July. Tree reaches a pyramidal 13.5 m (45 ft).

- Oriental stewartia is a superior tree when grown in a high-humus, lime-free soil that remains damp throughout the year.

Silk Tree

The silk tree (*Albizzia julibrissin*) is a native of the Orient. In summer the extended stamens produce a powder-puff-like flower, which is quickly devoured by birds. The stamens are numerous and evocative of silk, tinted pink, yellow or cream. Interesting seed pods follow the flowers.

The silk tree's phenomenal growth rate—as much as 3–3.6 m (10–12 ft) in a season—makes it ideal for the gardener who wants an immediate effect. Leaves are tropical in appearance, and often close at night, similar to the mimosa. This tree has a unique flat-topped shape, so it is best planted to be viewed from above, from a deck or hilltop. It does best when purchased in a container, at least a year old, and transplanted.

- *Albizzia julibrissin Rosea*. Produces deep pink flowers and tolerates cold winter weather. May develop as a large shrub on the coast. Grows to 9 m (30 ft) in hot, dry locations.

Tulip Tree

The tulip tree (*Liriodendron tulipifera*) is awesome in size when mature. The tree flowers when it is 15 to 20 years old. During July and August, curious cup-shaped green and orange-yellow flowers appear. They resemble open tulips. The leaves are saddle-shaped or squared off, light green or yellow in spring and summer, and brilliant gold in autumn.

The winter buds of the tulip tree have 2 outer scales, flat and broad, which resemble the valves of a clamshell. Pressure inside the bud pushes the scales open and out thrust the spring leaves. In

*Tulip tree (*Liriodendron*)*. Sandra Evelyn photo

winter, bare branches hold up broad champagne goblets to be admired in silhouette against the dark clouds. Transplant tulip trees while they are young: they resent root disturbances as they age.

- *Liriodendron tulipifera fastigatum.* Has a compact columnar growth habit, ideal for a large garden.

Autumn

The autumnal equinox on the West Coast brings a dazzling display of golds, browns, yellows, scarlets, reds, pinks and purples. Autumn trees and shrubs are resplendent in glowing leaves as they prepare for winter, and gnarled branches, patterned peeling bark, bright berries and brave flowers add pleasure to the fall scene. Each tree or shrub displays its particular colour—an inherited trait in many trees—and each individual plant has its own shade of that colour. The shade is influenced by climate and soil conditions.

Just before leaves drop in autumn, the nutrients they contain start to move back into the stems and roots of a tree. The green chlorophyll pigment stops being produced, and that which remains in the leaf is destroyed by light. Most leaves contain yellow colouring that is hidden during the summer by the green pigment. When the chlorophyll disappears in the fall, the yellow becomes visible. If no yellow pigment is present, the leaves turn brown. The development of orange, red and purple is more complicated. To display these colours, the leaves must produce another pigment, anthocyanin. The particular shade of orange, red, or purple is related to the acid or alkaline condition of the sap of the plant. If the sap is acid, the colour will be more red or orange. If it is neutral, the pigment is light purple. If it is alkaline, the colour tends to dark purple or blue.

The amount of anthocyanin depends on the accumulation of sugars and tannins in the plant. During warm, sunny weather, leaves produce sugar. In autumn, with night temperatures below 7°C (45°F), the sugars and tannins do not move into the branches for storage; more of them remains in the leaves to be converted into anthocyanin.

If the weather during the fall is quite cloudy, sugar production is reduced. If the nights remain warm, the sugars move to the branches and the foliage colour will be more dull. Sunny days and cool nights stimulate brilliant autumn colouring; cool, cloudy days and warm nights result in more drab colouring.

Arbutus

Virgil reveals in the *Aeneid* how the tender twigs of the arbutus were woven into the soft bier made to carry the body of Pallas home to his father. *Arbutus menziesii* is a native tree found along the coast of the Pacific Northwest, and the only native broad-leafed evergreen in Canada. The tree has smooth, reddish brown bark that peels from the tree in flakes. The evergreen leaves are a dull green in colour.

Spring finds large clusters of white to pinkish bell-shaped flowers on the tree. The flowers are followed in early autumn by bright orange and red berries, much loved by birds.

A. *menziesii* found in the wilds should be left there. You may find one at a specialty native nursery, but the tree is very difficult to transplant and reestablish in the home garden. A slightly acid soil and a place near the seashore are to its liking.

Arbutus. Bob Cain photo

- *Arbutus unedo*, or the **strawberry tree**, is a native of Ireland that is easily found in coastal nurseries. At maturity it outgrows its shrub-like habit and develops into a tree 6–9 m (20–30 ft) in height. Its evergreen leaves are thick, rough and green. Clusters of pinkish pendant flowers are evident from October to December, and strawberry fruits are produced at the same time. The fruit is edible as well as decorative.

- *A. u. compacta*. A newer introduction, with all the fine qualities of the older variety but more compact in growth and a heavy producer of flowers and berries. Suitable for planting in containers.

- *A. u.* 'Elfin King.' A tiny, picturesque form reaching 1.5–1.8 m (5–6 ft). Needs a soil rich in humus yet well-drained, and a sheltered but sunny site.

Flowering arbutus (Pacific madrone). Adam Gibbs photo

Arbutus bark. Adam Gibbs photo

Flowering Cherry

As the last spring-flowering bulb is tucked in under the earth, the Pacific Northwest gardener can look up through the branches of *Prunus subhirtella autumnalis*, the autumn- and winter-flowering cherry tree. Its appeal can be seen in its semi-double flowers in shades of pale pink to almost white. The tree is slender in outline and grows to 6–9 m (20–30 ft). The bark is a warm grey. As the tree matures, the bark roughens and becomes scaly. Along the lower parts of the branches are innumerable short, curving twigs filled with blossoms. Clouds of blossoms may be damaged by sharp frosts, but new flower buds continue to open whenever milder weather occurs through the winter and early spring.

Winter-flowering cherry. Sandra Evelyn photo

Ginkgo

The ginkgo tree shows well in autumn, developing into a picturesque form with a well-spaced open branching pattern. In early spring, two fan-shaped lobes unfold as light golden-green leaves. In autumn, leaves fall to the ground in a shower of gold.

Ginkgo trees are slow growing, but may eventually reach 18 m (60 ft) tall and 9 m (30 ft) wide. At the age of 30 to 40 years, the tree yields fruits or nuts, which appear as tiny buff plums. The outer husk of the fruit has an unpleasant odour and the nut, which is nourishing, tastes like rancid butter.

- *Ginkgo biloba* 'Autumn Gold.' Upright growth habit, golden yellow foliage in fall, a more pleasant form and scent than other ginkgos, and bright foliage.

Maple

The maple genus (*Acer*) includes a multitude of ornamental and diminutive forms appropriate for home gardens, many of which are as hardy as their relatives in coastal forests. Growing soil for maples should be lime-free or slightly acid. Small-growing maples are planted shallow, with the top of the root ball positioned only 3.5–5 cm (1½–2 inches) below the soil surface. Avoid handling the root ball. Gently set it intact into the planting pocket and fill in around the roots with fine soil. Pacific Northwesterners are most familiar with our native vine maple, or *Acer circinatum*. In autumn its slender branches glow with oranges and reds among the deep greens of the native evergreens.

Ornamental maples in autumn. Adam Gibbs photo

Vine maples grow with many slender stems, or clusters of stems, to a height of 6–9 m (20–30 ft). The tree's common name is descriptive of its twining, vine-like branches, which are characteristic when it grows in dense shade or when winter snows bend its slender limbs to the ground. Plant vine maples in shady corners of the garden. Their tall, arching branches will provide a natural bower for an underplanting of fern, dwarf azalea and rhododendron, along with native flowering plants.

A. palmatum, or Japanese maple, has more than 80 varieties. From this native of Korea, Japanese gardeners have created a wealth of foliage colours, shapes and textures.

A. palmatum septembobum 'Osakazuki.' Has the most consistently brilliant autumn leaf colouring and bolder foliage than most. 7-lobed leaves are bronze in summer, turning incandescent orange and red in late fall. Reaches a height of 6 m (20 ft).

A. p. dissectum 'Seiryu' (threadleaf maple). Superb for bonsai training, with slow, contorted growth and finely laciniated (fringed) foliage.

Acers with fine foliage include: *A. p.* 'atropurpureum,' with red-wine leaves in spring and fall; *A. p.* 'Nigrum,' striking in leaf colour of deep red; *A. p.* 'Beni Otake,' *A. p.* 'Kamagata,' and *A. p.* 'Ukigumo.'

*Japanese maple (*Acer palmatum dissectum*).* Sandra Evelyn photo

- *Acer rubrum* 'Red Sunset.' Twigs and branchlets are red, as are opening buds. Scarlet flowers appear before the leaves. The fruits are dull red. Fall foliage colour is brilliant scarlet. The tree is relatively low growing to about 12 m (40 ft).

- *A. platanoides* 'Crimson King.' Stretches skyward to 15 m (50 ft). Fall foliage is red-purple.

- Silver maple, or *A. saccharinum*. A huge specimen of 30 m (100 ft) or more. Leaves are pale green and shiny above and silvery beneath, so leaves flutter in the breeze like silver tinsel. Tolerates soggy, wet soils.

Oak

Quercus, or oak, is a noble, strong and long-lived tree. In some of the earliest English writings, these words appear: "In three centuries the oak grows, in another three it stays, and in three more it decays." Oaks are graceful in all seasons, with fine foliage, exciting fall leaf colour and patterns, interesting bark and strong branching habits.

- *Quercus garryana* (Garry oak). A native tree of the Pacific Northwest, varying in height from 7.5 to 23 m (25–75 ft). Its irregular branching habits make it a picturesque specimen.

- *Q. palurtis* (pin oak). Deeply lobed, large leaves turn reddish bronze each fall. Leaves stay on the tree all winter in drab brown tones. Tree is pyramidal when young and rounds out with age. Grows to 24–30 m (80–100 ft) and thrives in a soil that is dependably moist.

- *Q. coccinea* (scarlet oak). A slow-growing tree that thrives near the beach and may reach 15 m (50 ft). Brilliant red foliage in autumn.

Sourwood

The sourwood tree, or *Oxydendrum*, is appreciated for its ornamental form and brilliant autumn colours. The tree has a graceful pyramid shape and seldom exceeds 9 m (30 ft) in height. Laurel-like leaves are washed with shades of pink and coral as they unfold in the spring. Soon they turn bright crimson. Lacy panicles (loose, branching clusters) of white flowers open in late summer and remain attractive on the tree until seeds develop for winter display. Sourwoods prefer an acid soil, which makes them good growing companions to rhododendron and azalea.

Sumac

Particularly notable in autumn is the flameleaf sumac (*Rhus copallia*), an exotic tree with graceful stems, naked at the base, that support top-heavy tufts of luxurious leaves. Sumacs are naturals in coastal gardens. Their foliage is decorative and aflame with crimson and orange leaves in autumn.

- Staghorn sumac (*Rhus typhina*). Distinctive for dense, sticky hairs on its berries and twigs. In winter, angular branches suggest the hairy antlers of young stags. A small tree that will thrive in a rocky, infertile soil, and seems to enjoy neglect.

Sweet Gum

Sweet gum, or *Liquidamber styraciflua*, produces large, coarse, star-shaped leaves. They are dark green in spring, and in autumn they turn brilliant shades of orange and crimson. Scarlet berries decorate the tree during late summer and fall.

Sweet gums are compact, rounded trees that reach skyward to 24 m (80 ft). They need a moist, acid soil. 'Burgundy', 'Palo Alto' and 'Worpleston', three improved varieties of sweet gum, are readily available on the West Coast.

Winter

Japanese Quince

Japanese quince (*Chaenomeles japonica*) is precocious. It bravely displays its colours in the dark of winter and holds them into late spring. Open flowers are like apple blossoms in tones of cherry, red, coral, pink and white, with a combination of white, white and pink or pink and red blooms occurring on the same branch. Some flowers are double. Greenish yellow fruit follows the flowers. Train or espalier (see p. 172) the long-reaching plant on a wall or fence. Prune the branches heavily after flowering. Shiny oblong leaves are a bronzy green in spring and mature to a bright green. The branches are barren of leaves in autumn and winter. New hybrids include 'Crimson and Gold', with red blooms; 'Pink Lady', clear rose; 'Fire Dance', glowing red; and 'Nivalis', pure white.

Sweet gum. Adam Gibbs photo

Sasanqua Camellia

In winter, gardens sparkle with the scattering pink, red and white confetti-like blossoms of the sasanqua camellia. A native of Japan, it features twiggy, picturesque branches that grow to 5.4–6 m (18–20 ft). Its fragile single, semi-double or double flowers have the grace of wild roses. Bright golden stamens decorate the centres of the fragrant blossoms. Its glossy evergreen leaves are pointed and smaller than many other types of camellias. *Camellia sasanqua*'s slender, arching stems may be trained on trellises to form interesting patterns.

Sasanqua camellias will endure more heat and sun than other members of the camellia clan. Flowering is improved if the plants are exposed to all of the morning sun. Soil should be rich in humus, porous and fertile. Plant the camellias high, allowing their fibrous roots almost to show above the ground. Mulch over the root zone lightly with peat moss, humus or ground bark.

- 'Yuletide.' A compact upright grower whose bright red blossoms have yellow stamens in the centre.

- 'White Dove.' Sparkles with white peony-form, semi-double flowers.

- 'Momozono-Nishiki.' Has large semi-double rose and white shaded petals that twist.

- 'Showa-no-Sakae.' Striking with pink semi-double flowers.

Viburnum

No shrub among the winter-flowering types is more deserving of the classification than *Viburnum fragrans*. Reginald Farrer found this plant in palace and temple courtyards in China, and described it as having arching branches 3 m (10 ft) high and more than 3 m wide, with naked boughs that became a blaze of soft pink-lilac spidelets exuding an intense fragrance of heliotrope.

- *Viburnum bodnantense.* A cross between *V. fragrans* and *V. grandiflorum* and a winter marvel. Sweet-scented pink flowers smother long, stiff branches from November to March. 'Pink Dawn' produces deep rose blossoms, and long oval leaves that turn dark scarlet in autumn. Plant is nearly evergreen, with deeply veined green leaves and clusters of dark blue berries in autumn.

- *V. tinus* (Laurestinus). According to legend, flowers on the first day of the New Year, the feast of St. Faine, an Irish abbess of the sixth century. Here and now, flowers from September until early spring. An evergreen plant with large, glossy green leaves. Fragrant white to pink flowers grow freely on the ends of branches. Birds flock to abundant metallic blue berries. May grow to 4.5–6 m (15–20 ft) tall and broad. Tolerant of drought and suitable for seaside plantings. Needs a slightly acid soil. Often used for hedging as it endures severe shearing. Prune soon after flowering.

Winter Hazel

Winter hazel (*Corylopsis*) is often mistaken for witch hazel, and is less well known. The winter hazels bear their winter flowers in nodding clusters of small, yellow, finger-shaped blooms.

- *Corylopsis spicata.* A leafless shrub or small tree, the most ornamental of the winter hazels. Clusters of the brightest yellow flowers fall from every branch, reminiscent in scent of some primroses.

- *C. pauciflora.* A native of Japan. Pale yellow flowers are pendulous on slender branches. Leaves, which begin after the plant flowers, are rosy pink, then turn coppery and finally green.

- Chinese winter hazel (*C. sinensis*). Strong, upright tall-growing branches have winter flower buds covered with red husks. Light yellow flowers with red-brown anthers open in January and February.

Winter Jasmine

Winter jasmine (*Jasminum nudiflorum*) rushes over rocks in streams of gold. Its golden blossoms radiate light even on the dullest of winter days. Greenish arching branches, which may stretch 2.4–3 m (8–10 ft), are barren of leaves in late fall and winter. At a distance, winter jasmine is often mistaken for flowering forsythia. It is erratic in flowering: bright yellow in December, then defeated by a cold blast until a little January and February sun coaxes out more blooms. The plant has a tendency to become thin and straggly, so prune severely in spring after all the flowers have faded.

Winter jasmine. Sandra Evelyn photo

Wintersweet

Wintersweet (*Chimonanthus praecox fragrans*) is admired for its intricate blossom form, colour and fragrance. Each delicate yellow flower has an inner segment that is striped purplish brown. When the flowers are spread flat, they measure 3 cm (1 1/4 inches) across. These waxen bell-shaped blossoms, which permeate the air with the scent of honeysuckle, violet, almond and hyacinth, droop from the branches of the shrub at the beginning of December and fall from the plant in early March. Plant wintersweet on the south side of an evergreen shrub to catch the winter sun and provide protection from winter weather. Small, shiny green leaves cover the branches in spring and become a bright yellow in autumn. Then you might forget the shrub, until a sunny day in December when you first catch its spicy fragrance.

Wintersweet is aggravatingly slow growing when young but eventually reaches 2.4–3 m (8–10 ft) tall and 1.8–2.4 m (6–8 ft) wide. Flowering branches of *C. praecox fragrans* should be cut back by a third after blooming in early spring.

- *Chimonanthus praecox grandiflorus.* An improved form, with huge bright yellow flowers that do not have the purple streak on the inner petals.

Witch Hazel

It seems like June but it is really January when the branches of the witch hazel (*Hamamelis*) are spangled with threads of translucent gold. Curious, spidery yellow blossoms appear in clusters of 3 on the bare twiggy branches of this shrub or small tree. It is decorative in any season: winter finds it in flower, and in spring and summer thick green leaves cover the branches. Often a fair crop of small nut-like fruits appears in late summer or early autumn. After the orange- to reddish-coloured fall leaves drop, the attractive branching pattern is revealed. The shrub slowly grows to heights of 4.5–5.4 m (15–18 ft), and nearly as wide.

Plant witch hazel along a sunny wall or fence, where it will be protected from wind. It likes a slightly acid soil filled with organic humus.

Witch hazel blossom. Chuck Heath photo

- Ozark witch hazel (*Hamamelis vernalis*). Bears winter flowers smaller and duller in colour than the Oriental species, but it produces more flowers. Needs a moist growing soil. In nature it thrives along small gravelly streams.

- Chinese witch hazel (*H. mollis*). The show-off of the family. Golden flower petals are held up in wine-coloured goblets on the plant's bare branches. Leaves emerge bright green in spring, then turn the warm summer tones of ripe peaches.

- Japanese witch hazel (*H. japonica*). Outstanding for its spectacular winter flowers, which are pleasantly fragrant, and brilliant autumn leaves. Arborea, a newer variety of japonica, is extremely hardy and has a distinctive tree-like growth habit. Striking golden yellow flower petals are set in a maroon calyx.

Fruit Trees

Fruit trees are quite particular about their growing soil, and each type of tree has its own preferences. For example, pears grow and produce well in a heavy but well-drained soil; apples and plums prefer deep medium loam; peaches and cherries thrive in sandy loam.

For the best chance of success, buy young, locally grown nursery trees. They are more adaptable to native soil and climatic conditions on the coast. Nurseries often have standard, semi-dwarf, dwarf and espaliered specimens. Generally, nursery trees are ready for planting when they are 3 years old. A standard fruit tree normally begins to produce at 3 to 7 years. If you choose only one variety of each type of fruit, make sure that it is self-fruitful, or capable of pollinating itself.

Fertilize fruit trees around February 1 each year to boost the tree's growth, encourage fruit spurs, "set" the blossoms and improve the intensity of colour and the size of leaves and fruits. Apply about 2.3 kg (5 lbs) of a 5-10-10 fertilizer to each mature tree, or carefully follow the directions on the package. Apply the fertilizer in a wide band beyond the spread of the top branches. Water it deeply into the surrounding soil.

If you espalier your fruit trees, they will take up less garden space and you can regulate the fruit production. Apple and pear trees espalier particularly well, as they blossom and fruit over and over, primarily on spurs from the same branches.

Train fruit trees against a sunny wall if you can. The accumulation of heat on the wall, together with the shield it offers from chilly winds and frosts, produce an abundance of fruit.

Mixed plums (Prunus). Adam Gibbs photo

For the West Coast gardener, the double horizontal cordon is a simple espalier to train and maintain. Make a sturdy, permanent support or trellis for the espalier. For example, you can use 4 heavy wires suspended between strong posts. The lowest wire should be 30–45 cm (12–18 inches) from the ground; the next wire is about 30 cm (12 inches) above the first and the third and fourth are about 30 cm (12 inches) apart. Use thick galvanized wires for the middle, and pipes for end supports. Use vinyl-wrapped wire to tie the branches to the wires.

Espalier a dwarf fruit tree from a 1-year whip. In the spring, cut it to within 25–30 cm (10–12 inches) from ground level. From the uppermost top or growth bud, a new terminal shoot will grow. At about the end of June, cut this new terminal growth back to within less than 1 cm ($^1/2$ inch) of where it started. This will force at least 2 new shoots of equal strength to grow at the same level; cut out extra shoots that develop.

Tie the 2 shoots to the espalier support to keep them flat and horizontal. When they are 30 cm (12 inches) long, turn the tips upward to form a U shape if you wish.

The next spring and again in late June, after the turned-up branches have grown, cut both back to 30–38 cm (12–15 inches) above the bend and treat or train as the original shoot. This type of training will result in 4 uprights, forming a double U.

During the first few seasons, other shoots will start to grow. Cut all of them back to 5–7 cm (2–3 inches) from the trunk or branch from which they originated. They will become the fruiting spurs.

Prune espaliered fruit trees in winter, during their dormant period, and at least once during the spring or summer. Shoots or water sprouts that arise in the growing period should be cut back to the point of origin, unless needed for further development. Keep your design in mind at all times, and vigilantly pinch or cut back all errant shoots that interfere.

Cold spring weather and heavy frosts often damage fruit blossoms. Injured blossoms may appear normal after severe cold snaps in spring, but if the centre part or pistil of the blossom is killed, the tree will not bear fruit that season. Early-flowering fruit trees such as apricot, peach and sweet cherry are particularly susceptible. On cold, rainy and windy days, bees may not fly during the time the trees are in blossom, and you may have to use a blossom-set commercial solution.

Some fruit trees exhibit a biennial bearing tendency: they produce a heavy crop of fruit one year and little or no fruit the next. Thin the crop in the heavy year so that there is 15–20 cm (6–8 inches) between fruits. This will help keep the tree from exhausting itself.

Fruit trees vary in their fruiting habits and require individual pruning methods, but it is essential to develop a strong, well-balanced framework of branches when any fruit tree is young. Train the tree into the general shape of a funnel or inverted pyramid, with the centre well filled with fruit-producing limbs.

Apple

With the exception of Golden Delicious, most apple varieties are not self-fruitful. Plant McIntosh, Rome, Golden Delicious or Jonathan apple trees for pollination purposes. Winesap, Gravenstein, Baldwin and Northern Spy are poor pollenizers; a pollen bearer should be planted nearby for a full crop.

Apples to grow include Yellow Transparent, Red Gravenstein, King, Golden Delicious, Early McIntosh, Elstar, Empire, Jonatree, Mutsu or Crispin, and Spartan.

Crabapples to grow include Scheidecker, Transcendant, Dolgo, Norda and Radiant. The Dolgo crabapple has large, striking white blossoms in spring and produces bright red fruit in summer and fall, good for jellies and preserves.

Apricot

Apricot trees bear fruit in 4 to 5 years. Some varieties of apricots including Blenheim, Moorpark, and Tilton are self-fruitful.

The trees produce most of their fruit on short spurs along the branches, but a portion of the crop also grows on the 1-, 2- and 3-year-old spurs.

In general, prune the bearing apricot fairly heavily. Apricots are strong growers and prolific producers. Unless checked by pruning, fruit will grow too high in the tree. Thin new growth by a third to a half each year. Remove long, thin branches and keep the centre of the tree open.

Apple. Adam Gibbs photo

Peach

Peach trees bear fruit in 3 to 4 years. Most varieties are self-fruitful, except J. H. Hale and Golden Jubilee Peach, which need pollenizers.

Peach trees bear fruit differently than most types of trees. They have a tendency to overbear; therefore, pruning is essential. The most productive part of the peach tree is new wood 30–45 cm (12–18 inches) long. If the new growth is any longer or shorter, it produces few fruit buds. New fruit wood must be produced each year. Do not leave more than 3 main branches on the tree. Head back each of the main branches to a strong lateral or a sound outward-pointing bud, and cut the remaining fruit-bearing growth to 40 cm (16 inches) in length. Peach trees tolerate heavy removal of old wood, and it may be necessary to prune out as much as 50% of the previous year's growth.

If peach trees are not pruned properly the fruit will be produced on the terminal ends of the branches at such a height as to cause the limbs to break. Peach trees should be no more than 4.2–4.5 m (14–15 ft) high.

Once a peach tree has the desired height, it is necessary to practice renewal pruning. Allow new limbs to develop and grow from the 3 scaffold branches; in 1 to 2 years they will replace the older limbs. This type of pruning results in a continual supply of new fruiting wood.

Peaches to grow include Red Haven, Pacific Gold, Veteran, J.H. Hale and Renton.

Pear

Pear trees bear fruit in 4 to 6 years. They are often biennial bearers. Bartlett and Seckel pears require pollenizers such as Bosc or Conference.

Pears to grow include Bartlett, Comice, Anjou, Winter Nellis, Flemish Beauty, Bosc, Eddie and Highland.

Plum

Plum trees bear fruit in 4 to 6 years. Most varieties of plums are not self-fruitful. Toka, Superior, Climax, Burbank and Sultan plums are free bearers of pollen and will pollenize other varieties. European-type plums as Italian and Green Gage are self-fruitful.

Plums produce best from fruit spurs that appear on a branch after it is 2 to 3 years old. The spurs are small, gnarled, stubby growths that produce fruit year after year. When the tree is young, it is essential to develop a strong and orderly framework of branches. Head back the long, whip-like branches to about three-quarters their length, and set them no less than 30 cm (1 ft) apart. Save the oldest branches with fruit spurs.

Prune fruit-bearing plum trees heavily to maintain correct form and encourage growth of shoots, upon which new spurs and fruits are produced in the following years.

Plums to grow include Italian, Green Gage, Damson, Victoria, Burbank, Santa Rosa, Yellow Egg, Bradshaw and Bounty.

Sour Cherry

Sour cherry trees bear fruit in 4 to 5 years. Montmorency pie cherry trees are able to set fruit only when they are isolated from other cherry trees.

Young sour cherries require light pruning for the first 3 years; after that you must only thin the top, or fruiting wood, every winter. Sour cherry trees tend to develop many tangles of small twigs, which require annual pruning. Mature cherry trees normally require a minimum of pruning. The fruit is borne laterally on spurs. As a cherry tree ages, you may want to cut back the upper limbs on outward-growing branches. This encourages additional branching.

Sour cherries to grow include Montmorency, Early Richmond, English Morello, Olivet, and Stella.

Sweet Cherry

Sweet cherry trees bear fruit in 5 to 7 years. Varieties such as Lambert, Bing, and Royal Anne all require pollenizers. Black Republican, Windsor, Black Tartarian, Deacon, Sam and Van are fine pollenizers.

Early training is essential in pruning a cherry tree. Sweet cherries are tall-growing by nature and inclined to develop weak crotches when allowed to retain all their top growth. Generally young cherry trees are planted out as straight whips. At planting time each whip is cut back to within 63–75 cm (25–30 inches) of the ground. In the spring, select 3 shoots in the top 45 cm (18 inches) of growth; in that spring and the following one, cut these 3 shoots back, removing about a third of their season's growth. The next year select 2 more well-spaced shoots to let develop on each of the 3 framework branches. Repeat this training another year until a sturdy, well-formed tree pattern is set, with 3 or 4 additional framework branches.

Sweet cherries. Adam Gibbs photo

Sweet cherries to grow include Black Tartarian, Royal Anne, Bing, Lambert, Van, Deacon and Compact Stella.

Dwarf Fruit Trees

When space is limited, plant dwarf fruit trees, which are approximately one-fourth the size of standard trees. Their size makes harvesting, pruning, thinning and spraying much easier. Dwarf trees also bear fruit at an earlier age than standards. They remain small because they are grafted on naturally dwarf understock. (Dwarfing is accomplished by sap control: a desirable fruiting variety is grafted onto a rootstock, which limits the movement of nutrients and water and restricts growth.) A miniature dwarf may reach only 90 cm (3 ft) in height, true dwarfs will attain heights of 1.3–2.4 m (6–8 ft), while semi-dwarf and semi-standard fruit trees reach 4.5–5.4 m (15–18 ft). Standard fruit trees may grow to 6 m (20 ft) high.

Select dwarf fruit trees that are 2 years old. They generally begin to bear fruit in the third or fourth year after planting. The recommended planting distance between trees is 3–4.5 m (10–15 ft) in all directions. Prepare the dwarf tree for planting by cutting off damaged or broken roots. Prune a 2- to 3-year-old tree at planting time by selecting 3 to 4 of the strongest side branches. Prune these back by a third and cut off all other branches close to the trunk. Cut back young trees without side branches just above a growth bud about 90 cm (3 ft) up.

Before planting, find the graft union, a knob or slight swelling on the lowest part of the trunk. Place the tree in the planting hole so the graft union is 5 cm (2 inches) above the ground. If the tree is planted too deeply and the graft union comes in contact with the soil, a new set of roots may develop and the tree may cease to be a dwarf in either size or character. Applications of bark or other mulch material should be removed from the base of the tree each spring.

If garden space is limited, a semi-dwarf tree may be the right choice. Mature trees reach 4.5 m (15 ft) in height. They bear large fruit sooner and are easier to prune, spray and harvest than standard trees. A single semi-dwarf fruit tree will yield up to 6 bushels (290 litres/305 qts) of fruit annually.

Plant the semi-dwarf like the true dwarf, with the graft union 5 cm (2 inches) above ground level. Trees should be 3.6–4.5 m (12–15 ft) apart in all directions.

Grafts

Home gardeners with limited space for fruit trees can develop an "orchard" by grafting many varieties on to 2 or 3 trees. In fact, grafts make it possible to have as many varieties of a particular fruit—pear, apple, peach, plum, cherry or apricot as there are branches on a tree. Grafting is also useful on ornamentals such as dogwood, roses, quince, lilac and pyracantha.

Pyracantha. Chuck Heath photo

In each graft there is a scion and a stock. The scion, usually a bud or twig, is taken from the plant to be propagated, and it becomes the top part of the new plant. The stock may be only the root, or it may include the tree framework.

For a graft to be successful, the scion must be taken from a plant that is related closely to the stock. An apple will unite with other apples or a peach will grow on a peach, plum, almond, cherry, apricot or other stone fruit tree. However, a pome fruit, such as an apple, will not unite with a stone fruit, such as a peach.

The main principle of grafting is to make a strong bond between the cambium, or inner bark, of the stock, and the scion. The growing tissues of scion and stock must be flush.

Simple grafts, also called **whip grafts**, are used to propagate small shrubs or trees. They are successful either in winter or early spring. A section of 1-year-old growth about the thickness of a lead pencil is cut into sections, each of which contains 3 to 5 growth buds. Use a sharp knife and make diagonal cuts.

Then make a long, sloping cut on the stock—a branch or trunk the same thickness as the scion wood. Press the scion to the understock so that the cambium layer of bark of the two pieces is joined tightly at all possible points along the cut. Tie or bind the graft with raffia or tape and cover with grafting wax. (Exposed grafts invite insects, diseases and excessive moisture.)

Cleft grafting is perhaps the most common way to change a tree's variety. It is the method by which many fruit and ornamental trees are top-grafted. It is most successful with apples and pears, but difficult with plums and cherries and almost impossible with peach trees.

To do a cleft graft, cut off the stock, split the stump at the cut end and insert 1 or 2 wedge-shaped scions into the split. Begin by smoothing the edges of the cambium, the thin layer of cells between the outer sapwood and the inner bark, with a sharp, clean knife. Place a chisel on the centre of the stump and drive it into the stock 7.5–10 cm (3–4 inches) with a mallet. Choose 1 or 2 scions. They should be of the previous season's growth, from the outside of the tree where it is vigorous, and from a section where spaces between buds are relatively short. Cut off the tip of each scion and make a second cut 1 cm (1/2 inch) below the third bud, making a wedge at the lower end. Fit the scions snugly down into the cleft at the outer edges, so that the cambium bark of the scions meets that of the under-stock on the outside.

Remove the chisel and cover the cut area immediately with grafting wax.

Side grafting is simple. The stock is allowed to function more or less as it did before it was grafted, and when the union is complete, the head of the stock is removed just above the junction.

Select a stock branch 1–2.5 cm (1/2–1 inch) thick. Scions should be about 6 mm (1/4 inch) in diameter. Make 2 diagonal cuts, one slightly longer than the other, at the basal end of each scion at opposite sides, to form a gently tapering wedge. Make an incision in the side of the stock branch at an angle of about 20° and deep enough to permit insertion of the wedge.

Place the longer side of the wedge against the stock stem in such a position that the cambium of stock and scion are in close contact. By bending the stock so that the incision is opened, you can push the scion into position readily. Securely tie the scion to the stock, then seal all exposed surfaces with grafting wax. When the graft is complete, remove any lateral branches on the stub that might interfere with or crowd the graft.

Nut Trees

From the earliest days of human habitation in the Pacific Northwest, people have gathered nuts from indigenous trees for their food. Ounce for ounce, nuts have more protein, calories and other food value than anything else that grows.

As more settlers came from Europe, they brought other types of nut trees and bred them with native trees. Some of their efforts failed: European almond and hazelnut (filbert) trees did not succeed. But the introduced walnut and chestnut trees did prove fruitful. Extensive hybridization over the years has resulted in abundant yields and trees that are hardy in our region. Almond, chestnut, hickory, hazel and walnut are remarkably responsive to attention and correct cultivation.

Plant nut trees in late fall or early winter, when they are dormant. Select nursery trees that are 2 to 3 years old: mature nut trees often will not transplant successfully. But if large, mature trees must be moved, cut back a third of the top growth and a third of the roots before replanting. Nut trees have extremely long taproots. Do not cut or otherwise damage the taproot.

The type of planting soil is important. Chestnuts and hazelnuts thrive in acid soil; walnuts and some of the hickory nuts do best in a sweet or slightly alkaline soil. Good drainage is essential to all varieties. Select a planting site out in the open, with as much exposure to the sun as possible. Avoid low areas where spring frosts hover. If spring blossoms are injured by late frosts, often a poor crop of nuts will result. Avoid planting nut trees near apple trees or members of the heather family such as rhododendrons and azaleas. These plants may fail if they grow too close to a nut tree.

Dig a planting hole at least 90 cm (3 ft) in diameter and nearly as deep.

Drive in a sturdy support post. Add gravel or sand to the bottom of the planting area. Cover this with a light, sandy soil, and carefully place the roots of the tree in the planting area. Work additional soil in and around the roots. Tamp the soil firmly around the roots, and water it deeply. Stake and tie the tree to the support post, to prevent it from swaying in the wind.

Nut trees seldom require pruning. It is necessary to do only light trimming and shaping while the trees are young, and to remove dead or diseased wood. Prune nut trees in the fall while the sap is inactive. To make certain a tree is dormant, cut a small twig. If it does not "bleed" (if no sap oozes out) within a few minutes, it is dormant. If sap oozes from the cut, make no attempt to prune. Wait until the tree is inactive.

Almond

The almond tree is related closely to the peach. Failure to produce almonds is usually due to the tree's habit of flowering in early spring, when frosts may destroy the blossoms. Provide the almond tree with a sheltered spot, out of frost pockets. A light, sandy soil with quick and thorough water drainage is necessary. Give each tree 6–9 m (20–30 ft) of room to spread. Prune it lightly after one season's growth. Select 3 main branches, 15–20 cm

(6–8 inches) apart and spaced equally around the trunk, for the framework. Head these back by about a third and cut back the top to 75–90 cm (30–36 inches). In subsequent years, just do moderate thinning, and remove crisscrossing branches and dead or diseased wood.

Black Walnut

A popular garden tree is the black walnut, whose fruit is perhaps the most satisfying of home grown nuts. It takes fortitude to crush off the nut's juicy rind, which leaves indelible stains, and then to crack and pick the meat out of the rough, hard shell.

English or Persian walnut trees produce fine-flavoured nuts that are thin shelled.

- 'Carpathia.' An import from the Balkans and an improved strain of English walnut. Young trees bear from 4–6 bushels (145–220 litres/154–233 qts) of nuts annually, which generally fall free of their husks and need not be hulled.

- 'Franquette.' A self-pollinating walnut. Blooms late, making flowers less susceptible to frost.

- 'Thomas.' Bears large, thin-shelled nuts while tree is young, and continues to yield abundantly.

Chestnut

Native chestnut trees are too monstrous in size to fit in any but the largest garden. Indigenous varieties bear nuts that are smaller and less tasty than those of newer cultivated types.

- 'American Sweet.' A cultivated chestnut, fine as a shade or ornamental tree, and a producer of delicious nuts.

- 'Rochester.' An 'American Sweet' hybrid with a sweet kernel. Nuts ripen on the tree all at once and part from their burrs easily.

- 'Fort McNair.' A hardy deciduous flowering red chestnut (*Aesculus carnea*). Grows to 12 m (40 ft).

Hazelnut

Hazelnuts or filberts grow on a bush or decorative small tree related to the birches. Long catkins hang from the limbs during winter. The crown of the tree has several main shoots, which should be pruned back to keep the tree at 1.8–2.4 m (6–8 ft) high.

- 'Rush.' A superior variety, highly hybridized to produce improved kernels of fine flavour. Two hazelnut trees of different varieties are needed to ensure a full nut crop.

- 'Barcelona' and 'Daviana.' Both are excellent pollenizers.

- 'Royal.' Pollinates other varieties. Produces the largest nut of all, but is a shy bearer some seasons.

Hickory

The native hickories are close relatives of the walnut. They are lovely in their rugged symmetry and they are generous shade trees. Hickory trees were especially important to the early settlers of North America for both food and wood. The shells of indigenous nuts are thick and hard; improved hybrid grafted hickory trees produce kernels with shells that are easier to crack, or thin enough to break in your fingers. The flavours of the newer varieties are also sweeter. 'Hales,' 'Weiper' and 'Fairbanks' are recommended for home plantings on the coast.

Pecan and Hican

Pecans are traditionally southern trees, but new, improved hardy varieties such as 'Stuart' are being introduced. Promising hybrids between pecans and northern hickories, called hicans, are also available. They are small, attractive, useful trees, with fruits that resemble pecans in shell and flavour. Pecans and hicans are self-fertile, so you only need one tree for a crop of nuts.

Flowering Shrubs

Azalea

Our coast is aflame with azalea blossoms each spring and summer. Evergreen and deciduous azaleas, with their blossoms in burning orange, cool lemon and lime shades, pure white, or delicate pinks, vivid red or purples are in full recital from April through June.

Deliciously fragrant and designed like honeysuckle flowers, azaleas are a treasure. On most varieties of deciduous azaleas, leaves appear when the plant is in full flower or soon afterward. Spring-green leaves take on tints of bronze and red in autumn.

Azaleas belong to the Ericaceae, or heath family, which also includes heathers, pieris, blueberries and mountain laurel. They are classified as rhododendrons by botanists. Nursery people and home gardeners distinguish them as having smaller, flared flowers on smaller shrubs. Botanically, the two plants are separated by a combination of characteristics, one being that true rhododendrons usually have 10 or more stamens and the leaves are often scaly or have small dots on the undersides, whereas most azalea flowers have 5 stamens and the leaves are frequently hairy and are not dotted with scales.

A thin woodland setting is a good home for azaleas, whose simple basic needs are a fibrous-textured soil, slightly acid in reaction; generous amounts of water while blooming and during the early summer; a protective mulch over their shallow roots; morning sun; and an acid type fertilizer.

Azaleas in the rain. Bill Waldron photo

Incorporate organic humus into the planting soil to help it retain moisture and plant nutrients. Decayed logs or stumps, leaf mould or ground bark turned into the ground are beneficial before planting.

Deciduous Azaleas

Deciduous azaleas are tough. Many reach incredible sizes and live longer than a century. Tolerant of drought, sun, wind, cold temperatures and sheer neglect, deciduous azaleas are an excellent first choice for novice home gardeners.

Give deciduous azaleas a place in the morning sun in summer to aid in the formation of flowering wood and buds. Mulch over the root region in summer to help keep the roots constantly moist while the plants are actively producing.

Choose deciduous azaleas in the spring at a garden centre or nursery, where they are growing in containers. You can transplant them even when they are in full bloom. First water the plant deeply, saturating the dense, shallow mat of fine roots. Then slip the plant out, handling the roots carefully. Set the plant so the crown (where the main stem and upper roots meet) will be only about 2.5 cm (1 inch) deep. Spread 5–7.5 cm (2–3 inches) of mulch over the root area. Keep the mulch away from the main stem (the trunk).

In early spring, fertilize around azaleas with a rhododendron preparation (follow package directions). Mix equal amounts of cottonseed, fish, blood and bone meals and apply 250 mL (1 cup) of the mixture to each mature plant in the fall or early spring.

If you have an ungainly old plant, prune it by cutting back the stems drastically, to 20–25 cm (8–10 inches) from ground level, in spring or fall. The plant will recover in one or two seasons.

Corrective pruning may be done after the shrub flowers. If possible, remove all faded flower heads from the plant. Pinch off tip ends or cut back the growing twigs about halfway when the shoots are 10–12.5 cm (4–5 inches) long in early summer. This type of pruning induces branching and spreading, and makes a compact and busy plant.

Rhododendron occidentale, the western or Pacific azalea, is a native that has been introduced to home gardens with great success. Flower colour is variable from creamy white to bronze-pink, with orange or yellow blotches. The plant is tall-growing and flowers grow with the leaves in the spring, emitting a spicy, clove-like fragrance. The leaves turn brilliant autumn colours before falling.

Ghent azaleas (*R. gandavense*) can tolerate temperatures below –6°C (20°F). The plants may grow to enormous proportions and live forever. They resemble honeysuckle in form and fragrance. Flower colours include almost all hues and variations except true reds and purples. Spring blossoms vary from flaming orange to delicate pastel shades. Leaves are gold and red.

Mollis or **sinensis** hybrid azaleas are large-flowering deciduous plants. Pale pinks, yellows, soft flame, salmon and hot tangerine-red blossoms burst into full colour with virtually no foliage in evidence; green foliage follows, then gradually turns from yellow to bright red before falling in autumn.

The royal azalea of Korea, **R. schlippenbachii**, is a handsome plant with generous flowers and colourful autumn foliage. Pale to clear rose-pink flowers open before leaves appear, decorating the garden with delicate colour in April and May. This erect shrub grows to 3.6 m (12 ft) or taller at maturity.

When in flower, **pinkshell azalea** (*R. vaseyi*) looks like a small apple tree in full bloom. It is pale pink or white in May or early June. Blooms come in clusters of 5 to 6, scattered freely over the leafless shrub. Plants often grow to 4.5 m (15 ft) and are picturesque.

R. luteum is an ancient plant. It was used in the hybridizing of the Ghent azaleas. Its bright, clear yellow flowers are sweetly fragrant in May. When young, the plant is compact. As it ages it becomes more straggly and free-formed. It grows to 3.6–4.5 m (12–15 ft) in height. In autumn the leaves are brilliant.

Exbury azalea was introduced to gardens by the hybridization efforts of Lionel de Rothschild, in England. The plants are hardy and vigorous. Blossoms are orange, red, pink, yellow and white. Some measure 15 cm (6 inches) across and appear in trusses. Exburys are delightfully fragrant when in full flower. Spectacular leaf colouring in late fall adds to their beauty.

Evergreen Azaleas

Plant and maintain evergreen azaleas much as you would deciduous azaleas and rhododendrons.

Evergreen azaleas suitable for outdoor home gardens include:

- Gable's. Endures temperatures to –18°C (0°F). Fine examples include 'Elizabeth Gable,' rose-pink; 'Louise Gable,' salmon-pink; 'Purple Splendor,' orchid-purple; 'Rosebud,' pearl-pink; and 'Rose Greeley,' double white.

- Kaempferi. Tolerates cold weather well. Flowers cover the entire plant in spring. Varieties found locally at garden centres and nurseries are 'Fedora,' salmon-rose; 'John Cairns,' orange-red; 'Palestrina,' white.

Azalea 'Exbury 3.' Bill Waldron photo

- Kurume. A Japanese azalea, a compact, twiggy shrub, dense with small evergreen leaves. Fine examples are 'Adonis,' white; 'Gumpo White,' white; 'Gumpo Red,' pink; 'Gumpo Fancy,' dwarf, white-pink; 'Hinodegiri,' bright crimson; and 'Helena,' pink.

- Vuykiana. Taller and more open hybrids than most evergreen azaleas. Fine examples are 'Blue Danube,' violet-blue; 'Vuyk's Rosy Red'; 'Vuyk's Scarlet.'

Camellia

Camellias, like many other Asian plants, are at home on the West Coast. In the Far East, they are indigenous to forests, where rainfall is frequent and the soil is porous yet capable of holding moisture.

These reliable broad-leafed flowering evergreens bear exquisitely formed flowers that bravely display colour in late fall, winter and early spring. Flower form and colour vary widely. Some blooms are singles, with full stamens in the centre; others are compact doubles with overlapping petals. Colours include snow white, pink to crimson, and blends and shades including yellow. All hues except blues are represented.

Camellia japonica. Adam Gibbs photo

Trees and Shrubs

Camellia japonica. Adam Gibbs photo

Transplant camellias to the garden in any season, with care. At the nursery select well-branched plants with sturdy stems and many leaf buds. Avoid straggly plants with dull, rolled-back leaves that are off colour. Plant in an open woodland setting if possible. The protection of high-branching trees will give them shelter and ample light to set flower buds. You can also grow camellias in portable planters. Keep them in an area with filtered sunlight and sheltered from strong winds. Direct sunlight and winds burn and otherwise damage their foliage and flowers.

Camellias in their soil requirements are not too exacting. Soil should be woodsy in content, porous in texture and fertile.

Correct planting depth is a must. Prepare the planting pocket so that the top of the root ball will be about 2.5 cm (1 inch) above the surrounding ground. Mulch the surface roots with a few inches of peat moss, ground bark or compost.

Rainfall is sufficient on the coast for camellias, except in dry summers. In summer, wash the foliage frequently to maintain high humidity and slowly soak the soil twice a week.

In spring, when plants become more active, apply cottonseed meal or a special fertilizer that is acid in its reaction.

Camellias grow naturally into well-formed plants. If pruning is necessary, do it after the plant has flowered. Propagate camellias either by layering or by rooting cuttings. Layering is done in late summer. Take cuttings in July and August, as soon as the new spring growth has had time to harden. Select ends of twigs bearing 3 to 4 growth buds and remove all but 2 upper leaves. Dip the cut end of the branch in root-inducing hormone powder, then insert the cut end in several inches of coarse sand. Keep the planting in a warm, shaded place and water it every few days to keep the starting sand moist.

If the leaves turn yellow and the plant grows slowly, the cause may be poor drainage, lack of fertilizer, too much direct sun or an alkaline soil. A sooty mould sometimes develops on the leaves of camellias and other broad-leafed evergreens. This is a fungus that grows on the excretions of insects living on the camellia or companion plants. Control the insects with an organic insecticidal soap

Three species of camellias thrive on the coast.

Camellia japonica is the hardiest of the three. There are some 1,400 varieties of this species, including 'Bob Hope,' large, semi-double red; 'Alba Plena,' double white; 'Debutante,' light pink; 'Kramer's Supreme,' red; and 'Mathotiana Supreme,' red.

Varieties of **C. reticulata** suitable for growing on the coast are 'Buddha,' semi-double pink; 'Great Butterfly Wings,' semi-double light crimson; 'Shot Silk,' with fluted petals in pink; and 'Aztec,' a cross between *C. japonica* and *C. reticulata*, with iridescent rose-red flowers.

C. sasanqua is a common woodland plant that grows in Japan. Its twiggy, picturesque branches have a rampant horizontal growth. Fragile flowers resembling wild roses adorn the plant in fall and winter. Shiny, dark green leaves remain on the shrub during all seasons. A few good varieties are 'Yuletide,' a red single; 'Showa-no-Sakae,' pink semi-double; and 'White Doves,' white semi-double.

Ceanothus

Ceanothus, or California lilac, is a hardy deciduous or evergreen flowering shrub. Spreading out over dry, sunny hillsides, the plants provide brilliant covering.

Most varieties reach 2.4–3 m (8–10 ft) in height and width, but a few ground-hugging dwarf varieties, such as *C. gloriosus exaltatus* 'Emily Brown,' grow only to 60–90 cm (2–3 ft). In March and April, spike-like clusters of small flowers bloom, in colours that range from pure white through shades of pink and blue to deep violet.

Give the shrubs a light, sandy soil with a pH of 6.0. Frequent watering is needed only by newly transplanted starts: established, mature plants will endure droughts. Some varieties are sensitive to winter's severity. Protect them from cold winter winds and make sure water does not freeze around their roots.

Ceanothus *(California lilac)*. Adam Gibbs photo

Ceanothus is a rampant grower, requiring constant cutting back or trimming, and blooms appear on new wood. Prune severely in winter or very early spring to maintain a compact, flowering plant.

Propagate ceanothus by planting seeds, making cuttings, layering or grafting.

Tall varieties that do well on the West Coast include 'Gloire de Versailles' (deep blue); 'Marie Simon' (pink); and 'Blue Blossom.' Low growers include 'Emily Brown,' 'Mary Lake' and 'Royal Blue.'

Daphne

Daphnes are small, beautiful, low-growing flowering shrubs that are good choices for borders and rock gardens. Some remain evergreen, while others shed their foliage each autumn.

Daphnes tend to be temperamental. They object to being transplanted and sometimes die suddenly for no apparent reason. Give them an alkaline soil, well drained in winter, and light and sandy. Shelter them from cold winter winds and protect them from summer sun.

In autumn, place a handful of ground dolomite lime around the base of each mature daphne. Early in February, spread 250 mL (1 cup) of a fertilizer high in phosphorus and potash around each established plant. Mulch over the bases of daphnes with several inches of ground bark, old sawdust or peat moss in the spring. Keep the soil moist, yet not constantly saturated, through spring and summer.

Daphne odora. Adam Gibbs photo

Daphnes have a tendency to become leggy and weak if left unpruned. Prune them severely, when they have finished flowering, to keep them neat and well groomed. Cut each branch to an outside-growing bud to give the plant a more open, spreading shape. If a more upright form is desired, cut to an inside growth bud.

Daphne cneorum (pronounced nee-ORum), or rock daphne, is a low-growing, trailing evergreen shrub. It seldom grows taller than 25 cm (10 inches). Tiny, lilac-pink clusters of flowers clothe the end of each branch in March and April. The small, dark green leaves are lustrous on the upper portion and greyish beneath.

D. cneorum is reluctant to become well established if the soil and other growing conditions are not to its liking. Give the plant an open, sunny place and a well-drained soil filled with humus and sand. In the bottom of the planting pocket, place several inches of coarse sand for quick drainage. Gently set in the root ball and work around it generous amounts of humus-filled soil. Take care not to disturb the root system. Avoid lifting the plant by the top without support from below. If the top pulls away from the roots, the plant will fail. Container-grown plants must be treated with extra care. Make certain they have a sunny location and fertile, evenly moist soil.

D. mezereum (February) is an extremely attractive flowering shrub with a stiff, upright growth habit. Tight clusters of pink-lilac or white flowers bloom close to the stems each spring, followed by scarlet berries, which are poisonous. This is a slow plant to start, but once established it will grow to 1.2–1.5 m (4–5 ft) with a spread of about 90–105 cm (3–3$^{1/2}$ ft). The shrub is leafless in winter.

D. odora, the best known of the family, is originally from China and Japan. This shrub is a bit sensitive to cold wintry winds. Provide it with a sheltered place in the garden. Handsome glossy green leaves, some with a cream edge, decorate the plant all year round. Its spring flowers are pink to deep rose on the outside, with creamy pink throats. Each branch is heavy and graceful with blossoms. *D. odora* prefers a slightly alkaline soil. A handful of ground dolomite lime worked into the growing soil each spring and fall will benefit the plant. Poor soil drainage is the plant's death warrant, so do not let water sit around its roots or crown, especially in winter. *D. odora* has a tendency to become leggy and weak if not pruned annually. Prune this daphne when it is in bloom or immediately after flowering.

D. burkwoodii, also known as *D. somerset*, is a deciduous plant that becomes a compact, rounded bush about 90–150 cm (3–5 ft) wide and high. In May, fragrant soft-pink flowers appear on the shrub. Give this daphne full sun and a slightly alkaline soil.

Honeysuckle

'Honey baby' dwarf honeysuckle (*Lonicera*) is a small shrub that blooms through summer with fragrant pale yellow flowers. It grows to about 45 cm (18 inches) tall and wide at maturity. Honeysuckle is a fine addition to any shrub border. It will grow in full or partial sun and is naturally quite pest- and disease-resistant.

Hydrangea

Hydrangeas grew widely in ancient Japan, but they were unknown outside of Asia until a Swedish botanist, Carl Thunberg, brought specimens of the plant to Europe in 1775. Today hydrangeas are grown around the world for their brilliant display of colour and form.

Flower heads form flat, round clusters or pyramid-shaped panicles (loose, branching clusters). Plants may be tall bushes, low-sprawling shrubs or high climbers. Improved hybrids sparkle in vivid purples, carmine and other reds, blues, cream and pure white.

As growing companions to azalea, rhododendron, camellia and other shrubs that become dull and colourless in mid-summer, late-blooming hydrangeas are excellent. They are also decorative in borders, hedges and containers.

Semi-shaded areas with filtered light from high-branching trees or shrubs produce the best colours and glossy green summer leaves in hydrangeas. When they are exposed to the direct sunlight, flowers fade quickly and the leaves turn a pale yellow.

Hydrangeas are exuberant in producing enormous amounts of flowers and leaves in a season. It is essential to fertilize and to keep the soil constantly moist. As growth begins in the early spring, apply a 5-10-10 plant food. A mature hydrangea plant 1.2–1.5 m (4–5 ft) high requires approximately 900 g (2 lbs) of plant food at each feeding. The first application is made in the early spring and a second when the plant shows flower buds.

The word "hydrangea" comes from the Greek *hyder* (water) and *angeien* (vessel). The entire plant will wilt when water is lacking. If this occurs, drench the soil deeply and it will soon recover. Water deeply around the base of the plant twice weekly when there is little or no rain.

The flowers vary dramatically in colour, which is affected by soil acidity or alkalinity as well as the variety of hydrangea. Many gardeners have noticed the tendency of strongly acid soil to produce blue hydrangeas and alkaline soil to produce pink ones. You can treat the soil chemically to induce colour changes.

Bring out blue tones by watering the plant with a weak solution of alum in the early spring. Dissolve 5 mL (1 tsp) of alum or 85 g (3 oz) of aluminum sulphate in 4 L (1 gal) of water. Let the solution stand for at least 12 hours before applying it to the soil. Liberal applications of iron and rhododendron-type fertilizers will also encourage shades of blue.

For pinker blossoms, add 900 g (2 lbs) of dolomite lime to the growing soil of a mature hydrangea each spring and fall. Super phosphate deepens the pink colour almost to red.

Hydrangea macrophylla (hortensia), often called the florist's hydrangea, is the most commonly grown hydrangea on the coast. Two main types of flowers in this variety are the Lacecap and Hortensia. The Lacecap has large, flat flower heads with small, fertile, fragrant flowers in the centre and larger, sterile, ray flowers around the outer edge of the blossom. The Hortensia produces large, round flower heads that are full in form. Florists often force this one indoors to bloom early in the season; then it is planted out in the garden with success.

Lacecap hydrangea. Chuck Heath photo

H. macrophylla may be pruned incorrectly more often than any other shrub. In late summer it makes new growth, and next year's flowers come from the buds at the tips of these branches. But branches that did not have flowers this season will flower next year. So as soon as the flowers fade on the *H. macrophylla*, cut the stems back so that only 2 to 3 sets of leaves remain on each. Soon new growth will start up from the axils (topmost joins) of the top 2 leaves, and these new shoots will bloom the next summer.

PeeGee hydrangea (*H. paniculata grandiflora*) is prized for bud form and exquisite pink and cream blossoms. The flowers are heavy and conical, and cut blossoms keep indefinitely when dried for winter bouquets. The large shrub grows to 6 m (20 ft) tall and almost as wide. It grows coarse green leaves in spring and summer, and in fall the foliage is attractive with a bronze tint.

PeeGee tolerates heavy pruning in the winter or early spring while the shrub is dormant. Severe pruning insures large, upright clusters of flowers rather than small ones.

PeeGee hydrangea. Chuck Heath photo

Hills of Snow (*H. arborescens grandiflora*) is a hybrid from native plants. White flowers are produced in large, loose masses along the stems during the summer. Prune the branches to 20–30 cm (8–12 inches) from the ground during the winter or early spring. This hydrangea bears its flowers on the present season's growth.

H. quercifolia has foliage that differs from other hydrangea species. Enormous red oak-shaped foliage often grows to 15–20 cm (6–8 inches) long and turns vivid red and gold in autumn before falling. Massive white flowers are found on the shrub in late summer and fall. The flowers become purple with age. Prune the plant lightly each spring to keep it in an attractive shape.

H. petiolaris is a vigorous climbing vine, one of the few vines that will attach itself to stone, brick or wood walls by means of small aerial rootlets. Flat, white flower heads are 15–30 cm (6–12 inches) in diameter. July, August and September blossoms decorate the vine. Glossy green leaves make a bold pattern in summer, and the vine's reddish bark contrasts with the colours of the garden in winter. Prune the vine if it grows rampant in the early spring before new growth begins.

Kalmia

Low-growing native forms of kalmia are found at the edges of mountain lakes and meadows throughout the Pacific Northwest. Kalmia, an evergreen, is spectacular in all seasons. In summer it sparkles with tiny parasols of pink, red, yellow and white blossoms. Even in winter, its glossy green leaves do not droop in the cold and its red stems are brilliant against the grey sky.

Plants vary in height from a few inches to 4.5 m (15 ft), and almost as wide.

Purchase kalmias from a nursery or garden supply store. Kalmias make good growing companions for rhododendrons, azaleas and heathers. Give them similar care and growing conditions.

The best growing site is a place in the morning sun, to encourage full flowering and glossy green leaves. Full sun causes the leaves to become yellow or burned brown. Dense, dark shade causes the plants to develop tall, spindly growth with few or no flowers.

Kalmias may be transplanted at any season. They like moist soil enriched with organic humus, and like other members of the heath family, they require a slightly acid soil. Apply about 450 g (1 lb) of cottonseed meal to each mature plant in the autumn.

Never plant kalmias deeper than they were growing previously. Prepare a generous planting pocket, at least 30 cm (12 inches) deeper and wider than the root system. Add to the bottom of the planting area a shovelful of sand or fine gravel for quick water drainage in winter. Over the drainage material place several inches of oak leaf mould or peat moss and 250 mL (1 cup) of cottonseed meal. Cover this with an organic humus type soil, and work in more soil around the roots. Water thoroughly. Keep the soil moist until the new planting is well established.

Trees and Shrubs

Kalmia. Adam Gibbs photo

Mulching over the crowns and roots is important to the plant's survival. A mulch of oak leaves, ground bark or peat moss keeps the soil free of weeds, moist during dry summers and insulated from cold in winter.

After the shrub finishes flowering, or in early July, give it a light application of a rhododendron fertilizer. Apply 225 g (1/2 lb) per mature plant. Water the fertilizer into the soil.

Mature kalmias, like other broad-leafed evergreen shrubs, often become tall and leggy. Prune assertively in spring by cutting them back to within a few inches of the ground. This stimulates the growth of new shoots, which will be more productive in time. After this operation, fertilize and water the plant deeply and frequently to force new growth quickly. Flowering will be delayed one or two seasons, but the plant will be invigorated.

Propagating kalmias is difficult even for the skilled grower. The most successful method is to layer a low-growing branch in October.

Several species and varieties of kalmia are available to home gardeners of the coast:

- Mountain laurel (*Kalmia latifolia*). One of the east coast's most ornamental native flowering evergreens. Native people used the branches to carve utensils, hence its common name "spoon wood." Grows to 4.5 m (15 ft) high and 3–3.6 m (10–12 ft) wide. Produces spring flowers in shades of pink, rose, purple, red, yellow and white. Dull red berries follow the flowers and remain until birds find them in winter. Leaves are glossy green and similar to English laurel, but smaller.

- Sheep laurel (*K. angustifolia*). Thrives in wet, boggy ground where few other plants will survive. Grows to 90 cm (3 ft) tall with a spread of 45 cm (18 inches). Crimson red or purple flowers grow in lateral clusters around the stems in June and July.

- *K. a. rubra.* A rare dwarf crimson flowering form.

- Bog laurel (*K. polifolia*). A low-growing, straggly shrub less than 60 cm (2 ft) high. Blossoms appear in shades of rose and purple. In among the flowers are long, narrow evergreen leaves.

- *K. microphylla.* A miniature that grows over the ground as an almost flat mat. Flowers are pink.

Lilac

Lilacs are popular, fragrant spring-flowering shrubs that can be grown as single plants or hedges. Tinkerbelle lilac, *Syringa* 'Bailbelle,' is a neat, compact, highly ornamental shrub. Its tresses of wine-coloured buds open into deep pink blooms with a spicy fragrance.

Nandina

In Japan the shrub **Nandina domestica** is planted near the entrance of homes to ward off evil spirits and bring good fortune. People tell their bad dreams to the plant to keep them from coming true, and the head of the household tells the plant all of his or her troubles before entering. Perhaps it is appropriate that this small shrub is slow-growing and long-suffering.

In China the plant is known as the Chinese sacred bamboo. It looks like a member of the bamboo clan, with its delicate, bamboo-like year-round foliage, but botanically it belongs to the Berberidaceae family.

Erect stems of *N. domestica* stretch to 1.8–2.4 m (6–8 ft) and 90 cm (3 ft) wide. The slender woody stems are clothed with delicate, feathery leaves, which remain on the small shrub all year round. In summer the plant may have pinkish and copper-red leaves at the same time. Autumn leaves are red. The shrub flowers in small white panicles (loose, branching clusters) 30 cm (1 ft) long. These are followed by red or purple berries that linger all winter (or until found by the birds). White and yellow-fruited forms can be found, but they are rare. Fruits remain on the plant all winter.

Purchase nandinas at a nursery or garden supply store. Either sun or shade is satisfactory for this plant, but it needs shelter from strong winter winds. Nandinas prosper in a soil generous in leaf mould or humus. Keep the soil constantly moist.

Apply fertilizer in early February and continue to fertilize lightly every 6 weeks during spring and summer. Use a complete 5-10-10 commercial fertilizer, 450 g (1 lb) annually for each mature plant 1.5–1.8 m (5–6 ft) tall.

The nandina plant requires cross-pollination to produce berries, and commonly fails to achieve this. Plant several shrubs in a group to encourage berries. A commercial blossom-set hormone spray also helps. Apply it on the open flowers in spring.

Prune the plant in the early spring by cutting dead branches to the ground, and trimming or thinning branches if the plant becomes too tall or wide.

N. domestica can be propagated easily from seedlings that often appear beneath an established older plant. If you sever a rooted shoot that has developed by the side of the mature plant, a new plant may grow. Cuttings of the shrub are slow and almost impossible to root. In an extremely cold winter, a nandina may be cut down, yet the roots usually survive to reappear in spring.

The miniature **N. domestica compacta** grows to a height of 25 cm (10 inches). It is ideal for containers, rock gardens and borders, or as a bonsai plant.

Pieris

John Fraser, the eighteenth-century adventurer and botanist, introduced many valuable plants to the world. **Pieris floribunda**, a native of China, was among them. Pieris shrubs, also called andromedas or lily-of-the-valley trees, are handsome flowering evergreens, treasured in gardens of the Pacific Northwest.

Sprays of unopened flower buds form a lacy pattern in winter, ready to open on the first bright spring day. Clusters of urn-shaped white or pinkish flowers drip from the shrub anytime from February to May. They are followed by a myriad small, light green fruits that later turn brown. The leaves of the pieris are red in spring and change to glossy green and copper in summer. Some varieties have yellow and green variegated leaves.

Pieris shrubs are of the Ericaceae clan. They are available in many varieties at garden supply stores. They like the same type of soil and growing conditions as rhododendrons: a somewhat shady, sheltered spot with acidic soil, ideally a pH of 4.0–5.0. (However, too much shade will result in few flowers.) A moist, well-drained peaty soil with the addition of 7.5 cm (3 inches) of oak leaf mould is to their liking.

Fertilize the plants in February, April and July. Apply 450 g (1 lb) of a specially formulated acid-type fertilizer to each mature plant 2.4–3 m (8–10 ft) in height and width. In fall, an application of manure, bone or cottonseed meal is beneficial.

After the shrub has finished flowering, it may be pruned lightly. Thin overcrowded branches in the centres of older plants and trim back capricious shoots. You can prune pieris in either the spring or fall.

Seed collected in the fall and sown indoors, in January, will germinate in 2 months. Set seedlings outdoors in late spring. For the first winter after that, take the young plants into a cold frame or cool greenhouse.

Pieris may also be propagated from semi-hardwood cuttings. Take the cuttings in midsummer and root them in a mixture of half sand and half peat moss. Pieris strikes roots from cuttings slowly but surely.

Layering the plant is simple and a sure method of propagation. Choose a long, low branch, make a long, shallow slit on the underside and insert a small rock to keep it open.

Rub a bit of rooting hormone powder in the slit to induce rooting. Then bend the branch down and hold it under several inches of sandy soil with a brick or with a wooden peg shaped like a hairpin. Keep the layering evenly moist for rapid root development. When the roots are evident, cut the layer from the parent plant and transplant it out on its own in a protected place in the garden.

P. japonica develops into a small tree or shrub that grows to a height and width of about 3–3.5 m (10–12 ft). It is a gracefully flowering evergreen with a rather open centre. Glossy green leaves are decorated in spring with drooping clusters of ivory-white flowers.

Pieris japonica. Adam Gibbs photo

Dwarf varieties include *P. pygmaea*, only 30 cm (12 inches) high; *P. crispa*, small-growing and compact with wavy-edged leaves.

- The 'Flamingo' variety, which originated on the West Coast, is a favourite with its flowers of deep pink.

- 'White Cascade,' 'Valley Rose' and 'Red Mill' are also excellent varieties.

P. forresti is a Chinese pieris with vivid rosewood-red young leaves and new shoots early in the spring. This native of the Himalayas stretches upward and outward to 2.4–3.5 m (8–12 ft). White or pinkish flowers grow in pendulous clusters 15 cm (6 inches) in length in early February.

- 'Bright Red' is an excellent example of *P. forresti* varieties.

P. taiwanensis, an import from Formosa (Taiwan), has translucent red leaves in spring. Creamy white festoons of flowers are held high above the leaves. The shrub averages 2–2.4 m (7–8 ft) in height and width.

Rhododendron

The rhododendron plant has evolved over many millions of years. Botanists surmise that they descended from a strain of ancient magnolias. The beginning of the rhododendron appears to have been in the Himalayan Mountain areas of Asia. Spreading slowly eastward, they reached into almost all of China, Korea, Taiwan and across the sea to the islands of Japan. They then crossed the ancient land bridge near the Bering Sea and followed the Alaskan range of mountains into western Canada.

Arbutus, King George rhododendron, Magnolia soulangeana, *blue rhododendron 'Augustin,' sword fern,* Anemone nemerosa. Sandra Evelyn photo

Full-size Plants

Native varieties are found along the West Coast. **Rhododendron albiflorum** is found only above 750 m (2,500 ft). It is deciduous, 1.8 m (6 ft) high, and produces small white flowers. It grows to almost an impenetrable thicket in some parts of the Rocky Mountains and in northern British Columbia.

Another alpine, **R. lapponicum**, grows to only 30 cm (12 inches) in height, with long purplish flowers. This dwarf from Arctic tundras and cold mountaintops is cultivated by rhododendron connoisseurs.

West coast rhododendron R. macrophyllum can reach 6 m (20 ft). It is decorated with large, rose-purplish flowers. It grows from California to BC. In BC it can be seen near Parksville on Vancouver Island, and on the Hope-Princeton highway on the mainland.

Coast gardens of the Pacific Northwest are naturally suited to rhododendrons. Native soil is often rich in organic humus and acid in reaction. If your soil is lacking in organic material, add leaf mould, peat moss, compost or decomposed manure.

Select rhododendrons with healthy foliage, a strong branching pattern, and evident buds or new growth.

Select a site with protection from excessive wind and sun. Large flowering hybrids need morning sun for the formation of flower buds, and semi-shade for the longest part of the summer day. Dense shade will promote lush foliage but fewer flowers. Strong winds will be harmful to the plant structure, particularly to leaves. Avoid planting the shrub against a dry, hot wall or nearer than 90 cm (3 ft) to concrete or brickwork, as the lime from such structures will make the soil more alkaline.

One of the most critical requirements of rhododendrons is quick water drainage. If the planting area is drained poorly, raise the planting level by placing several inches of coarse sand or fine gravel in the bottom of the planting area.

Rhododendrons require plenty of moisture during their active growing season in the spring and summer. In late summer and fall give them less water, to help prepare them for winter. (Watering and fertilizing late in the season results in soft growth that is easily winter killed.) In dry periods of spring and summer, soak the soil slowly with water twice a week. During hot weather (above 21°C/70°F), water the foliage in the early morning.

Rhododendrons may be planted at any time of the year, even when in full flower. When transplanting a rhododendron, take every precaution to prevent soil from falling from the root ball. Prepare a generous planting pocket at least twice the size of the root ball. Sprinkle root-inducing hormone powder on the root ball. Set the plant in the hole so that the surface roots are only about 3–5 cm (an inch or two) below the soil level. Fill in around the roots carefully with equal parts of moist peat moss, sandy loam and compost. Allow a slow trickle of water from the garden hose to soak the planting.

Mulch over the planting lightly with a woodsy soil containing leaf mould from oak trees and peat moss. Avoid mulching around the trunk of the plant. Water the mulching material thoroughly.

With a special rhododendron fertilizer containing blood meal, cottonseed meal, acid phosphate, trace minerals and other necessary elements, fertilize the plants each year on about March 1. Apply a second feeding at the end of April and one last feeding in early summer. Do not fertilize after midsummer.

Remove the flower heads when they fade. Take the old cluster between your thumb and first finger and snap it off carefully. Do not injure the tender growth behind the flower head.

Prune the shrub just after it flowers. This will give the rhododendron time to ripen new wood and promote the formation of flower buds for the next season. Prune the plants only to maintain desirable shape, compactness and size. If you have old, over-grown rhododendrons that need shaping, cut back the stems to an area where the leaves occur in whorls, usually at the end of each growth. In the axils of the leaves are growth buds, which remain dormant unless they can be forced into growth by the removal of the stem beyond them.

The leaves of rhododendrons turn yellow in the early spring, usually because of temperatures unfavourable for chlorophyll formation. But there can be other causes of chlorosis, such as incorrect soil cultivation, which destroys some of the shallow feeding roots, or insufficient mulch, or deficiency of iron in the soil. As the earth warms in spring, apply to the soil a rhododendron fertilizer that contains iron, or spray a solution of ferrous sulphate directly on to the foliage to give the leaves a bright green appearance. Formulations of chelated iron also are used to "green" the leaves.

It is not unusual for a large plant to wilt and die from root-feeding grubs or weevils. Root weevil larvae feed upon the roots in fall and spring. They chew holes along the edges of the leaves, but not in the midribs. To control weevils, use slug bait containing metaldehyde. Apply the bait several times in spring and fall. Insecticides containing malathion sprayed on the leaves and soil also destroy the insects.

The lace bug is a serious enemy of the rhododendron. Lace bugs appear as a whitish mottling of the leaves, with brown droplets forming on the undersides of the leaves. The insect winters in the leaf tissues as eggs, which hatch in early June. Plants growing in full sun are more likely to become infested. Begin to spray with sevin or malathion on June 1 and repeat the treatment in 2 weeks, or whenever the insect is detected.

Hybrid rhododendrons available on the coast include:

- In shades of pink or rose: Alice, Jan Dekens, Linda, Albert Close, Scintillation, Pink Pearl, Irene, Bel-Air, Anna Rose Whitney.

- In shades of blue and purple: A. Bedford, Anah Kruschke, Blue Ensign, Blue Japy, Lee's Dark Purple, Purple Splendor, Purple Lace, Blue Peter.

- In shades of apricot, orange and yellow: Sonata, King of Shrubs, Evening Glow, Goldsworth Orange, Harvest Moon, Hotei.

- In shades of red: America, Vulcan, Trilby, Thor, J.M. de Montague, Lord Roberts, Nova Zembla, O.B. Jantzen, Shames Ruby, Wilgen's Ruby, Holden, Caractacus.

Rhododendrons: Pink Pearl, with Bow Bell in background. Sandra Evelyn photo

Smaller Plants

Rhododendrons measured by inches rather than feet perform well in small gardens and containers. A few just creep and scramble over rocks. Cozy in containers, they may be grown where only a balcony or deck is available. Miniature or dwarf rhododendrons have distinctive foliage and flowers. Many have aromatic leaves and some have scented flowers.

Rhododendron impeditum is a noteworthy dwarf species. This small, compact plant may reach 45 cm (18 inches) at maturity. In April it is startling with lavender-blue flowers. Its grey-green evergreen leaves are tiny.

R. pemakoense forms a low mound about 45 cm (18 inches) high and wide. Purplish-pink flowers appear in late March. Small-leafed foliage is bronzy green. This plant is a natural for being tucked in a rock crevice, and as a companion to alpine plants.

R. radicans is extremely ground-hugging. It is adorned with bright green leaves and dainty purple flowers. One of its dwarf forms attains a maximum height of only 2.5–5 cm (1–2 inches) in old age.

R. tessa is one of the earliest small rhodos to flower in spring. Soft, rosy red blossoms are found on the plant in trusses. Leaves turn a copper colour in the spring. This small evergreen reaches 60–90 cm (2–3 ft) in height.

Humming Bird has bell-shaped flowers in loose trusses. They are carmine in bud and open to a deep pink. April is more colourful when Humming Bird appears.

Bow Bell has bright pink cup-shaped flowers that cover a compact, round-leafed plant. It thrives in the sun.

Moonstone is small and tight-growing. When young it begins to show large creamy cups of blossoms with faint red markings.

Jock is a rose-pink dwarf rhododendron that does well in the sun. Its flowers open to a trumpet shape. The plant forms a rounded, tightly compact mound 60–90 cm (2–3 ft) high.

Blue Diamond grows to 90 cm (3 ft) in 10 years. Leaves are evergreen and light blue-green. Deep blue flowers decorate the plant in May. It loves sun.

Blue Tit, another of the blue-shaded dwarf rhodos, is an early May dazzler. Rock gardens are to its liking. Blue-green foliage and clear blue flowers reward gardeners in April and May.

Bric-a-Brac is a round-leafed, low-growing rhododendron. In March, sparkling white flowers with a chocolate throat cloak this hardy plant.

R. cilpinense shows funnel-shaped blooms of apple blossom pink, fading to white. The plant flowers in March and thrives equally well in sun and shade. Growth is slow and low.

Naomi blooms vary from pink to lilac. Neat and compact in growth, it reaches about 90 cm (3 ft) in many years. Flowers grow in trusses of 4 to 5.

Carmen is a late-May flowering dwarf rhododendron about 30 cm (12 inches) tall. Its red bell-shaped flowers grow in clusters.

Rose of Sharon

Hibiscus syriacus, or rose of Sharon (althaea) blooms in summer or early fall. The shrub needs full sun and well-drained soil. Prune well-established plants in early spring by removing about a third of the old wood.

- 'Diana' rose of Sharon has lovely large, single white flowers with yellow centre stamens.

- 'Hamabo' rose of Sharon has showy single pale pink flowers with bold red centres.

Summer Sweet

Hummingbird summer sweet, *Clethra alnifolia* 'Hummingbird' is a recently developed ornamental shrub. Fragrant upright panicles of flowers grow in mid-summer, complemented by glossy green foliage. The leaves turn golden in autumn. Summer sweet needs full sun and neutral or slightly acid soil.

Viburnum

Viburnum is the city cousin of the honeysuckle family. Evergreen and deciduous types are grown with ease in the Pacific Northwest. They are easy to care for and tolerate heat, drought, wind and neglect.

Plant viburnum in a fertile, humus-enriched soil and generously water in summer. The plants will respond vigorously.

Avoid planting them near rhododendron or other plants that demand an acid-type soil. Viburnums appreciate the addition of dolomite lime. Use 450 g (1 lb) of lime to each mature plant about 1.5 m (5 ft) tall. Adding super phosphate increases berry production and plant hardiness.

Fertilizers encourage new growth, glossy foliage and berry production. Make the first application in spring, when the growth starts. Another organic type fertilizer is needed in late summer. Apply 900 g (2 lbs) of a 5-10-10 fertilizer per 9 m² (100 sq ft) of planting area and water it deeply into the soil. In autumn give the plants a light feeding of super phosphate.

Prune viburnum either in early spring or immediately after the shrub has flowered. Reach into

Viburnum carlesii. Sandra Evelyn photo

the centre of the plant and cut out any dead wood. Trim the whole plant to give it a well-groomed yet natural appearance. Young plants require only a light pruning.

Viburnum may be propagated or increased by cuttings or layers. Take cuttings and root them in June or July. Bend branches to the ground to form layers in May or June.

As with hydrangea, the flower heads of several species of viburnum are composed of two types of flowers. One is showy but sterile, incapable of producing seed. You will need both a male and a female plant of this type if you want fruit or berries. The other flower head is less conspicuous but complete with stamens and pistil, and therefore is fertile and self-fruiting. If you cannot plant several types of viburnums, spray the open flowers with a fruit-hormone spray when the plant is in open bloom, to insure a crop of berries.

- *Viburnum fragrans*. Originally found only in palace or temple courtyards in China. A tall, lanky shrub with branches that tend to droop; often called the pink snowball bush and indispensable for fragrance and winter colour. Spicy-scented ball-like flowers of white touched with pink are scattered among leafless brown branches from November through February. Blossoms withstand severe frosts without injury. Leaves turn bronze-red before falling.

- *V. carlesii*. A native of Korea, popular for exquisite fragrance and vivid fall colouring. A low, rounded form ideal for small home gardens. Flowers are soft-pink in bud and white when fully open in late winter and early spring. Choose a permanent place: it resents transplanting.

Viburnum bodnantense. Sandra Evelyn photo

- *V. burkwoodii*. A hybrid cross of *V. carlesii* and *V. utile*, almost an evergreen, with an open, arching habit of growth. Glossy dark green leaves remain on the plant until early spring, when new leaves emerge. Maximum height and width is 2.7–3 m (9–10 ft). Round clusters of waxy white, pink-budded, fragrant flowers bloom January to April. Winter hardiness is improved by watering less frequently in the late summer and fall.

- *V. bodnantense*. A cross between *V. fragrans* and *V. grandiflorum*. Nearly evergreen with scented pink flowers. Shrub grows stiff to about 180 cm tall and 90 cm wide (6 x 3 ft). Dark blue berries grow in fall and are taken quickly by birds. The variety 'Pink Dawn' is superior, with very fragrant rose-coloured flowers.

- *V. tomentosum plicatum grandiflorum.* A gaudy but free-flowering shrub with pure white, sterile flowers. Blossoms crowd the branches in May and June. Needs shelter in the garden for full development of flowers.

- *V. opulus,* or Guelder rose. A native of Europe. White, round blossoms open in May and June. Leaves and berries are red in autumn. When mature, *V. opulus roseum,* the common snowball, grows to 4.5 m tall and 3–3.6 m wide (15 x 10–12 ft). *V. opulus nanum,* the dwarf European cranberry, has bright green leaves. Shows well in a rock garden. Grows to 60 cm (2 ft) tall and wide. Leaves turn rusty red before falling.

- *V. rhytidophyllum,* or leather leaf viburnum. Striking with coarse, crinkly leaves. The hardiest of the evergreen species, tolerating freezing temperatures if very well drained and protected from cold winter winds. Flowers are white, followed by red berries that gradually turn to black.

- *V. tinus robustum,* or laurustinus. A tall, rangy, luxuriant evergreen. Reddish flower buds form in late summer; white and rose flowers bloom in winter and early spring. Metallic blue berries appear in spring and summer.

Viburnum davidii. Adam Gibbs photo

- *V. davidii.* A low-growing evergreen shrub with dark green, deeply creased leaves. Clusters of white flowers bloom in May and June. Steel-blue berries appear in late summer and stay all winter. Plant male and female plants near each other for a full crop of berries.

- *V. cassinoides* 'Witherod.' Dark green foliage becomes orange, red and purple in fall. White flowers appear in June, followed by spectacular red fruit in fall.

Willow

The clatsop willow, *Salix hookeriana* 'Clatsop,' is brilliant in spring with showy 10 cm (4 inch) catkins on a leafless shrub. New spring twigs are covered with dense soft hairs, and the dark green leaves are downy on the undersides. Grow this shrub in full or partial sun.

Trees and Shrubs

Vines

Nature provides vines with the means to weave a tapestry: they climb or creep in various ways, clinging to surfaces with root-like growths or tendrils as they go.

Every vine is useful in the garden. They decorate walls, fences and trellises, and enclose areas with lacy foliage and brilliant flowers. Vines provide shelter from winds, protection from summer sun and a screen to filter sight and sound.

The trick with vines is to choose carefully and keep them contained. Many are ruthless growers and can overwhelm the garden. Confine the roots in a sunken metal or plastic bucket, which helps contain overzealous growth.

Clematis

Clematis vines are spring and summer stars of the garden. Bell-, bowl- and lantern-shaped flowers decorate vines with spectacular shapes and colours. Claret, pink, blue, lilac, deep purple and sparkling white blossoms unfold among the green leaves. Members of the clematis clan will scramble up trellises, ramble around fences, stretch over stumps and clothe naked twigs and branches.

Clematis montana. Adam Gibbs photo

Locate the vine in an area where the top of the plant is in the open sunlight and its roots are shaded and sheltered. Clematis prefer light, sandy soil with good drainage, that has been enriched with organic material, such as leaf mould, peat moss, wood ashes and compost. Plant clematis in any season, even when in full flower.

Select a container of clematis from the nursery, a plant at least 2 years old that is growing on its own roots. Such a plant will become established quickly and will flower sooner than a younger vine. Avoid transplanting in the heat of the day; wait to plant until evening and preferably on a cloudy, rainy day. If the clematis is in full flower, take extra care in moving it. The root system should be disturbed as little as possible.

Dig a generous planting pocket, put in a handful of dolomite lime and set the roots in gently. Plant the crown (the point where the roots branch out from the stem) 5 to 7.5 cm (2–3 inches) below ground level. Too shallow a planting will cause many varieties to die back near the soil line. Water the leaves and the soil faithfully each day until the plant is growing well on its own. Each fall, sprinkle lime around the clematis, at the rate of 1 cup (250 mL) to a mature vine. Each spring, fertilize the vine with 5-10-10 fertilizer. Apply 250 mL (1 cup) around each established vine.

Begin to train and prune clematis vines at an early age. As new shoots appear, tie them in place. Cut out unwanted shoots to redirect the plant's strength. When the vine has reached the coverage you want, prune it regularly and ruthlessly.

Large flowering clematis hybrids that bloom before the middle of June on wood from the past season's growth, such as the florida, patens and Montana groups, include 'Duchess of Edinburgh,' 'Belle of Woking,' 'Edouard Defosse,' 'Miss Bateman,' 'Montana alba,' 'Montana rubens,' 'Nellie Moser' and 'Lucie Lemoine.' Prune them before spring, usually in February or early March.

Vines belonging to the jackmanii, viticella and paniculata classifications, which flower on new wood produced in the same growing season, include 'Crimson Star,' 'Gypsy Queen,' 'Mrs. Cholmondelay,' 'Hauldine,' 'Little Nell,' 'Minuet,' 'Mme. Edouard Andre,' 'Jackmanii' and 'Comtesse de Bouchard.' Established vines should be cut each spring to within 60 cm (2 ft) of ground level.

The evergreen clematis, *C. armandii*, is vigorous and needs judicious thinning and shortening during February (bearing in mind that the flowers are produced on the previous year's shoots).

Interesting varieties include *C. tangutica* 'Golden Tiara,' with large lanterns of buttercup yellow outside and chocolate brown inside; 'Mrs. M. Thompson,' with violet-blue flowers highlighted by vivid scarlet bars and dark red stamens; 'Multi-Blue,' with a spiky central tuft of blue petals, the tips of which vary in colour from white to various shades of red or green; 'Pink Fantasy,' hybridized in Canada and showy with deep pink bars and chocolate anthers; and a new winner,' Veronica's Choice,' which produces large, frilly double blossoms in early summer and single lavender flowers in the fall.

The following are excellent choices for planting on the West Coast: 'Asao,' with deep pink flowers in June; 'Bees Jubilee,' which produces bright deep pink blossoms with red centre stripes during May and June;

Kathi Linnman's Clematis jackmanii. Bob Cain photo

'Belle of Woking,' showy with double flowers of lavender in May and June; and 'Comtesse de Bouchard,' with large mauve-pink blossoms in June.

'Duchess of Edinburgh' bears striking white flowers from June through August; 'Ernest Markham' has red flowers from July through September; 'General Sikorsky' produces lavender-blue flowers with red stripes from June through September.

'Hagley Hybrid' has glittering shell-pink flowers from June through August; 'Henryi' has sparkling white flowers from June through August; and a coastal favourite, 'Jackmanii,' produces dark purple blossoms from June through August.

Clematis 'Ernest Markham.' Sandra Evelyn photo

C. jackmanii Rubra produces red flowers from June through September. 'Lady Betty Balfour' has deep purple flowers from August through October. *C. lanuginosa* Candida, with white blossoms from June through September, is a treasure.

C. montana Rubens is adorned with light pink blooms in May and June; 'Nelly Moser' has pale pink blossoms with red stripes in August and September; 'Niobe' produces deep red flowers from June through September; *C. paniculata* has creamy white flowers in September and October.

'The President' is showy from June through September with deep blue flowers; 'Ramona' has light lavender flowers from July through September; 'Star of India' is covered with purple blooms with red stripes in July and August.

'Ville de Lyon' is radiant in red from June through September. *C. viticella* 'Etoile Violette' has velvet purple blossoms from June through October. *C. viticella* 'Mme. Julia Correvon' has flowers red as wine, with twisted petals that decorate the vine from June through September.

Clematis are propagated easily by layering. Choose a shoot of the present year's growth, as close to the ground as possible so that each joint will touch the soil. Dig out 10 cm (4 inches) of soil and replace with a light, sandy soil mixture or half sand and peat moss. Do not remove any leaves.

Split the stem with a sharp knife above and below a stem joint or node. Rub into the split a root-inducing hormone to speed propagation. Peg down the shoot and cover with 5 cm (2 inches) of sandy soil or half sand and half peat moss. Water the finished layer. The stem should root successfully within 3 to 4 weeks. After rooting takes place, cut the stem from the parent plant and set it out on its own.

Passion Vines

Passion vines were one of the treasures found by the Spaniards in the New World. To early missionaries devoted to botany, the open blossom suggested the Passion of Christ. The ten petals represented the ten apostles present at the crucifixion (Peter and Judas being absent). The plant's corona, or crown, represented the crown of thorns. Five anthers were suggestive of the five wounds or marks of hammers used to drive nails; three stigmas represented the three nails piercing hands and feet; the tendrils were the cords or whips and the digitate leaves were the hands of the persecutors.

In coastal gardens, passion vines are spectacular in growth and flower. The vines are vigorous and reach high places quickly. Large, leathery leaves cover the vine. Intricate blossoms vary in colour, including blues, pinks, yellows, reds and sparkling white. They stay open all day and close at night. Many produce edible fruits, which are rarely larger than an egg in size, and dull purple when ripe. The pulp may be eaten directly from the fruit and they flavour jellies, sherbets and candies.

New vines may be started from seeds or cuttings. Take seeds from the fruit and dry in a shady place out of doors for several days. Then plant them in pots filled with vermiculite, or sand or half sand and half peat moss, covering the seed lightly. Keep the seeding moist, warm and in a light place. The seed will germinate any time from a few weeks to several months later. In the late spring, transplant the young seedlings to the garden.

Plant passion vines in a sandy, well-drained soil. Full exposure to the sun encourages them to produce flowers spontaneously.

Or you can take cuttings of passion vines in August or September, when the vine is mature but not too woody and the stems are hollow. Cuttings should be 15–20 cm (6–8 inches) long, with 2 to 3 leaf nodes each. Plunge the cuttings into a rooting medium of sand, vermiculite, or a mixture of one part sand and one part peat moss. Then put them out in sterile pots, in bright indirect sunlight. Transplant them to the garden in May. Cuttings taken from a mature vine in late summer usually flower the next spring and summer.

Passion vines are extremely energetic in growth and demand large amounts of water and nutrients. Begin

Passion flower. Adam Gibbs photo

fertilizing in the early spring and continue to feed the plants once a month through the summer. Apply a plant food high in phosphorus and potash. Use approximately 225 g (1/2 lb) of a 5-10-10 fertilizer to each mature vine at each application. Water the vines often in summer.

If a severe winter is expected, remove the vine from its support in the late fall and bury it in the soil 12.5–15 cm (5–6 inches) deep. Cover with 7.5 cm (3 inches) more of an insulating mulch such as ground bark, old sawdust, leaves or compost. Remove the mulch in the spring after the danger of heavy frost has disappeared. You can also bring the vine indoors during severe winters. The vines thrive in a cool, light room.

Passiflora caerulea is a wild flower native to South American forests, where it grows in festoons from the branches of tropical trees. The vine is adorned with fragrant flowers, each measuring 9 cm (3 1/2 inches) in diameter. The flower has a greenish-white sepal, with spines at the tips and white petals. The rays of the corona, in two rows, are blue at the tip and white in the middle, shading to deep maroon. Each leaf has 5 slender lobes. *P. caerulea* is one of the hardiest of the passion vines. It can endure winter temperatures just below 4°C (40°F). The fruit is not edible.

P. coriacea has 5 flower petals and no sepals. The 3.5 cm (1 1/2-inch) twin flowers are golden yellow, and the golden fence around the stalk encloses a maroon floor. The foliage is mottled and light.

The cuttings of this species root easily. They often bloom from a rooted cutting started in water only.

P. violacea produces exquisite flowers 9 cm (3 1/2 inches) in diameter, brilliant violet-lavender in colour. The filaments have coloured tips. The foliage is 3-lobed and more slender than other varieties. *P. violacea* is a hardy vine that grows well in the Pacific Northwest.

Wisteria

Wisteria vines hold the blue ribbon among hardy flowering vines. They weave a tapestry that inspires feelings of romance and nostalgia, and they grow fast, live long and resist drought.

In May, wisteria produces clusters of flowers that fall from the vines like bunches of grapes in an extravagance of pink, white, lavender and mauve.

At the nursery, select plants that are propagated by cuttings or grafts, not seeds. Grafted, container-grown plants will flower within 1 to 2 years of planting, whereas seedling plants can take 15 years or more to flower.

Plant wisteria in early spring before the vine starts into new growth. Wisteria is not particular about soil. A fertile soil enriched with organic humus is ideal and full sun encourages flower production. These vines resent being transplanted, so remove them from the nursery container carefully. Plant the crown (collar) about 5 cm (2 inches) below the surface of the ground. Firm the soil around the roots and water the new planting

Wisteria. Mary Palmer photo

deeply and thoroughly. Water the new planting generously until it becomes re-established. Keep the soil slightly moist through spring and summer to keep the vine producing flowers.

Each summer, after the vine is well established, apply a fertilizer low in nitrogen and high in phosphorus and potash. (Too much nitrogen encourages soft, green leaves at the sacrifice of flowering wood.) An application of super phosphate in the autumn after the leaves have fallen will increase flower production. At each application of fertilizer, use 125 mL (1/2 cup) for each mature vine.

Train wisteria vines to trellises, arbours, walls, posts or fences. Start when the vine is young, tying new growth until it begins to twine around its support.

Wisteria is energetic and sometimes defiant. Keep the vine in check constantly by pruning regularly. In summer, prune out any long, straggling growths, except those required for covering. In late summer, after the new shoots have grown several feet, cut them back by a half to a third of their length, to encourage the production of short spurs from which the next season's flowers will grow.

Stubborn vines that refuse to flower are sometimes encouraged by root pruning. With a sharp shovel, dig a trench or ditch around the base of the plant at a radius of 90 cm (3 ft). Go down 45–50 cm (18–20 inches) deep and cut all roots that the shovel touches.

Over time, wisteria vines produce quantities of large stems that tangle in knots. As the stems grow and expand, the knots become tighter and the vine can be strangled. Avoid this by reducing the number of major stems when the vine is young, and by training the young growth so that it does not become twisted.

A wisteria vine may be shaped into a tree form. After setting out a young plant, allow only a single upright branch to remain. Tie desired points onto the main stem, which should be 90–120 cm (3–4 ft) tall. Side branches more than 90–120 cm long can be drawn to the main stem to form a well-balanced head. Each spring, cut back any unwanted shoots or branches. Some support can be provided by attaching the framework to the central leader in maypole fashion. Continue to thin the young tree by removing all twining growths from the top. In time you will have an umbrella-shaped tree with a strong trunk.

Wisteria sinensis *(Chinese blue)*. Sandra Evelyn photo

Wisteria floribunda *and* Viburnum japonica. Adam Gibbs photo

Chinese wisteria (*Wisteria sinensis*) form long flower clusters 30 cm (12 inches) long. These develop about 2 weeks before the leaves unfold. The following varieties are recommended for the coast: *W. s.* 'Amethyst,' light rosy purple; *W. s.* 'Blue Sapphire,' lilac-mauve; *W. s.* 'Caroline,' lavender mauve; and *W. s.* 'Royal Purple,' light rosy purple.

Japanese wisteria (*W. floribunda*) is spectacular with flower tresses 25–50 cm (10–20 inches) long, which appear at the same time as the leaves. This wisteria has many outstanding varieties: *W. f.* 'Macrobotrys' is well known for its exceptionally long flower clusters, up to 90 cm (3 ft). Flowers open from the base downward to the tip and arrive each spring along with new foliage. *W. f.* 'Kyushaka' produces lavender tresses; 'Longisima alba' bears white clusters of flowers; 'Geisha' is clothed in long tresses of blue and lavender.

W. venusta 'Alba' is breathtaking when trained into a tree form. The plant drapes itself in long, fragrant blooms. *W. v.* 'Violacea' is striking with fragrant purple-blue flowers. Leaves of *W. venusta*, which often flowers in early April, are broad and have silky hairs.

Other Vines

Honeysuckle (*Lonicera*) has a sweet fragrance and honey that are especially enjoyed by hummingbirds. There are many cultivated varieties and *Lonicera cilosa* grows wild in many coastal areas.

The foliage of honeysuckle is usually evergreen. Clusters of orange, red or yellow trumpet-shaped flowers decorate the vine in summer.

This vine will endure drought, strong winds and poor drainage. Grow it in a sunny site to encourage rapid growth and spectacular blossoms. Mulch over the growing soil with organic humus such as peat moss, aged manure or compost. Regular pruning is unnecessary; prune only to keep the vine in a desirable shape.

A new introduction from University of British Columbia Botanical Garden, 'Mandarin,' shows winning characteristics. Its large clusters of long flowers are burnished red-orange on the outside and golden orange inside. Dark purple-brown stems and young copper leaves that become glossy green as they mature add to the vine's beauty. This vine will endure cold temperatures with ease.

'Dropmore Scarlet,' another Canadian introduction, is extremely hardy and relatively fast growing, with scarlet flowers from midsummer to fall. Another excellent honeysuckle, 'Belgica,' produces clusters of tubular, soft yellow summer flowers.

Trumpet vine (*Campsis radicans*), also known as the hummingbird plant, climbs or clings by its aerial roots, requiring no support. Yellow, deep orange or red

Honeysuckle. Chuck Heath photo

blossoms are long and funnel-shaped. Hot, sunny days encourage the plant to flower fantastically.

The vine will travel 9 m (30 ft) in a season. Often it overgrows and requires heavy root pruning. If you plant the trumpet vine with its roots enclosed in a metal or plastic container, you can prevent its roots from spreading wildly. A deep freeze may cut the plant back, but with just a few warm spring days, it will reappear. Prune this vine hard each fall. Cut it to within 2.5–5 cm (1–2 inches) of the base of the previous year's wood.

C. radicans 'Flamenco' is a vigorous, hardy grower with summer trumpet-shaped flowers in deep orange-red. In *C. r.* 'Flava,' deep yellow trumpets decorate the vine in summer. *C. tagliabuana* 'Guilfoylei' is an extremely hardy vine for the coast region. Salmon-red flowers drape the vine in summer and fall.

Actinidia (Chinese gooseberry, or kiwi vine) is a climber with uniquely coloured leaves. Bronzy young growth in spring turns striking shades of pink, then becomes white in the middle and green at the base. Single plants are ornamental; you must have both male and female plants for the production of fruit. Self-fruitful varieties are not often available and are rarely successful.

The fruit is the shape and size of a hen's egg, and coated with brown fuzz. The taste is reminiscent of melon, strawberry or banana.

The vine is most colourful when planted in a sunny site. Plant the vine near a sturdy trellis, arbour or fence for support. Each spring, prune the vine to shape and control it.

Give *Actinidia* a fertile, moist soil. Fertilize the vine in early spring by applying a handful of 5-10-10 formula to the soil to keep the plant vigorous and colourful. Keep the roots moist through spring and summer. Well-established plants will stretch 6 m (20 ft) in height and width. Some actinidia to consider:

- *Actinidia arguta* 'Issai' is a female kiwi with fragrant white blossoms and delicious fruit.

- *A. chinensis*, a female, is a fast grower, producing creamy white blossoms and large leaves.

- *A. kolomikta* has leaves drenched in white and pink. The vine is extremely hardy to cold.

- *A. chinensis* 'Blake' is a self-fruitful variety of the kiwi family, best grown for restricted coverage, as it grows slowly and unpredictably.

Silver lace vine (*Polygonum auberti*) is a rampant twining vine, not recommended for confined areas. It will cover over 30 m (100 ft) in one season and is invaluable as a quick screen.

The leaves are about 5 cm (2 inches) long, heart-shaped and glossy green. Late in summer, the vine becomes covered with foaming sprays of green-white or pink tinted flowers. The leaves remain on the vine until late fall. The vine will tolerate poor soil and drought, which makes it especially useful by the sunny seashore. If it is top-killed by severe winters, it will develop rapidly in the spring from the rootstock. If necessary, it can be pruned back to ground level in the fall and will return quickly by spring. Consider:

- *Polygonum reyoutria*. A select variety with foliage that becomes bright red in autumn. Flowers are light pink.

Virginia creeper (*Parthenocissus*) stretches out and spills over walls, trellises and tree trunks or covers the ground. Autumn is ablaze with its colourful leaves. The vine clings by means of discs at the end of the tendrils. Avoid planting it near shake or shingle siding, as vines can creep under the wood, and note that at painting time it is difficult to

Trees and Shrubs

Virginia creeper. Sandra Evelyn photo

remove the clinging tendrils from the painted surface of a house. But the vine is useful in controlling erosion on a steep bank. *Parthenocissus* thrives in dense shade or a place in the sun; colours are more spectacular in the shade. Plant the vine in an organic soil that retains water well and keep the soil moist in summer. A complete 5-10-10 fertilizer used in the early spring is beneficial.

- *Parthenocissus quinquefolia* 'Engelmannii.' Features deeply cut 5-lobed leaves that become brilliant in autumn.

- *P. tricuspidata* 'Beverly Brooks.' Adorned with bronze-green leaves that are smaller than most varieties. Plant in partial shade for bright fall colours.

- *P. henryana* 'Silvervein Creeper.' Leaves are dark green variegated with silvery white along the veins. A striking climber that produces small, dark blue fruits.

- *P. tricuspidata* 'Vietchii.' The ideal Boston ivy for self-clinging on brick or masonry walls. Leaves take on a vivid red tint in fall.

Roses

Roses growing in our coastal gardens are the result of seventy million years of history. Fossils of roses have been found that date back to ancient times. Original species of roses found in nature usually have single 5-petalled flowers, in white, pink, crimson or yellow. They are decorated in fall and winter with large red rose hips or seeds. The plants bloom briefly in early summer, with no recurrence of flowers.

Modern roses are found in many forms, from climbers reaching skyward to miniatures 7.5–10 cm (3–4 inches) tall. They have been hybridized to need minimal

Pat Collin's rambler rose 'Albertine.' Bob Cain photo

maintenance and to bloom for a long season. With a little attention, roses can be floriferous on the coast from May until December.

Choose plants with thick, straight stems that are well branched. Roses need a sunny site with plenty of elbow room. Plant them where their roots will not compete with those of trees or large shrubs. Space hybrid tea, grandiflora, polyanthas and floribundas about 90 cm (3 ft) apart in all directions. Shrub roses are spaced about 1.5 m (5 ft) apart. Climbers and pillars are planted 1.8–2 m (6–8 ft) apart. Standards are set 1.3–1.5 m (4–5 ft) apart in all directions.

Pling advised in 77 A.D.: "Dig the rose bed deep." Deep and thorough preparation of rose-planting soil is essential. Spade to at least 45 cm (18 inches). Turn into the earth organic materials such as decomposed manure, peat moss, or compost. Prepare individual planting pockets deeper and wider than the spread of the root system. Put a mound of soil in the bottom and centre of the planting hole, then press it into a firm cone with your hand. Set the centre of the rootstock on the centre of the cone and arrange the roots so they spread naturally over the cone. Fill in around the roots with fine soil. Firm the soil against the roots. Hold the graft union (a knot-like growth on the end of the stock and above the root system) about 5 cm (2 inches) above ground level, as the soil is filled in around the roots. Flood the planting hole with water, and allow the water to drain completely from the planting before adding the rest of the soil. The graft union should be about 2.5 cm (1 inch) above ground level when the planting is finished. Keep the soil around the new planting moist until the plant is well established.

The number and quality of rose blossoms depend on the condition and quantity of leaves on the plant. Rose plants must produce and retain enough energy to thrust forth healthy leaves, flower buds and long, sturdy stems.

Roses are adversely affected by insects, diseases, lack of available nutrients, shade, incorrect watering, improper cutting of flower stems and other inadequate environmental or cultural procedures.

In the early spring, just as the new leaves unfold, begin a program of pest control. Every 2 weeks apply a multipurpose rose spray or dust to keep roses free of insects and disease. Avoid waiting until a rose is infested with pests before taking action.

Systemic insecticides are absorbed and carried into all parts of the plant, dealing a lethal blow to aphids, spider mites, thrips, leaf miners and other insects. Dry granules are distributed evenly over the soil surrounding the base of the plant. Water the material into the soil down to the roots.

Rose hips. Bob Cain photo

These insecticides are effective for 6 weeks after each application.

Diseases such as black spot and mildews can be serious during humid summer months. Black spot appears as round black dots, frequently surrounded by yellow halos, on the leaves. In time the plant can be almost completely defoliated. Prune and burn the infected canes and leaves. Discourage black spot and other diseases with a dormant spray of lime-sulphur; apply before new growth begins in early spring.

Mildews may form on young leaves, shoots and buds of rose plants. Young shoots may become swollen or distorted and foliage may be stunted. Mildew is spread by wind and water. It overwinters on fallen leaves and in infected bud scales and flower stems. In winter, use a liquid lime-sulphur spray to control mildews.

Roses grow best in a soil that is slightly acid with a pH of 5.5–6.5. Coast soils tend to be deficient in calcium, which can cause the margins of the rose leaflets to die. Eventually entire leaves die and drop off, and flowers may become deformed with brown spots near the margins of the petals. When calcium is deficient, add dolomite lime to the soil, using 450 g (1 lb) for each plant.

Roses improve dramatically with the correct type of fertilizer applied in adequate amounts. A 6-8-12 or 5-10-10 formulated commercial fertilizer is satisfactory. Apply it at the rate of 1.3 kg (3 lbs) to 9 m^2 (100 sq ft) of rose bed, or 1 handful of fertilizer in a ring around each rose plant. Water the fertilizer deeply into the soil immediately. Apply rose fertilizer in the early spring as growth begins, again after the first flush of flowers in early

Pat Collin's 'Betty Boop' floribunda. Bob Cain photo

June, and again in July. Do not fertilize roses after the middle of August. Late summer fertilization stimulates soft new growth that may be killed in winter.

Organic fertilizers such as decomposed manure, blood meal, fish meal or bone meal are helpful in early spring. Super phosphate is especially beneficial to rose plants. In February, place 125 mL ($1/2$ cup) of super phosphate around the base of each plant and water it into the soil.

Yellowing of leaves often indicates a lack of nitrogen or iron. Foliage turns greyish green from lack of phosphorus; a browning of leaf margins indicates a lack of potash.

Rose roots must have an adequate supply of water through the summer. Even when summer rains are frequent, deep waterings are beneficial. Slowly seeping water that penetrates to a depth of 45 cm (18 inches) once or twice a week is appreciated by roses. Avoid wetting the foliage of the plants late in the afternoon or evening, as this encourages mildews, black spot and other common rose pests. Mulches will hold moisture for the plants during summer, and help prevent weeds as well.

Prune rose bushes to promote healthy, vigorous growth that will bear the maximum number of quality flowers. Prune a hybrid tea bush rose to a well-balanced framework of 3 to 5 husky main stems, free of twiggy growth at both the top and the base of the plant. Each main stem should have about 5 well-spaced buds.

Drastic or low pruning will encourage the root system to channel its energy into producing fewer roses, but of spectacular size. Light pruning—between 30 and 45 cm (12–18 inches)—will result in more plentiful flowers of smaller size. Remove any growths or suckers that appear from below the bud union (the point where the top part is grafted to the rootstock).

Hybrid Tea Roses

Some recent hybrid tea roses include:

- 'City of Welland.' Unique light apricot-coloured blooms grow high on long stems, complemented by glossy, deep green foliage. A 2001 winner.

- 'Gemini.' A 2000 hybrid with a mild, spicy fragrance. Deep cream flowers edged in coral pink grow on long single stems, occasionally with 2 or more blooms growing on a stem. Leaves are deep green.

- 'Golden sceptre.' A 2001 hybrid tea with spectacular amber-gold blooms and leathery green leaves.

- 'Henry Fonda.' Pointed buds open into deep yellow flowers with a light fragrance, amid shiny green leaves. A 2001 winner.

- 'Opening Night.' A 1998 winner and already a classic. A long-stemmed beauty whose deep red flowers are mildly fragrant.

- 'Rebekah.' Tea-like buds open to fragrant, deep pink flowers reminiscent of old-fashioned roses. The plant is hardy and the stems are long and graceful.

- 'Women's Institute.' A 2001 winner with fragrant pink blossoms and rich, dark green leaves on a well-formed plant.

Other hybrid tea roses of merit include 'Artistry,' coral-orange; 'Bewitched,' pink; 'Brandy,' apricot; 'Honor,' white; 'Intrigue,' purple-red; 'Lady X,' mauve; and 'Peace,' lemon yellow and pink. Prune them severely.

Grandiflora Roses

These plants are tall, vigorous bushes that produce large clusters of flowers of good size on the ends of long, sturdy stems. Prune grandiflora plants in the early spring along with hybrid tea roses. Cut them back lightly. Remove small twigs or laterals. Prune to an outside-pointing bud below the old flower cluster. In late summer, remove the old bloom sprays to the first 5-leaflet leaf.

- 'Candelabra.' New in 1999, with striking coral and orange flowers that flicker brightly against a background of glossy dark green leaves.

Other grandifloras include 'Queen Elizabeth,' 'Ole' and 'Arizona.'

Tree (Standard) Roses

These roses are produced by grafting or budding the top part of a hybrid tea, grandiflora or other rose plant on a standard or stem of a hardy variety that makes a straight, firm cane. This type of budding or grafting produces roses at different heights instead of all near the ground. Tree roses are available at heights starting at 45, 60 or 90 cm (18, 24 or 36 inches). Some are standard weeping forms. Prune weeping standards after flowering: as the flowers fade, cut back the laterals on which the flowers were borne to within 2 to 3 buds of the main canes.

In spring, prune out all dead, spindly or weak growth. Tree roses require severe pruning. Often their heads become proportionally too large for the structure of the plant. In early spring, cut back the top branches to healthy green wood. Leave 3 to 5 well-spaced main branches, each with at least 3 to 4 growth buds. Trim the finished main branches back to 20–30 cm (8–12 inches). In summer, trim any long shoots that develop.

Try 'Crimson Bouquet,' with brilliant clusters of bright red flowers, a winner in 2000. Glossy green foliage covers a tall, upright plant, and blooms are lightly fragrant.

Rambler Roses

These plants, including old favourites such as 'Dorothy Perkins,' have fallen out of favour because of their limited flowering season. If you do grow them, remove the branches that produced blooms as soon as flowering is over. Enough young basal growths are produced to replace the old flowering canes.

Shrub and Groundcover Roses

Shrub and groundcover roses, such as 'Bonica,' 'Nozomi' and 'Surry,' play an invaluable part in the garden. Many provide bright red hips or seeds in fall; others are colourful in hanging baskets or other containers, or tumbling over steep, sunny banks. If you want rose hips, do no pruning until the hips disappear.

Treat each plant individually. In most cases, flowers are most likely to be produced on growths formed the previous year, so encourage any tendency to produce strong stems from near the base. Shoots that have flowered poorly may be removed even in summer after flowering to provide room for strong basal growths; in February, thin any old flowering wood. Some grow to outlandish proportions and may be shortened by a third in early spring.

'Kaleidoscope' is a 1999 winner. Its uniquely coloured flowers have tan centres, shading to mauve at the edges. The plant is vigorous and a free bloomer.

Polyantha Roses

These roses, examples of which include 'Mothersday,' 'Cecile Brunner' and 'The Fairy' are distinguished from the floribundas by their large clusters of small flowers, on low plants that bloom intermittently. In early spring, remove any dead canes or twiggy growth, and give all canes a light trimming. Polyanthas constantly develop new canes from the base, and a few of the older ones die to the ground each year. Cut these off at ground level each season.

Floribunda Roses

Floribundas are essentially flowering summer shrubs with clusters of blooms borne continually. Prune them early in the season, along with hybrid tea roses, but cut lightly. If they are treated severely they may take a full season to recover and come into bloom. Trim only to maintain a pleasing form, cutting back about a fourth of the previous year's growth. Like polyanthas, these plants constantly develop new canes from the base; cut off the older ones at ground level each season.

'Betty Boop' has a sweet, fruity fragrance and abundant semi-single blossoms of ivory-yellow with red edges, amid rich green leaves.

Also consider 'Betty Prior,' carmine pink; 'Valentine,' bright red; and 'Sun Flare,' bright yellow.

Climbing Roses

Climbers of the large flowering types are vigorous sports of the bush-type hybrid tea roses. Keep pruning to a minimum; just remove dead wood, weak spindly twigs and side

Climbing rose 'Blaze.' Bob Cain photo

shoots that have flowered. Remove only 1 to 2 of the oldest canes each season, and slightly shorten the remaining ones to encourage new growth.

Cut off old flower heads just above the first bud or eye in the axil of a leaf (its join with the stem) and the climber will give more flowers in summer.

'Fourth of July' was an All-American winner in 1999, and the first climber in twenty-three years to win an AARS award. Velvety red-and-white-striped, semi-double, ruffled blooms grow on long climbing stalks.

Other climbers to try include 'Don Juan,' 'Tropicana' and 'New Dawn.' Prune these varieties in early March.

Pillar Roses

These roses are actually extensions of the bush rose, with a rigid growth. Pillar roses are planted to grow against fences or posts. Prune them in early spring. After 2 to 3 years the plants form thick, hard canes that will be shy about sending out laterals or side shoots over their entire length. On these laterals the flowers grow. Retain five or six of the most vigorous young shoots and cut away any remaining old shoots. Shorten any long laterals by a third. Summer pruning consists of shortening new shoots that are overadventurous. 'Golden Showers' and 'Joseph's Coat' are good examples.

Miniature Roses

This special group of plants are used in border edging or grown in containers. They produce a mass of twiggy growth each year. Cut the centres out, and severely cut back very weak and thin growths in early spring. Some Miniatures produce shoots naturally from the base; these new shoots will replace any older weak growths.

Desirable Miniature roses include 'Baby Darling,' orange-pink; 'Cinderella,' pink; and 'Masquerade,' yellow-red. All-America Rose Selections, an association of rose growers, constantly tests new varieties by growing seedlings in trial grounds, for a 2-year period. The best in the field are designated as worthy of recommendation to gardeners, and are promoted with the symbol familiar to gardeners. Select AARS winners whenever possible for superior results.

The Gift of a Greenhouse

Most coast gardeners find a greenhouse indispensable. There seeds can be started, cuttings can be made, tender, tropical plants can "winter over," experiments with plants can be done, and you can simply experience the joy of working with your plants.

After a few years of living on a coastal island, my husband Al and I installed a lean-to greenhouse over the front veranda of the house. Later, when we moved away from the island, we made arrangements with Vern Mann, one of the young fellows who had grown up on the island, to remove the greenhouse and move it to his home. Our friends loaded us aboard their two fishing boats to take us to Nanoose, BC, with our animals, plants, tools, piano, furniture and other flotsam. We left the greenhouse for Vern to pick up later.

Then one day we received a phone call telling us that the greenhouse on the island was being dismantled. Al rushed to the nearest RCMP office to report the theft. Dutifully he filled out the necessary forms and gave the officers pertinent information.

When he returned, I asked him how it had gone, and he said he thought it wasn't going to be taken very seriously.

"What do you mean, not taken seriously!" I yelled. "Give me the keys to the car." I jumped in and put my lead foot to the pedal. Lucky for me, no patrol cars were in the area. In the spirit of Bellona, the Roman goddess of war, I stormed into the detachment office and shouted, "Who's in charge here?"

continued...

A calm, efficient officer asked, "May I help you, ma'am?"

"Help, that's what I need." I was now pounding on the counter and demanding action. "Do you people realize that we lived on an isolated island and we never bothered you once or asked for help? Now we need you."

The courteous, calm officer asked, "What do you want us to do?"

"Stop the beggars from tearing down the greenhouse on Jedediah Island," I said.

"Okay, lady, we'll check it out when our boat goes by there in a few days."

"What do you mean, in a few days?" Oh, I was really beginning to push my luck. "I'm not leaving this office until you send over a detachment in pursuit of the perpetrators."

The officer put in a call to the Vancouver RCMP and requested a helicopter to check out the problem. He promised to call us immediately when he had heard from the helicopter crew. I made my way home more slowly than I had left.

After several hours, the phone rang. "Is this Mrs. Palmer?" the caller asked.

"Yes."

"We wish to report to you and your husband that we have the fellow in hand that is tearing down your greenhouse. He says his name is Vern Mann."

I fell into a chair, stuttering stupidly that I had given him the greenhouse months ago, and never dreamed it was Vern who was taking it down. Would the caller please apologize to Vern on our behalf, and to the crew of the helicopter?

A few days later, although I hoped they had forgotten me, I went to the RCMP office, ate humble pie and asked forgiveness.

CHAPTER 5

In the House and Around the Yard

Container Gardening

TURN AN OLD STRAW HAT UPSIDE DOWN, line it with plastic or foil, load it with soil, plant a 'Tiny Tim' tomato in the middle, and you have a container garden!

If you are one of the many gardeners who have only a small balcony, deck, windowsill or doorway to grow plants, the answer is containers. They can be colourful and productive in all seasons, and they also have a significant advantage over permanent gardens: they can be moved—in and out of the sun, in and out of shelter—as needed by each plant.

In the yard. Evelyn Heath photo

Container gardening. Adam Gibbs photo

Containers come in many sizes; the trick is to match the plant to the container. If you build your own, use heavy, durable construction material. Several weeks prior to planting, treat the insides and bottoms of wooden containers with a preservative. Check the labels first—creosote, for example, is very toxic to plants.

As the roots of the plant will be restricted, the growing soil should be porous, fertile and filled with organic material. Mix equal parts of peat moss, leaf mould, compost, garden loam and sand. Add aged manure, bone meal and a commercial 5-10-10 fertilizer to the mixture. To each bushel (36 litres/38 qts) of soil, add 250 mL (1 cup) *each* of manure, bone meal and 5-10-10. Set the container, 2.5–5 cm (1–2 inches) off the ground on blocks, bricks or saucers with casters on the bottom. There must be room for air to circulate and water to enter and drain.

The soil in the container must be kept moist but not waterlogged. Overwatering is common. Excess water causes wilting, a dark decay of underground parts and sudden leaf drop, plus yellowing or spotting of leaves. A lack of water often results in leaf scorch, stunting and root damage, as well as premature leaf and flower drop. A general rule for container-grown plants is to water when the topsoil feels dry. Wet the soil deeply and do not water again until the topsoil feels crumbly. On hot, windy summer days, plants such as fuchsia and tuberous begonia may require several waterings. Avoid getting water on the foliage of plants such as rose, tuberous begonia and caladium.

Plants growing in containers often require lighter yet frequent applications of fertilizer. Flowering, fruiting or berry-producing plants thrive when they are fertilized every 10 to 14 days with a liquid food high in phosphorus and potash.

Sun-loving container plants include chrysanthemum, geranium, hyacinth, marigold, nasturtium, pansy, dusty miller, cockscomb, petunia, portulaca, rose, sedum, snapdragon, tulip, verbena, sun rose and zinnia.

Container gardening. Adam Gibbs photo

Container gardening. Adam Gibbs photo

Nicotiana and lobelia in a container. Adam Gibbs photo

Shady garden corners can be brightened with containers of lush caladium, begonia, fuchsia, impatiens, coleus, fern, hosta, balsam, lobelia, vinca and lily-of-the-valley.

Some needled and broad-leafed evergreens to try are dwarf Mugo pine, yew, juniper, euonymus, pieris, dwarf holly, pittosporum, camellia, azalea, rhododendron, bamboo, podocarpus and mahonia, and miniature fir, hemlock and spruce.

You can even grow a mini-garden of vegetables in containers. Tomato, cabbage, onion, chive, carrot, beet, cucumber, kale, leek, leaf lettuce, parsley, pepper, radish, summer squash, Swiss chard and turnip can all be grown successfully in containers.

Berry plants thrive in containers. Ripe red strawberries tumbling out of a strawberry jar, hanging basket or wooden box are a delight all summer. Raspberries, dewberries, loganberries and boysenberries may be trained on wires or trellises and grown in containers out in the full sun.

Dried Flowers

Nature is generous to those who walk through woodsy areas, stop along the roadways, climb mountains and meander through meadows and tidelands to discover a world of material for winter cheer. Weeds, reeds, leaves, seed pods, cones, berries, ferns, unusual stones, pieces of driftwood or mossy tree limbs add warmth to the winter scene.

Garden plants, trees and shrubs yield berries, fruits, seed pods and blossoms that can all be tapped to capture the beautiful colours of summer, simply by being dried and preserved.

Whether it is wild or home-grown, select only mature material. Gather blossoms while they are fresh and full of vivid colour. Harvest flowers, leaves and grasses on a sunny day when there has been no rain or artificial watering for at least 24 hours.

Remove all unnecessary parts from the plant for efficient drying. Strip flowers of their foliage. Cut a weak flower stem 2.5 cm (1 inch) below the blossom, then thrust a piece of fine support wire through the flower and fashion a stem from it. Make sure all plant material is clean, dry and free of excess foliage before it is preserved.

Several methods are used for the preservation of plant material. Drying time varies from 1 to 3 weeks, depending on the material, drying medium and method of drying. You can dry flowers naturally by scattering flower heads loosely on newspapers. Keep these outdoors in a dry, shady place. Baby's breath, larkspur, delphinium, heather, geranium and many grasses retain their natural colours and remain perfect when dried this way.

Bunch short-stemmed flowers such as strawflower, statice, hydrangea and Chinese lantern, and hang them upside down to dry completely, until crisp. Most flowers dry in 1 to 2 weeks, depending on size, type, temperature and amount of dry air circulation.

Some plant material requires special methods and materials for preservation. Sand, laundry borax, cornstarch, alum and white cornmeal are all useful in the dried flower cupboard. Uniodized salt helps plant material to retain bright colours. Add 45 mL (3 tbsp) of it to each litre (qt) of preserving material.

Select a drying box or container large enough to accommodate the blossoms without crowding. A box 40 x 28 x 35 cm (16 x 11 x 14 inches) will take care of 12 to 15 flowers of average size. Line the container with waxed paper. Cover the bottom of the box with 2.5 cm (1 inch) of drying material such as sand, borax or alum. Lay blossoms in the box with their petals smoothed out naturally. Place flowers with large heads, such as dry chrysanthemums, face down and stems up. Place stalk-like flowers such as gladiolus in a horizontal position or head down. Flowers like tulips and poppies should be opened and their petals spread out.

Using your fingers or a small cup, sift the drying material gently over the blossoms to a depth of 2.5 cm (1 inch), making certain it works itself in between all the petals, until the flower is covered completely. Leave the cover or top of the container off during the drying process. Most flowers require 6 to 7 days to dry by this method. Small flowers like violets will be ready for arrangements in 2 to 3 days, daffodils in about 4 days, azalea flowers 5 to 6 days and marigolds and zinnias 4 to 5 days. Larger flowers may take as long as 3 weeks to dry completely.

To determine whether the flowers are dry, gently remove the drying material from one blossom. If it is firm and brittle, the flower is ready. If you won't be using the dried material immediately, store it in moisture-proof containers. It is essential to keep delicate blossoms and other plant parts absolutely dry, so protect them from humidity and other dampness.

Floral prints may be designed from pressed flowers, ferns or leaves of trees and shrubs. Gather the material for pressing on a dry, sunny day. Place it between layers of absorbent paper towels, tissues or blotting paper. Set a heavy weight on top. Another method of pressing leaves is to smooth them flat and place between sheets of waxed paper with the waxed side of the paper against the leaf. Then weigh them down until the leaves are dry and crisp as taffeta.

Prepare a solution of 1 part glycerine and 2 parts water and cover leaves of *Magnolia grandiflora*, aucuba, ivy, beech, photinia and rhododendron with this liquid. Let the leaves soak until the liquid is absorbed. They will assume coppery brown and red tones, or an intense green colour. Submerge soft-leafed plants such as ivy in the glycerine solution for 4 to 5 days. For branches of shrubs, first scrape the lower part of the branch or stem with a knife to provide more penetration area, then submerge the cut stems in the solution to a depth of 7.5–10 cm (3–4 inches).

The time required to colour and preserve foliage varies greatly. Beech, holly and osmanthus will be ready in a few days. *Magnolia grandiflora* may require 2 to 3 weeks. Rhododendron, aucuba and plants with long leaves often need 4 to 6 weeks to absorb the solution fully.

For the glycerine and water treatment, choose leaves that are fresh and crisp. Cut the branches of fall-tinted leaves when the leaves are beginning to dry on the tree and are in the early stages of colouring. Wash the leaves well and pound or crush the bottom 5 cm (2 inches) of the stem to maximize absorption. The leaf is preserved when tiny drops of moisture appear on it.

Large-bladed grasses, reeds and leafy branches are treated by placing cut stems in clear water. They absorb the water quickly. No additional water needs to be given and the material dries gradually.

Care and Cutting of Garden Flowers

One of the great pleasures of gardening is that you can bring its sparkling beauty indoors and share it with friends by gathering fresh flowers. Plan a flower garden that will produce continuous colour from the earliest crocus to the last chrysanthemum. Early spring-flowering bulbs planted at 2-week intervals provide flowers over a longer period of time than if they are all planted at once.

Plant gladiolus every 10 days, beginning in April and continuing through June, for a long-lasting display. Sow seeds of candytuft, lupin, godetia, pansy, stock, petunia, snapdragon, pinks and sweet alyssum indoors in March and April. They will be ready for transplanting after the spring-flowering bulbs have faded. Zinnia, marigold, verbena, rudbeckia, larkspur, cosmos and calendula may be seeded in the open ground in May for cut flowers in August, September and October.

Delphinium, phlox, snapdragon, verbena, campanula, zinnia and many other plants may be forced to produce more flowers by cutting back or pinching out the top main stem. This practice results in stockier, more productive plants.

For the freshest crisp cut flowers, harvest the blooms at the proper stage. Snip gladiolus when the second floret is open; iris when the first bud is nearly open; peony when half-open; poppy in the bud stage just before opening; rose when the outer petals begin to loosen; dahlia when fully open. Water lily and passionflower should be cut one day before opening. Drop warm paraffin wax into the centre of the bloom to hold open the petals of these and other open flowers that tend to close quickly. Remove the centre stamens of lilies and other flowers to extend their life.

Cut the flower stems in the late afternoon or early evening. Flowers produce their food through photosynthesis during the day and use that food during the night. Blooms taken in the morning will not last as long as those cut late in the day because their energy is lower. Flowers should be cut, not pulled or torn from the plant. Use a sharp cutting tool. A dull-edged tool tends to block the water conduction tubes in the stems.

Most flowers wilt a few minutes after they are cut if not quickly plunged into warm water. Remove all foliage that will be under water after the flowers are arranged. Foliage causes bacterial growth, which clogs the water-conducting tissues in the stems. Woody-stemmed flowers such as rose, lilac, stock, chrysanthemum and rhododendron should be stripped of most of their foliage before arranging. Cut rose stems diagonally, split them and scrape them, and plunge the bottom third of the stems into water. If cut roses wilt, they may revive if you place their stems in very hot water and let stand until the water is cold.

Dahlia, poppy, calla lily, hydrangea, poinsettia, zinnia and other flower stems that exude a milky substance can be conditioned by inserting their cut ends in boiling water for 30 seconds before being placed in warm water.

Some arrangers sear the cut end of each stem with a candle flame. After they have been seared, immerse the stems in cold water. Water will be taken in along the stock above the part that has been sealed.

Lilac, dogwood, flowering cherry and other woody branches hold their flowers fresher longer when the bark is peeled back, or the branches are bruised or crushed 5–10 cm (2–4 inches) from the cut ends. Leave the stems in cold water overnight before arranging.

Coloured foliage will keep its colour longer if it is kept in a solution of equal parts water and glycerine.

To keep orchids over a long period, lift their stems out of the water for 1 to 2 hours every day. Orchids tend to absorb too much water, and this causes petals to become transparent and waterlogged.

A freshly cut flower stem absorbs water freely. Old cut ends tend to seal off the stalk, shutting off the supply of water. With a sharp knife or shears, cut off a bit more of the stalk every other day, and fill the container or vase with fresh warm water. Avoid crowding flower stems into a vase or other container. Keep the water level high, except for zinnias, whose stems decay rapidly in water. Place the cut ends of zinnias in 5 cm (2 inches) of water at the most.

Commercial flower preservatives are available to provide food for cut flowers. They also contain acidifiers and mild fungicides to prevent micro-organisms from clogging the stems. Cut the stems just before adding the preservatives. Many gardeners use a homemade formulation for keeping flowers fresh: to each litre (qt) of water, add 30 mL (2 tbsp) of white vinegar and 15 mL (1 tbsp) of sugar.

Forced Flowering of Trees and Shrubs Indoors in Winter

Close the curtain on the dreary, grey days of winter and bring out an armload of spring-flowering branches. Suddenly it's blossom time! The bare limbs of many flowering shrubs can be taken indoors in winter and forced into early bloom. These include forsythia, dogwood, cherry, crabapple, magnolia, quince, pear, camellia, pieris, wisteria, peach, plum, blueberry, almond and red maple. You can usually recognize flower buds because they are more plump and rounded than the slender, tapering buds of leaves. Material cut for pre-seasonal bloom should be vigorous, firm and bursting with buds. Pick 1-year-old branches at least 60–90 cm (2–3 ft) long for best results.

You can obtain branches or twigs for forced flowering during a light, corrective early spring pruning operation, when the plants are slightly shaped and thinned.

Take branches from several plants to avoid denuding a single plant. Harvest them on a mild day after a rain, when the outdoor temperature is above freezing. Frozen branches will not produce colour when taken indoors. Working with care so as not to alter the form of the branch, make clean diagonal cuts with sharp pruning shears to prevent injury to the remaining plant. (A diagonal cut also lifts the stem end off the bottom of the vase so that there is more water absorption.)

Immediately after cutting the branches, submerge them entirely in tepid water for 24 hours. Then crush the ends of the branches, or make a new clean cut on each end, and place them deep in cool water. Keep the branches at an indoor temperature of 16–18°C (60–65°F). In the early stage of forcing, the branches need not be placed in a light room. But when the flower buds have become plump, move the branches into a location with daylight, allowing the colours to develop naturally. When they show a touch of colour, you can place them in arrangements.

Forcing times vary with the plant. Red maple produces small, orange-red flower clusters in about 2 weeks. Flowering almond and pussy willow usually force in 2 weeks. Forsythia takes 1 to 2 weeks and flowering quince 3 to 4 weeks.

Grape hyacinth. Deb McVittie photo

If you want to accelerate the flowering process, place the branches in a plastic bag, saturate a cloth with household ammonia, place the cloth in the bag with the branches, close the bag tightly and leave for about 30 minutes. Be sure to work in a well-ventilated area during all stages of this process. Remove the branches from the bag and place them in a deep container of water. Sprinkle the branches with water every day.

Spring-Flowering Bulbs for Indoors

Prolong the gardening season with indoor plantings of golden daffodils, sweet-scented hyacinths and bold goblet-shaped tulips. When started indoors in the fall, these and other spring-flowering bulbs may be encouraged or forced to flower indoors in late December, January and February.

Begin by selecting quality bulbs that are suitable for forcing indoors. Daffodils and narcissus for forcing include 'King Alfred,' 'Golden Harvest,' 'Carlton,' 'Gold Medal,' 'Rembrandt,' 'Geranium,' 'Cheerfulness,' 'Cragford,' 'Thalia' and 'Paper Whites.'

Tulips suitable for indoor growing include 'Cassini,' 'Bing Crosby,' 'Paul Richter,' 'Apricot Beauty,' 'Merry Widow,' 'Preludium,' 'Levant,' 'Christmas Marvel,' 'Charles Pax,' 'Bellona,' 'Madame Spoor,' 'Clara Butt,' 'Prince of Austria,' 'Zwanenburg,' 'Krelage's Triumph,' 'Orange Wonder,' 'Atom,' 'First Lady,' 'Hibemia,' 'Princess Beatrix,' 'Copland's Favorite,' 'Insurpassable,' 'William Pitt,' 'General Eisenhower,' 'Gudeshnik,' 'President Kennedy' and 'Queen of Sheba.'

Hyacinths to bloom indoors during winter are 'Jan Bos,' 'Anna Marie,' 'Eros,' 'Lady Derby,' 'Ostara,' 'Bismark,' 'L'Innocence,' 'Edelweiss,' 'City of Haarlem,' 'Delft Blue,' 'King of the Blues,' 'Queen of the Pinks,' 'Carnegie,' 'La Victoire' and 'Amethyst.'

Crocuses for forcing include 'Pickwick,' 'Joan of Arc,' 'Grand Maitre,' 'Peter Pan,' 'Enchantress,' 'King of the Striped,' 'Remembrance' and 'Yellow Mammoth.'

Freesia, scilla, anemone and other spring-flowering bulbs and corms also may be forced to flower indoors.

Forcing will be successful only if the bulbs go through a cold rooting period of 6 to 10 weeks. This procedure, which helps to keep the bulbs dark as well as cold, can be done outdoors or in a refrigerator.

To root, prepare an outdoor trench 30–35 cm (12–14 inches) deep, about 30 cm (12 inches) wide, and long enough to hold all of your pots or other containers. Place 7.5–10 cm (3–4 inches) of gravel in the trench to ensure perfect water drainage. The size of the planting container depends upon the type of bulb planted. A container 12.5–15 cm (5–6 inches) in diameter will accommodate 3 to 5 hyacinths, tulips or small narcissus. A dozen crocus or grape hyacinth bulbs will fill a 15 cm (6-inch) container.

Set bulbs close together but not touching, in planting soil that consists of 2 parts garden loam, 1 part peat moss and 1 part sand or charcoal. Plant daffodil (narcissus) and hyacinth with their necks slightly exposed. Crocus, snowdrop and grape hyacinth should be set about 2.5 cm (1 inch) below the soil. Water the plantings thoroughly, then place on top of the drainage material in the outdoor trench. Fill around and over the pots with soil.

If the weather is dry, water the planting in the trench to make certain that the bulbs do not dry during their rooting period. Forced bulbs need an evenly moist soil at all times.

Over the planting, place insulating material such as heavy building paper, evergreen boughs or thick burlap. Sink the planting in the trench so the brim or top of the container is covered with insulating material to about 20 cm (8 inches).

Indoor gardeners without the luxury of an outdoor cooling area may pre-cool their bulbs in a home refrigerator for 6 weeks at a temperature of 4°C (40°F). Then place them immediately in soil or water and pebbles. Keep in a semi-light, warm place of about 10–13°C (50–55°F) for 2 weeks to encourage slow growth and a sturdy root system. Then move them into a lighter and warmer area until the buds begin to open. When the buds show colour, move them out of the direct sunlight and keep the planting at a temperature of 18–20°C (65–70°F).

After you take potted bulbs from the outdoor trench, move them to a place with light but no sun, and a temperature as near to 10°C (50°F) as possible, for about 2 weeks. Keep the soil constantly moist. When the flower buds show, move the plants to a warmer and lighter place to flower. Turn the planting around every few days so the flower stems and leaves grow tall and straight. Continue to maintain a moist soil.

After the flowers fade and the foliage turns yellow and withers, cut down on watering to cure the bulbs properly: water only enough to keep the leaves from shrivelling. After severe spring frosts are finished, move the bulbs, container and all, into the garden. When the leaves and stems pull away easily, clean the top growth from the bulbs, take them out of the containers and plant each bulb in the garden permanently. Some will recover and flower in the garden the following season; others may take another year; a few will not return.

Native Gardens

One of the great excitements of spring on the West Coast is discovering drifts of native plants. Take a walk among the majesty of the mighty evergreens. Under the forest giants snow lingers; melting slowly, it feeds springs and rivers. Deep in the woods, along slow-moving streams and scrambling over rotten logs, indigenous plants explode with colour.

Search out the native plants and observe the conditions they like. What type of soil do they grow in? Do they live in shade or sun? Are their roots growing in wet, spongy ground or clinging to barren rocks? The objective is to provide native plants with approximately the same conditions in the home garden as they enjoyed in the wild. Imitate their original habitats as closely as possible and they will thrive.

Ideally you will search seed catalogues and specialty nurseries for your native plants. Sometimes you can salvage them legally from areas that are about to be developed for roadbuilding or construction. If you do collect specimens from the wild, practise conservation. Remove only 1 or 2 plants of each type from an area, only after ascertaining that they are not endangered species. Remember: other plants and animals may be relying on your specimen for food or shelter.

Old-growth Douglas-fir in Helliwell Park on Hornby Island, BC. Bob Cain photo

Root-prune large plants in the season before you plan to take them from the woods. To root-prune trees or large shrubs, use a sharp shovel and take a brush hook or axe along as well. Dig a circle around the tree at least 3 times the diameter of the trunk in all directions. For example, if the trunk is 7.5 cm (3 inches) in diameter, cut a circle 23–45 cm (9–18 inches) around the tree. Cut as deeply as possible, but do not move the plant until the next season.

Take bulbs and flowering plants after they have bloomed. Whenever possible, mark the plants you want in spring or summer and return to claim them in the fall or early winter, when they are dormant. Dig native plants after a heavy rain, using a heavy digging fork, shovel and pick. As the plants are removed, wrap the soil and the root ball in wet burlap, moss or wet newspaper. Dig only as many as can be transplanted the same day they are taken. When you have brought them home, plunge the roots into water for a few hours or overnight. Never pull a plant bare-rooted from its habitat.

Take to your garden as much of the woodsy soil as possible from the surrounding area. If the plants have been growing in a clay or sandy-type soil, try to duplicate it in the home garden. Set native plants slightly deeper than they grew naturally, and keep the soil around the transplants moist until their root system is re-established. After the plant begins to take hold, you may apply organic fertilizers. Bone meal, blood meal, fish meal, cottonseed meal and dried manure work well. Fertilize native plants sparingly in early spring.

Design your native garden to imitate the original surroundings of the plants you like. For a backdrop use indigenous conifers such as hemlock, fir and cedar. Dogwood and vine maple work well as accents.

No spring wildflower garden is complete without trilliums. Western trillium (*Trillium ovatum*) has stems up to 45 cm (18 inches) tall and white flowers which fade to pink. Trilliums are threatened species in some parts of North America, so buy them from a wildflower specialist rather than taking them from the wild. Many species are available from growers.

The lady's slipper (*Cypripedium*) is a true aristocrat of the wild garden. It needs light shade and a humus-filled soil. The variety *pubescens*, a country cousin of the orchid, grows along mountain streams. Deep yellow and brown, its fragrant flowers grow in the shape of slippers.

False Solomon's seal is found in shaded woods. From April to June, a sweep of white blossoms decorates an arching stem. When exposed, the roots show "scars" left by growths of previous years; these scars resemble ancient seals. Ruby red berries appear in autumn.

The observant woods walker often will spot a weird, white, almost ghostly plant with waxy blooms that suggest an upside-down meerschaum pipe. This is Indian pipe (*Monotropia uniflora*), a saprophytic plant: it feeds on decayed organic matter. Its ghost-

Indian plum. Adam Gibbs photo

like appearance is due to its lack of green colouring, or chlorophyll. The plant pushes up through gloomy, dank forest floors and rarely reaches 30 cm (12 inches) in height.

Yellow dogtooth violet (*Erythronium grandiflorum*) is a subalpine native. The golden-yellow flowers appear in April and May, nodding on thin stalks. *Erythronium oregonum*, the white fawn lily, blooms in the woods in spring.

Shasta lily is a spicy, sweet-scented flowering California native. Blooms grow in clusters with 2 to 20 flowers on a stem. They do best when grown in a damp, humus-filled soil and under the high shade of conifers.

Bunchberry (*Cornus canadensis*) grows under conifers and may be found creeping over rotten logs. Tiny, white starflowers similar to those of the gigantic dogwood appear on this evergreen ground cover in April, May and June. Bunchberry thrives in a shady area in an acid-type soil.

Swamp laurel (*Kalmia polifolia*) grows in sphagnum bogs along with native cranberry. The leaves are evergreen and the rose-purple flowers are saucer-shaped. Below the edges of the petals are 10 shallow pockets, in which are caught the tips of 10 curved stamens. When an insect lights upon the floral cup the stamens pop out from their retaining pouches, showering the intruder with pollen. Swamp laurel is poisonous.

Monkey flower (*Mimulus*) bears small trumpet-shaped blossoms. Some varieties have yellow flowers, others range from rose-purple to pink. Monkey flower grows in damp, shady locations.

Bearberry, also called kinnikinnick (*Arctostaphylos uva-ursi*), is found in dry soil in open sun. A West Coast aboriginal name for the plant was *sacacomis*. The French made a pun by calling it sac-a-commis, from *sac* ("bag") and *commis* ("clerk"), since the clerks of the Hudson's Bay Company habitually carried the dried leaves (which they smoked) with them in pouches.

Trillium ovatum. Sandra Evelyn photo

The native rhododendron (*Rhododendron macrophyllum*) was recorded in 1792 by Archibald Menzies, a botanist-naturalist with Captain George Vancouver's expedition. Flowers are orchid pink and leaves are long and evergreen.

In spring, flowering currant (*Ribes sanguineum*) bursts into bloom, covering its deciduous foliage with clusters of bright crimson or pink flowers. Rufous hummingbirds buzz and chase each other from bush to bush for the nectar. Bird and bush are inseparable in springtime.

Ocean spray (*Holodiscus*) is also known as ironwood because of its strength and hardness. The Native people of the coast hardened the wood further over a fire and used it for digging sticks. It is also known as arrow wood because arrow and spear shafts were made from its long branches. Stems are covered with foam-like creamy flowers in June. The plant can attain a height of 2.4–6 m (8–20 ft). Foliage is light green. The shrub makes an excellent windbreak. It likes full sun and almost any soil.

At the edge of a pool or along a meandering stream, violet, fern and marsh marigold will accompany iris, lily and wood anemone.

*Yellow dogtooth violet (*Erythronium grandiflorum*).*
Adam Gibbs photo

In dark corners of a native garden, plant Indian pipe, wild ginger, false Solomon's seal and gaultheria. Lily-of-the-valley, mayapple and jack-in-the-pulpit are some cultivated plants that will also perform well in the shade.

Wild roses, native honeysuckle (*Lonicera ciliosa*) and California poppy blend in with cultivated garden plants like dusty miller and lavender in hot, dry, sunny situations. Sunny, moist sites are excellent for penstemon, columbine, lupin and aster.

Seaside gardeners should consider wild rose, oceanspray, bearberry, lupin, goldenrod and rosy plectritis (sea blush).

Oregon grape, azalea, alpine fir, pine, spruce, juniper and aspen are also available for the native garden.

Yellow Monkeyflower and Rosy Plectritis. Adam Gibbs photo

Lawn Seeding and Sodding

Spring or early autumn is an ideal time to start a new lawn. Lawn seeds germinate quickly and sod roots become well established in the warm, moist soil.

The first rule of lawns is: A turf is only as good as its foundation. Before laying sod or seeding a turf, establish grade on the site. Make certain that the contour slopes away from the home or other buildings. A slight pitch (as little as 15–20 cm/6–8 inches per 30 m/100 ft) lets excess water run off and discourages puddles and wet spots.

Whether a lawn is seeded or sodded, it will need a well-prepared base sod or seed bed. First, cultivate the lawn area with a mechanical tiller or heavy spade. After turning the soil to a depth of 30–45 cm (12–18 inches), remove large stones, sticks and other debris. Rake the area clean and level. Drag a heavy plank to level the surface even more. Spread on a layer of organic material, such as compost, peat moss, or aged manure, 7.5–10 cm (3–4 inches) thick. Add ground dolomite limestone at the rate of 22.5 kg (50 lbs) to each 90 m² (1,000 sq ft). Water this into the topsoil. Rake into the topsoil a commercial fertilizer formulated for new lawns with approximately 3 parts nitrogen, 1 part phosphorus and 2 parts potash. Next, roll the surface with a heavy lawn roller to smooth any humps or hollows. Roll firmly enough so that walking over the ground will leave no footprints.

Lawn seed mixtures containing bluegrasses, bent grasses and fescues work well in coastal areas. Use 900 g (2 lbs) of mixture to cover 90 m² (1,000 sq ft) of seed bed. Spread the seed evenly with a mechanical spreader. Divide the seed in half. Spread one half back and forth across the area in one direction; then spread the rest at right angles to the first seeding.

Rake the seed into the topsoil lightly, enough to cover it by 6 mm (1/4 inch), or mulch over the seeded area with 6 mm (1/4 inch) of fine peat moss. Roll with a lawn roller about half filled with water, and lightly sprinkle the finished planting with water. Keep the seeded area slightly moist during germination. Greening will begin in 10 to 14 days.

Mow the newly seeded lawn for the first time when it is 5 cm (2 inches) high. Use a sharp mower, and cut only when the grass is dry and the soil firm. Set the mower to cut off 1 cm (1/2 inch). Mow the lawn in one direction. Leave the mower set at 1 cm and cut it again at right angles to the first cutting; then mow it a third time on the diagonal. Leave the clippings on the turf: they provide valuable mulch.

The result of uneven seeding and fertilizing. Peter A. Robson photo

Sodding a new lawn gives a home garden or commercial site an instant turf. Before sodding, thoroughly prepare the soil, as for seeding, and provide for drainage.

Unroll the sod strips carefully and lay them on the prepared soil bed. A 2x4 pressed firmly against the side of the turf will push it firmly against the adjacent strip and eliminate any seam between strips. Stagger the sod strips as you would stagger courses of bricks on a wall. This will strengthen the turf, promote uniformity and help prevent visible seams. If the sod is installed on hills or inclines, drive small stakes through the sod to hold it in place.

After the sod is in place, roll it with a lawn roller half filled with water. This compacts the sod and encourages it to adhere to the subsoil. Water the new sod deeply. Continue to maintain a moist sod bed until the roots are well established.

Lawn Maintenance

There is no single secret to growing and maintaining a beautiful lawn. A weed-free and disease-free lawn requires precise soil preparation, adequate fertilization and correct mowing and watering practices.

Soil fertility is one of the most important factors in producing and maintaining a fine-quality turf all year round. When the soil lacks necessary nutrients, inferior grasses and weeds dominate. The soil becomes increasingly acid in its reaction, and moss and other unwanted plants thrive. The soil becomes more impervious to water and less resistant to injury from drought and insect attacks.

Gardeners can choose from many formulas, types and brands of lawn fertilizers. Following are a few pointers on selecting the right fertilizer for your garden.

Fertilizer analysis, showing the percentages of nitrogen, phosphorus, potash and other essential elements, is printed on all packages. Nitrogen is added for bright green colour and leaf growth; phosphorus stimulates root development; potash increases the vigour of the grass and makes it more resistant to diseases. In a lawn fertilizer labelled 6-2-4, each 45 kg (100 lbs) of fertilizer material contains 2.7 kg (6 lbs) of nitrogen, 900 g (2 lbs) of phosphorus and 1.8 kg (4 lbs) of potash. (The rest is a carrying medium.)

Nitrogen is the key element. It must be supplied at a constant and uniform rate to keep a turf vigorous and green. A good lawn fertilizer is formulated with multiple sources of nitrogen, each source designed to release its nitrogen at different times to avoid overstimulation, with a surge of growth and greenness all at once rather than over a long period. Overfertilizing with a very high-nitrogen fertilizer would create mowing problems, low disease resistance and thatch buildup. Apply nitrogen to lawn soils each year, at the rate of 2.7 kg (6 lbs) per 90 m^2 (1,000 sq ft).

Apply lawn fertilizers with a mechanical spreader when the turf is dry, and water it in immediately after application.

Frequent mowing is also essential. Grass should be cut often enough to ensure that not more than 8 mm (about 1/3 inch) of leaf is removed at a single mowing.

On an established turf, the question of whether to rake up lawn clippings or leave them where they fall is a subject of continuing debate among gardeners. Grasses differ in their patterns of growth and mowing requirements: bluegrasses and fine fescues arch sharply upward from underground stems, for example, and do not ordinarily build up a mat of old stems or thatch. They are best mowed to a height of 3.5–5 cm (1 1/2–2 inches). Stoloniferous grasses, such as bents, have trailing runners that do best when mowed short—about 2 cm (3/4 inch). If bent grasses are allowed to grow tall, brown stubble develops underneath. Whatever the grass varieties in the lawn, the lawn mower should be kept sharp.

Controlled watering in spring and summer is important. Avoid frequent light sprinkling, especially in the late afternoon or evening. Moisten the soil to a depth of at least 20 cm (8 inches) twice a week in dry weather. Thorough watering aids in the development of deep, vigorous roots. Light watering encourages shallow roots and weeds.

Ground Covers

Bright, luxurious ground cover plants will carpet areas where a lawn is impractical. Low-growing plants lend a natural appearance to a garden and need minimum maintenance. As well, often they help prevent soil erosion, protect the roots of trees and shrubs, and provide an aesthetically pleasing setting for larger plants.

Ground covers lend a quality to the landscape that may be impossible to create with turf or other plantings. Low-growing plants provide variation in plant height, texture and colour. They give strong definition to ground patterns and are often the most significant unifying element in a total planting composition.

When selecting ground cover, consider how rapidly different plants spread, how much shade and/or sun each one prefers, what moisture they need, and whether they tolerate traffic. Many cover plants have definite requirements, which are usually listed on tags attached to the plants. (See suggestions for plants at the end of this section.)

Hardly a muddy finger need be lifted in caring for ground cover plants if their planting soil is prepared well. Turn and work the soil to a depth of 25–45 cm (10–18 inches). Spade in generous amounts of peat moss, ground bark, compost and aged manure. If the soil is compacted and drains poorly, work in generous amounts of coarse sand as well.

Level the planting area and rake a 5-10-10 commercial fertilizer into the top few inches, at the rate of 1.3 kg (3 lbs) to 9 m² (100 sq ft) of planting area. Water the fertilizer well into the soil.

Spacing depends on the plant: small growing plants are placed 15–20 cm (6–8 inches) apart. Vine-type plants are set 30–38 cm (12–15 inches) apart. Small shrubs are generally placed 90 cm (3 ft) apart on centre. The closer the spacing, the quicker the covering. Stagger the plants in a diamond shape pattern rather than row-on-row squares.

Set the plants into the soil so that the crown is even with the surface. Firm the soil around the roots and water the planting thoroughly and often until the plants are established. Watering and mulching are especially important in new plantings. Once established, a ground cover requires only normal rains on the West Coast. In hot, dry weather, when additional watering is necessary, soak the ground deeply once a week. Avoid frequent light sprinklings of water.

It often requires 2 to 3 years for ground cover plants to carpet an area and become well established. If they become leggy or straggly, prune them severely. Pruning may be done either in early spring or in autumn, according to the habits of the particular plant.

To encourage healthy, vigorous growth, apply a 5-10-10 fertilizer in the spring. If weeds spring up around ground covers before they are well established—a common problem—avoid the use of weed killer. Instead, control weeds by pulling them and covering the area with a heavy mulch. After the plants are well established, a weed killer such as Casoron may be applied. As with any chemicals, always read and follow the directions carefully.

Ground cover plants suitable for dry, sunny areas include: sedums, *Mahonia repens*, cotoneaster (low-growing species), creeping thyme, potentilla, winter jasmine, broom, aubretia, *Phlox subulata, Euonymus fortunei*, kinnikinnick, Mugo pine, creeping ceanothus, dwarf junipers, wild strawberries and heathers.

Wild strawberry. Adam Gibbs photo

Hen-and-chickens. Adam Gibbs photo

Deep shade-loving cover plants include fern, *Andromeda polifolia*, gaultheria, dwarf rhododendron and azalea, *Cornus canadensis*, ivy, *Viburnum davidii*, pachysandra, alpine epimedium, primrose, violet, ajuga, vinca, hosta, hypericum and mosses.

Traffic-tolerant plants include creeping thyme, baby's tears, mint, moss and chamomile. Many of these plants give off a wonderful scent when stepped on.

Ground covers adaptable to moist conditions include forget-me-not, dwarf phlox, violet, lily-of-the-valley, *Sarcococca humilis*, pachysandra, ajuga, vinca and fern.

Infrequently watered areas can be covered with kinnikinick, heather, sedum, veronica, creeping phlox, berberis, sun rose, ice plant and thyme.

Garden Pools

The sound and sight of water adds a refreshing note to the garden landscape. Pools bubble with life, nourish aquatic plants and fish, and attract birds, and they give gardeners the opportunity to grow many lovely and uncommon plants that they could not otherwise hope to raise.

Jim and Pam Gordon's pickerel weed. Bob Cain photo

In the House and Around the Yard

Creating a water garden can be as simple as sinking a watertight keg in the ground, or as spectacular as installing a crashing waterfall. Whatever the form—pool, stream, fountain or waterfall—it must be planned as an integral part of the general landscape. Give careful consideration to the site, type and design.

The form or shape will depend largely upon the general plan of the garden. Formal gardens call for geometrically designed water gardens or sculptured pools. Smooth-surfaced materials such as tiles, slate, bricks or finished concrete and formal plantings are in keeping with geometrical or sculptured designs.

The more naturalistic West Coast garden emphasizes a flowing natural outline. Weathered rocks, rugged contours and native plants belong in such a setting.

Whatever a garden's style, construction of the pool or stream should be as inconspicuous as possible. A low area is an ideal site for a pool. Other major considerations are watertightness, drainage and water supply, including the control of inlet, outlet and overflow. Concrete gives excellent results in construction of a pool. Fibreglass and heavy black plastic sheeting are also good materials, and they are more economical.

Jim and Pam Gordon's 'Escarboucle' in flower. Bob Cain photo

If you build a concrete pool more than 4.5 m long and 5.4 m wide (15x12 ft), you must reinforce the sides with steel rods or heavy wire. Pour half the concrete, then place the reinforcement. Trowel the concrete and leave the surface rough on a natural pool. To give the pool a more rustic appearance, work in small, flat stones while the concrete is still wet.

Fibreglass pools are made with glass-fibre cloth and polyester resins. Fibre cloth is available in rolls and can be cut and fitted easily. Cover the bottom and walls of the pool with the glass-fibre cloth. Extend the cloth over the edge of the excavation and overlap the pieces. With a paintbrush, thoroughly soak the cloth by brushing on the polyester resin (which is also a catalyst).

Many garden centres, nurseries and building supply outlets offer heavy plastic or fibreglass ready-to-install pools. To install such a prefabricated pool, place it in the excavation so that the rim is 5–7.5 cm (2–3 inches) above the ground. Fill in around and beneath the container with fine gravel, and conceal the rim with an overhanging edge of patio blocks, bricks or stones. Add low-growing plants along the edge.

Pool water should be drained frequently. A plastic pipe drain is flexible and easily sends water in the direction you want it to go. Put it in place at the time the pool is constructed. The inlet pipe may be brought in below the surface of the water. Fill the pond with water and let it stand for 3 to 4 days, then drain. Repeat the procedure four times before allowing fish or plants to enter the pool.

Few landscapes have a natural flow of water on the site. Recirculating electric pumps are available that return water to the upper part of a pool after it cascades down.

It takes some self-control for a gardener not to overplant the pool site by crowding plants into the pool. Allow for open spaces. Water plants such as lilies do not grow well in moving water: they need a quiet home, so do not plant them near fountains or under water currents.

Water gardening provides a means for the cultivation of exotic water lily, lotus, hyacinth and other aquatic plants. With a source of water, you can grow these plants as easily as you can grow a head of lettuce in the garden. Water plants perform best where they receive sunlight the greater part of the day.

Grow water lilies in half-barrels, boxes, tubs or plastic or concrete containers with dimensions of at least 35x45x25 cm (14x18x10 inches).

To plant, half fill the container with garden loam enriched with decomposed manure and compost. Press the roots of water lilies into the soft soil and cover the planting with fine gravel to keep the water clear. Give water lilies 15–30 cm (6–12 inches) of water over their roots. Support their containers with bricks or stones to bring the roots to the correct depth.

In spring, feed the lilies with a 10-8-6 fertilizer. Add 250 mL (1 cup) of fertilizer to each container of lilies annually. Hardy water lilies have rhizomes—heavy, half-buried horizontal stems from which roots grow. Plant the blind end of the rhizome in a corner with the growing shoot aimed out into the open soil. Bury the blind end, but leave the end with the eyes—or perhaps young leaves—sticking above the soil slightly. Cover the planting with fine gravel 2.5 cm (1 inch) thick.

Hardy water lilies can survive coastal winters, provided their roots do not freeze. If a severe winter is expected, cover the plants with heavy burlap and drain the pool of water. In late autumn, cut off the foliage as it deteriorates. Divide and replant hardy lilies every 2 years.

Tropical lilies are splashy, exotic beauties. They are fragrant and come in almost every colour. Many hold their blooms high on stems 30 cm (12 inches) or more above water level, and their flowers may be more than 30 cm in diameter. These lilies are either diurnal or nocturnal. Canny gardeners utilize both. The night-blooming ones stay open early in the morning and close at about the time the day bloomers begin to unfurl. Lily flowers grow on erect stems several inches above water level. Plant tropical lilies in the centre of the container. This plant has no true rhizome, but a sort of knob with fleshy roots growing from it. Spread out the roots naturally and cover them, leaving the eyes or growth buds exposed.

Water lily. Deb McVittie photo

If the garden pool is small, miniature or pygmy lilies are appropriate. These tiny gems are found in both tropical and hardy varieties. Pygmies produce tiny leaves and glistening flowers in shades of blue, purple, yellow, pink and sparkling white.

The lotus is among the most fascinating of water plants. The plant holds its giant leaves 60–90 cm (2–4 ft) out of the water and its stems support fragrant blooms 25–35 cm (10–14 inches) in diameter, high above. The lotus blooms when planted in a tub or half-barrel set on top of the ground, but it is at its best in a pool of water, planted in a large box 90 cm (3 ft) square and 30 cm (1 ft) deep.

The container should be half filled with garden loam, enriched with decomposed manure and compost. Plant the lotus shallow: no deeper than 5 cm (2 inches). Water 15–20 cm (6–8 inches) deep generally covers the planting.

The lotus plant forms tubers in the fall, and winters over in this condition. Don't disturb the tubers; wait until the water warms in the spring before transplanting. Each spring fertilize lotus plants with a commercial 10-8-6 plant food.

Some aquatic plants float on the surface of the water with their roots hanging downward. Duckweed, with its small, bright green leaves, looks like polka dots floating on the water. Duckweed is an excellent fish food.

Water lettuce, with velvety green leaves, looks something like garden lettuce. It keeps down algae by starving it out. Young fish hide in its bushy roots. Water lettuce produces oxygen in the water and absorbs carbon dioxide released by fish, thus keeping the water healthy.

Water poppy is a small plant that ambitiously produces large, poppy-like flowers with 3 petals. The roots of this aquatic plant must be planted in soil.

Water hyacinth has inflated leaf petioles that enable the plant to float and grow without its roots in soil. Lavender-blue blooms decorate the plant. Its roots catch and protect goldfish spawn.

Parrot feather trails over the water surface lightly. Its feathery, bright green foliage adds grace to a pond.

Fish make a pool more lively with their colours and flashing movements. They are scavengers and they eat mosquitoes. Snails and tadpoles complete the balance of nature in a pond or pool.

The Gardener's Calendar

AS THE SAYING GOES, A GARDEN IS A THING OF BEAUTY and a joy forever. One of the secrets to good gardening is to look after the garden all year round. Give it some regular attention and your garden will reward you in all seasons.

January

January is a month of anticipation on the coast. With just a few days of sun, winter's adversities are soon forgotten as the scents and sights of spring emerge. This is an excellent time to take a stroll in the garden, combining the pleasure of a winter walk with a good look at the garden and its overall shape and layout.

Snow on Pyracantha coccinea. Adam Gibbs photo

- Move or discard old and outgrown shrubs and trees. Select new plants that will enhance the landscape.

- Search for egg bands of tent caterpillars. These often appear on twiggy growths of leafless fruit and ornamental trees, as dark grey or brown bands about 2.5 cm (1 inch) wide. You can loosen them from the bark easily with your thumbnail and remove them before destroying. (Take a minute to examine a band under a magnifying glass before you discard it: these bands are a marvel of natural design.)

- Finish pruning grape vines and fruit trees. Apply a dormant oil spray.

- Repair hollow areas in lawns with soil and sod. Avoid unnecessary traffic on the turf while it is saturated with water or frost. Clear lawns of fallen leaves, twigs and debris.

- Cut the lawn short when conditions permit (avoid cutting a turf when it is soggy). Apply a fertilizer formulated for spring turf rebuilding. Apply generous amounts of dolomite lime to the lawn.

- Remove all fallen leaves from the foliage of low-growing alpine, heather and juniper. If leaves are left for the winter, they will be matted down and block light and air from the plants, possibly causing decay.

- Clean all old leaves from your rose plantings. New leaves will develop soon. Spray roses with a dormant oil spray. Make certain all leaves or twigs lying under the plants are picked up and destroyed: these harbour insects and disease spores.

- Plant living Christmas trees out in the garden immediately after the holidays. Ensure that plants growing outside in dry areas under overhangs or eaves receive adequate moisture. Place gift plants such as poinsettia and azalea in a cool, bright indoor area.

- Plant fruit trees, ornamental flowering shrubs and roses if the ground is not frozen or soggy.

- If spring-flowering bulbs such as tulip, daffodil and hyacinth are starting to push through the ground, protect the exposed tips with 2.5–5 cm (1–2 inches) of mulch.

- Mulch rhubarb and asparagus plantings with aged manure.

- Plant lily bulbs if weather permits and ground is workable.

- Plant raspberry, currant, gooseberry and other vine berry plants.

- Seed an outdoor cold frame with vegetables such as early cabbage, spinach, turnip, radish, lettuce, kale, cauliflower, Brussels sprout, broccoli and collards.

- Seed indoors, on a sunny windowsill, half-hardy annuals that require a long growing period. Sterilize soil for indoor seeding by baking it in the kitchen oven for 1 hour at 82°C (180°F).

- Divide, separate and replant any perennials that were not tended to last fall. Dig the roots from the soil and gently pull the plants apart: each division needs a few vigorous roots, a sturdy crown and healthy leaves. Replant each section and water into the soil a weak solution of a 5-15-5 transplanting formula.

- Inspect bulbs, corms, tubers and other roots stored for winter. If any are shrivelling from dryness, place a wet cloth over them to restore moisture. If they are too damp, ventilate the area and lower the storage temperature. Discard deteriorated material.

- Inspect indoor plants for signs of mealybug in the axils of leaf and stem joints. Wipe them with a piece of cotton dipped in rubbing alcohol. If the pests persist, take the plant outdoors and spray with an indoor plant insecticide.

February

- Prune filbert trees lightly as soon as catkins are obvious. Shorten long growths and remove any suckers at the base of the tree. Cut back side growths not bearing catkins to within 2 buds of their base. Continue to prune and apply dormant lime-sulphur sprays on leafless fruit trees, berry plants and deciduous ornamentals.

- Trim or shear evergreen and deciduous hedges to improve shape, reduce size and thicken growth.

- Prune late-summer-flowering clematis.

- This is the time to treat mossy lawns. First rake out as much moss as possible with a heavy steel rake or power rake. Then apply a commercial eradicator containing ferrous-ammonium sulphate. A week after using an eradicator, apply generous amounts of dolomite lime to the lawn. Established lawns may require aeration and dethatching if they are matted.

- Firm into place any rock plants and other small perennials that frost and thaw have heaved from the ground. Lightly mulch with sand over the crowns.

- Apply a complete fertilizer in areas where spring-flowering bulbs are planted, and around trees and shrubs.

- If broad-leafed evergreens such as camellia, rhododendron and pieris have pale yellow leaves, give them a generous application of chelated iron.

- Clean wood ashes from stoves and fireplaces often, and spread the ash around the bases of roses, lilacs, *Daphne cneorum* and vegetable garden areas.

- Set out young starts of rhubarb and asparagus. Replant resting indoor gloxinia tubers. Plant each tuber concave side up, so that its top is nearly level with the surface of the soil. Gloxinia may also be started indoors from seed.

- Start outdoors in the vegetable garden: endive, lettuce, peas, radish, kale, spinach and broad bean. As soon as the young seedlings of vegetables that were started in cold frames in January show 2 true leaves and are sturdy, transplant them to the garden outdoors.

- Plant sweet pea, day lily, tigridia, montbretia, canna, ranunculus and anemone outdoors.

- Slugs have begun to do their damage. Set bait for them.

- Start tubers of begonias indoors, in moistened peat moss. Keep the planting area at 21°C (70°F). When roots and leaf growth develop, transplant the tubers into individual containers filled with a woodsy, fertile soil.

- Thin vegetable seedlings started indoors in January.

March

- Prune hybrid teas, *Floribunda* and other roses that flower on the current season's wood.

- Prune shrubby perennial herbs by cutting twiggy branches back to new growth. Sage, thyme, rosemary and rue are ready to be trimmed.

- Graft fruit trees.

- Start a new lawn from seed or sod. Renovate established lawns by raking, mowing, applying fertilizer and removing thatch.

- Plant deciduous and evergreen shrubs.

- Fertilize camellia, azalea, rhododendron, pieris and other broad-leafed evergreens with an acid-type fertilizer containing cottonseed meal.

- Apply a 5-10-10 fertilizer to the growing soil of asparagus and rhubarb.

- Plant out young starts of rock garden plants such as aubretia, iberis, helianthemum, creeping phlox and primrose. Many are showing bright colours at garden centres and nurseries.

- Plant ground cover plants such as periwinkle, ivy, gaultheria, hypericum, pachysandra and kinnikinnick.

Primroses. Deb McVittie photo

- Plant strawberry starts. Remove the blossoms the first year to prevent berries from forming so that the energy of the plant is directed into root and crown development. Berries may be produced the second season. Some gardeners remove only a few blossoms the first year to allow for the production of a few berries.

- Plant out flowering primrose, early iris, spring-flowering heather and other bright and colourful plants offered at nurseries.

- Plant early gladiolus spikes for June flowering.

- If summer- and fall-flowering perennials such as chrysanthemum and phlox are overcrowded, divide and replant them. Give them a boost with blood meal or a complete fertilizer.

- Continue succession planting in the outdoor vegetable garden: peas, spinach, leaf lettuce, Chinese vegetables, onion sets, potato and turnip. Garlic can be grown along with shallot, leek and onion in the full sun. Plant individual sections of the garlic bulb 15 cm (6 inches) apart and 5 cm (2 inches) deep.

- Scatter seeds of forget-me-not, poppy or verbena among daffodils, tulips and other spring-flowering plants to cover their yellowing foliage. Do not cut, tie or braid the bulb foliage until it has turned brown and withered.

The Gardener's Calendar

- Sow outdoors seeds of candytuft, clarkia, poppy, nasturtium, larkspur, baby's breath, coreopsis and alyssum.

- Some of the seeds sown indoors last month will have produced seedlings ready for thinning and transplanting. Plant them in a screened soil made of 3 parts compost, 1 part peat moss and 1 part coarse sand. Give the seedlings a weak solution of plant food once a week and make sure the soil remains moist.

- Harden young seedlings before transplanting out in the garden. Expose them to cool temperatures gradually by placing them outdoors during the day and bringing them indoors at night. They will be conditioned within 7 to 10 days.

- Before seeding root crops outdoors, dust the soil with a safe insecticide such as Sevin.

- Sow tomato, pepper, eggplant, cucumber, melons and other tender vegetables indoors.

April

- Remove the dead ends and straggly tips of clematis vines that flower in the spring and early summer. Late-blooming varieties can be pruned quite severely, as their flowers will be on new shoots produced this year.

- Clean outdoor lily pools. If you must divide water lily plants because of overcrowding, lift and divide just as the new shoots appear.

- Sharpen the hoe and destroy encroaching weeds.

- Maintain a healthy green lawn with frequent mowings, soil sweeteners and spring lawn fertilizers.

- Plant conifers, rhododendron, heather, and camellia.

- Give support to blackberry, loganberry and boysenberry plants. Fertilize their soil with an acid-type plant food high in phosphorus to insure a good crop.

- Increase stock of rhododendron, camellia, azalea and other shrubs by layering low, long branches into the ground.

- Punch holes around the outside perimeter of fruit and shade trees and pour a complete fertilizer into the holes. Use approximately 2.3 kg (5 lbs) of fertilizer for each large, mature tree.

- Fertilize garlic planted in March.

- Pinch out the tips of flowering annuals such as snapdragon, schizanthus, sweet pea, annual mum and salpiglossis when they reach a height of about 7.5 cm (3 inches). The plants will be bushier and lower-growing, full of blooms and more wind-resistant.

- Pinch out the tops of broad beans to discourage insects.

- Plant bedding plants or young starts of vegetables and flowers, ready at garden centres this month.

- Plant young indoor begonia starts at the end of the month or when the weather is warm.

- Plant summer-flowering bulbs, corms, tubers and rhizomes of canna, day lily, Peruvian daffodil, summer hyacinth, hardy gloxinia, lily and tuberous begonia.

- Plant a succession of gladiolus corms every 2 weeks for continuous summer colour. A few corms set out at intervals from early spring until mid-June will produce plants with generous amounts of blooms.

- Sow outdoors hardy annuals such as snapdragon, candytuft, godetia, Shirley poppy and mignonette.

- Sow the seed of Russian sunflowers. The seeds are highly nutritious and the flowers are decorative.

- To attract pheasants, ducks, geese, doves, quail and songbirds, sow millet in otherwise empty garden spaces. Plant smartweed around a pool or pond to attract waterfowl.

- Sprout dahlia tubers in a moist, warm atmosphere indoors. Shoots that appear will provide cuttings to increase your supply of favourite varieties.

May

- Cut flowering wood from currant, forsythia and flowering almond.

- Shear rock garden plants such as aubretia and alyssum after flowering; they may flower again.

- Give the lawn a feeding of a turf-formulated fertilizer high in nitrogen. Apply a combination weed killer and fertilizer, plus an insecticide if the lawn is weedy and infested with lawn moths.

- Bearded iris is ready for lifting and dividing if the planting is finished flowering and is overcrowded.

Compost in February. Deb McVittie photo

- Add to and work the compost heap so that plenty of material will be ready for fall use. Ample material is available now from cutting back of faded perennials and the removal of early pea vines (see below) along with loads of grass clippings.

- Take cuttings to increase your stock of pink, pansy, fuchsia, aubrietia, iberis, arabis and helianthemum. The parent plants will benefit from being trimmed for cuttings.

- Keep vegetables growing vigorously with applications of a 5-10-10 commercial fertilizer. Water the fertilizer thoroughly into the soil. Thin vegetables as needed.

- Add bone meal, fish meal or decomposed manure to the growing areas of spring-flowering bulbs to help them develop for the next season.

- On windy days, frequently water plantings in tubs, pots, hanging baskets and other containers.

- Hill up the soil around the bases of corn, potato and bean plants.

- To discourage root weevil invasion around the base of rhododendrons and other broad-leafed evergreens, apply ground garlic, hot pepper or thyme, or a sticky band of "tanglefoot" as a preventative.

- Set geraniums outdoors.

- Pull up early pea vines when they are finished producing, and seed leaf lettuce in their place. When the lettuce is harvested, seed peas again for later use.

- Plant or transplant *Lilium candidum*, the madonna lily. Set the bulb in the soil no deeper than 5 cm (2 inches).

- Sow outdoors: corn, squash, bush and pole beans.

- Seed herbs outdoors.

- Sow a succession of lettuce, spinach, radish, pea, kale and late cabbage.

- Vegetables seeded now will provide food for late fall and winter. Sow bush bean, carrot, beet, spinach, winter radish, parsley, lettuce, onion, parsnip, turnip, rutabaga and kohlrabi.

June

- Summer-prune espalier trees and vines.

- Prune wisteria vines lightly and repeat regularly through the summer.

- Cut finished blooms from rose plants.

- Frequently trim top growth and flowers from chives to encourage continued green tops.

- Cut the lawn weekly to 3 cm (1^{1}/2 inches), Rake off the cuttings and add them to the compost pile.

- Turn and work the compost heap.

- Tend climbing plants such as roses and ornamental vines. New adventurous shoots need to be tied and trained into place. Apply a general 5-10-10 fertilizer to keep them growing well. Water well in periods of dry weather.

- Take cuttings of spring-flowering shrubs such as forsythia, kerria, quince, choisya, ceanothus, pieris, spireas and viburnum. They will root easily at this time of year.

- Thin apples, pears, peaches, plums, figs and grapes by removing small fruits so that the rest of the crop can grow bigger and better. Prune fruit trees—this is a light, leisurely chore in summer. As the fruit becomes well set, trim the young growth to obtain more fruiting spurs for the next season.

- If cabbage heads begin to crack, slow their growth by bending over the stems until the roots break on one side.

- Pinch out side shoots of single-stemmed tomato plants. Keep them staked and tied. Fertilize with a 0-10-10 compound and spray the open blossoms with a hormone preparation to set their fruits.

- Fertilize and water deeply twice a week: squash, cucumber, pepper, eggplant and melon. On dry days, water the soil and foliage of rhododendron, azalea, camellia and other broad-leafed evergreens thoroughly, but always early in the morning.

- Apply rapid-acting liquid plant food to fuchsia, geranium, begonia and other flowering annuals, biennials and perennials. For continued blooms, use liquid foliar fertilizers that are low in nitrogen and high in phosphorus and potash. Begin to fertilize after the plants start active growth in the spring and continue to feed every 2 to 3 weeks while they flower.

- Select fall- and winter-flowering heathers and heaths at nurseries and garden centres.

- Set indoor foliage plants outdoors. Sink their containers in a fertile, sandy soil in a sheltered area of the garden. Water frequently and apply a liquid plant food once a month.

- Select and plant flowering and vegetable transplants. Fertilize them regularly with liquid plant foods and water them frequently.

- Plant outdoors: tomato, cucumber, eggplant, squash, peppers and melons.

- Plant corms of colchicum, fall crocus and *Fritillaria imperialis*.

- Sow seed of perennials for next season: columbine, lupin, delphinium, Solomon's seal, sidalcea, meadow rue, nepeta, heucher, campanula and astilbe.

- For a generous amount of cut flowers in fall, sow seeds of larkspur, cosmos, annual mum, rudbeckia and giant zinnia.

- Sow seed of biennials outdoors: foxglove, honesty, campanula, hollyhock, Canterbury bells, forget-me-not and pansy.

July

- Prune conifers for shape or to promote a more compact, dense shrub or tree.

- Keep Ghent, mollis and Exbury azalea vigorous and productive by cutting out old, senile wood, thus encouraging new shoots. Prune the plants soon after they finish flowering. Remove the seed heads.

- Remove canes of rambler roses that have flowered.

- Thin and prune wisteria vines.

- Dig and store spring-flowering bulbs such as tulip, daffodil and hyacinth.

- Regularly cut the faded flower heads of gladiolus, dahlia, rose, begonia, sweet pea and geranium.

- Remove the top growth on tall-growing tomato plants.

- Resist the impulse to cut back the foliage of peonies. Let frost deal with it.

- Water lawns deeply twice a week and keep them cut short.

- Water plants faithfully and deeply.

- Transplant Oriental poppies with care.

- Harvest zucchini and runner beans.

- Dig early potatoes.

- Dig shallots, and use or store them.

- Pick and dry flowers for winter colour.

August

- Make notes on changes needed in the arrangement of perennials, shrubs or other garden plants, and of new ones you need for specific purposes. Remove weeds from the bases of shrubs, trees and perennials.

- Use chemical fertilizers sparingly from this time on: any fertilizer left in the soil will become available to roots of garden plants after the heavy rains of fall. New growth in that period has little chance of hardening off before winter. (*Note:* You may use bone meal, for it is slow-acting and does not induce soft, new growth.)

- On fig trees, the fruit that formed at the beginning of the growing season will not ripen by winter; however, tiny, embryonic figs that form from now on may over-winter successfully and provide fruit next season.

- Remove the old cropping canes of brambleberries such as blackberries, logan-berries and boysenberries. Remove all but 4 to 5 new fruiting canes for the next season.

- Deadhead lavender and other perennials, biennials and annuals.

- Turn the compost heap, and keep adding material to be used later this fall and next spring.

The Gardener's Calendar

- Take semi-ripe cuttings of shrubs, following the procedure for softwood cuttings. Take cuttings of ceanothus, dogwood, buddleia, philadelphus, deutzia and berberis.

- Detach runners from strawberries and plant them on their own.

- If rhododendrons have produced flower buds for next year, they may need one more soaking at the roots, after which they should receive only enough water to prevent wilting.

- Dahlia, gladiolus and chrysanthemum are in full colour; they require soaking around the roots.

- Select and plant fall daffodils or *Sternbergia lutea*. Plant them 10 cm (4 inches) deep. Flowers will appear on the plants before the heavy fall frosts.

- In a cold frame or sheltered sunny spot, sow winter lettuce, endive, cress, green bunching onion, Swiss chard, winter spinach and winter radish.

- Start lifting the main crop of potatoes if the foliage is turning yellow and brown.

- Harvest ripe melons. Test for ripeness by pressing the end opposite the stalk with your thumbnail. If it gives slightly, it is ripe.

September

- Prune espalier shrubs and trees lightly to keep them in the desired shape.

- Trim overanxious vines and tie their growths neatly to avoid damage from winter winds.

- Shear ground covers such as St. John's wort and pachysandra close to ground level.

- Prepare new lawns. Fall-planted lawns are the most successful on the coast.

- Gather fallen fruits, overripe vegetables and the tops of finished flowering plants. Add them to the compost, along with fallen leaves.

- Remove seed pods, fallen flowers and leaves from the ground around tuberous begonia. Wait until the first frost to clean the tubers and take them indoors for winter storage.

- As soon as gladiolus leaves are yellow, lift the corms, cut off the leaves 2.5 cm (1 inch) above the corms and dry them for winter.

- Root conifer cuttings in a sandy soil mixture and plant in a cold frame.

- Prepare the soil for planting broad beans during October.

October

- Inspect blue spruce and other spruce trees for spider mites. Needles of infested trees turn yellow, then rust colour, and fall. The centre of the tree becomes "browned out," then the insects work their way to the outer branches. Spray or dust the trees with a miteicide several times in late fall and early spring, and again in midsummer, to destroy the mites.

- Apply a dormant spray to leafless trees and shrubs.

- Rake maple, alder and other large leaves from the lawn and garden. Large, heavy leaves tend to form mats that exclude light, air and moisture from the soil.

- Mow the lawn if it grows higher than 1 1/2 inches. Add clippings to the compost.

- Plant fruit trees and other deciduous shrubs, trees and berry plants and vines.

- Lift, divide and replant peony, day lily, iris, astilbe, delphinium and hosta.

- Spray peach trees for leaf curl, and add iron and other trace elements to the soil to help prevent peach leaf curl. Trees planted under the protection of eaves or overhangs usually are free of this condition; rain seems to spread the spores of the blight.

- Lift and take in all bulbs, corms and tubers, including begonia, dahlia and gladiolus. Fuchsia and geranium plants should be brought indoors.

- Dig a few strong young clumps of rhubarb with large balls of soil around their roots. Plant them in a tub or wooden box indoors to force new shoots to be ready in winter and early spring. Keep the roots well watered to encourage new stalks.

- Cut back the tops of perennials, including delphinium, to ground level.

- Apply a top dressing of dolomite lime to the lawn and vegetable garden.

- Clean flower beds of old stalks, leaves and weeds. After a light frost, mulch over growing areas with peat moss, ground bark or aged sawdust.

- Select and plant winter-blooming heath and heather, winter pansy, early-flowering bulbs and winter jasmine.

- Biennials such as foxglove, wallflower and forget-me-not that were started earlier from seed are ready for planting out in their permanent place in the garden.

- Plant outdoors: tulip, daffodils and other spring-flowering bulbs.

- Tulip, narcissus, hyacinths and crocus may be planted in containers plunged into the ground for a cool rooting period of about 8 weeks. Bring them indoors to a cool, light area to flower.

- Sow seeds of early peas and broad Windsor beans out in the vegetable plot for early spring use. Plant seeds of parsnip and Swiss chard as well.

- Plant fall rye in empty vegetable beds and annual flower beds.

- Keep the birds well supplied with winter food.

- Hardy water lilies may be left in the pool over winter. Store tropical lilies in shallow containers in a place that is cool yet frost-free. Cover with moist burlap.

November

- Tie together loosely branched conifers to protect them against damage from wet snow.

Jay with peanuts. Chuck Heath photo

- Transplant and prune deciduous trees and shrubs, and apply a dormant spray.

- Prune roses slightly. (Wait until March to do major pruning on hybrid teas and floribundas.) Cut back only excessively long shoots. Apply a dormant spray.

- As chrysanthemum flowers fade, cut the plants down to ground level.

- Complete bulb planting. There is still time to plant tulip, daffodil and hyacinth.

- Clean, oil and store garden tools that will not be used during the winter. Replace broken handles. Remove gasoline from mowers and other power equipment.

- Order rose plants or select them from garden centres and nurseries for Christmas gifts.

- Reduce the amount of water given to indoor plants. Watch for tiny webs and nests of insects. Remove them, and take the plant outdoors to wash with soap and water, then rinse. Leave the plant outdoors until evening.

December

- Prune grapevines. Use the cuttings of 1-year-old shoots to increase the stock. Cut the shoots to 25 cm (10 inches) in length, and bury them in the ground so that a third of their length is above ground level. In time new plants will grow.

- Continue to prune fruit trees. Collect the prunings and burn them.

- Start pruning late-flowering clematis such as *jackmanii.*

- Give azalea and citrus fruits frequent sprinklings of warm water from an atomizer. Keep them in a cool, light room.

- Bulbs that were planted in containers outdoors to root are now ready to bring indoors to flower.

- Select a live Christmas tree for the holidays. Keep it indoors for only a few days. Evergreen needles dry out quickly in a warm room, so line the container with damp moss or sawdust, fill with water and add water to the container every day. Plant the tree out in the garden as soon as possible after the holiday.

- If roses or other bare-rooted plants arrive as gifts, select a sheltered spot in the garden and heel them in. Dig a trench and place the plants so that their roots slant into the trench. Water if the soil is dry, then fill the trench with soil. Leave the plants in the trench until garden conditions are right for permanent plantings.

- Make sure to water indoor gift plants generously.

- Purchase a soil testing kit to analyze your soil needs for spring.

- Plan the vegetable garden for next season, making sure to rotate crops.

INDEX

A

abelia (*Abelia*), 20, 30, 31, 32

Abies balsamea (balsam fir), 147

Abies (fir), 29, 32, 147

Abies procera (noble fir), 147

Abutilon (flowering maple), 30, 31

Acacia (mimosa), 29, 30, 32

Acer circinatum (vine maple), 164–65

Acer (maple), 29, 30, 164–66, **165**

Acer palmatum (Japanese maple), **165**, 165–66

achillea, 106

acid soil, 19–21

acidanthera, 133

aconite, winter (*Eranthis*), **112**, 112–13

Actinidia arguta, 210

Actinidia chinensis, 210

actinidia (kiwi *Actinidia*), 29, 30, 210

Actinidia kolomikta, 210

Adiantum pedatum (maidenhair fern), 139, **139**

Aesculus (horse chestnut), 32

African daisy, 23

African marigold, 95, **95**

agrostemma, 100

Ailanthus (tree of heaven), 32

ajuga, 102, 239

Albizzia julibrissin (silk tree), 161

Alcea (hollyhock), 103

alkaline soil, 20

Allium cepa (shallots), 61

Allium sativum (garlic), 59–60

Allium schoenoprasum (chives), 59

almond (*Prunus*), 158, 178–79

alpine epimedium, 239

alpine wallflower, 110

althaea (rose of Sharon *Hibiscus syriacus*), 199

Amaryllis lutea. See lily of the field (*Sternbergia lutea*)

Ampelopsis (blueberry climber), 30, 31

Andromeda polifolia (bog rosemary), 29, 30, 31, 239

Androsace lanuginosa (rock jasmine), 29

anemone (windflower), 106, 113, 229, 246

annuals, 75, 92–101

apple, 20, 173, **173**

apricot, ornamental (*Prunus mume*), 157, 173

aquatic plants, 241–42

aralia (*Fatsia*, 31, 32

arborvitae (*Thuja*), 27, 29, 30, 32, 145

arbutus (*Arbutus menziesii*), 29, 162–63, **163**

arbutus, trailing (*Epigaea repens*), 31

Arbutus unedo (strawberry tree), 31, 32, 163

Arctostaphylos (manzanita), 29, 30, 31, 32

Arctostaphylos uva-ursi (kinnikinnick), 233, 238, 239, 246

artemisia (*Artemisia*), 31, 106

artichoke, globe, 20, 39–40

artichoke, Jerusalem (sunchoke), 40–41

Arundo donax (giant reed), 140–41

Asiatic lily, **129**, 130

asparagus, 19, 20, 41, 244, 246

aster, 93–94

astilbe, 20, 106

Athyrium filix-foemina (lady fern), 140

aubretia, 238, 246

Aucuba (spotted laurel), 29, 31, 32

autumn crocus (*Colchicum autumnale*), **124**, 124–25